C0065 71263

D1340265

JOHN McAVOY

REDEMPTION

FROM IRON BARS TO IRONMAN

WITH MARK TURLEY

First published by Pitch Publishing, 2016
Paperback edition, 2019

Pitch Publishing
A2 Yeoman Gate
Yeoman Way
Worthing
Sussex
BN13 3QZ

www.pitchpublishing.co.uk
info@pitchpublishing.co.uk

© 2016, John McAvoy and Mark Turley

Every effort has been made to trace any copyright.
An oversight will be rectified in future editions at the
earliest opportunity by the publisher.

All rights reserved. No part of this book may be reproduced,
sold or utilised in any form or transmitted in any form or by
any means, electronic or mechanical, including photocopying,
recording or by any information storage and retrieval system,
without prior permission in writing from the Publisher.

A CIP catalogue record is available for this book
from the British Library.

ISBN 978 1 78531 600 5

Typesetting and origination by Pitch Publishing
Printed and bound in India by Replika Press Pvt. Ltd.

Contents

The events described in this
book are all true.

Some names have been
changed for legal reasons.

Prologue

21 September 2012

'I don't know why you do this to yourself'

I HAD never run more than 10km before, but my need to stretch boundaries overrode common sense. Everyone around me had doubts. 'You haven't trained for it, running is a new discipline for you, start small and build up,' but fun-running held no appeal. I'm not even sure what fun-running means.

I heard that on an ultra-run (classified as anything above marathon distance) physical and mental pain took you to a whole new place, sometimes dark or sometimes joyous, deep within yourself but connected to nature. People described it as a 'spiritual awakening'. Maybe that's what I was looking for.

We assembled at six on a chilly, autumn morning, me and the other 300 entrants for the London-to-Brighton footrace. Our starting point was on Blackheath, a large, flat, treeless plain, criss-crossed with roads and ringed with bars and restaurants in the south-east of the city. A few ghosts hovered around, memories of coke-fuelled binges, robberies, a kid nearly bleeding to death in the back of my car. The area was one of my old hangouts, but it felt good to be back.

As the top of the sun crested the skyline I looked around. Most of the others seemed edgy, shuffling, biting their lips. I was already high, head surging with the dew and air and people. 2012 was the last purists' race, the final self-navigated year on that route. Now they have signposts and maps, even guide runners to lead you along. Back then it was you, your provisions and a compass. The starting pistol fired and *bang!* Off you went, 106km cross-country, from the capital to the sea, as quickly as you physically could.

For the first third everything was smooth and under control, the boring bit. There's no challenge in running comfortably.

My hips began complaining on a grass trail in Surrey after about five hours. It originated as a dull ache, either side of my lower-waist before sharpening into intense pain over the next four or five kilometres. That's when it got interesting. My pace did not slow.

Endurance sport hinges on pain, which is why it attracts a certain kind of athlete. You begin an event with your fitness and strength but you finish it only with stubbornness. Hip ache was just a teaser of what would come. I ate a couple of flapjacks, drank some of the flat cola from my backpack and pressed on. The throbbing stayed with me and grew worse, steadily joined by stabs from every other joint below my ribs – *good*. If you're not hurting, you're not trying.

I got lost in the fields after East Grinstead and started following a wide-eyed beanpole from Holland. He had that craziness about him, the absorption of the hopeless addict, but he claimed to know what he was doing and I believed him. We meandered way off course, along a winding hedgerow, before finding a gap into a farmer's field. The old guy spotted us and jumped out of his tractor, swearing, gesticulating wildly. His big, woolly dog barked its head off. The two of us scampered away laughing like schoolboys.

By the three-quarter mark, on a towpath near Haywards Heath I had left the disorganised Dutchman long behind and felt deliriously, insanely happy. The body's internal drugs are as powerful as any you can buy. This kind of event teaches you that.

Endorphins erupted, adrenaline surged, while birds sang and breeze laced with wild flowers tickled my sweaty skin. It was mid-afternoon by then and I had been running for nine hours straight, most of it alone.

16km from the sea I drew level with a woman, the first fellow runner I had seen in a while. She wore the number 76.

'I think I'm in second place,' she coughed, looking sideways, grim-faced. 'I'm struggling though. My back is torture.'

I had banished all my pain by then, locked it away, a trick I learned to perfect. 'Come on,' I smiled, 'we'll run together.'

'Thanks.' She eyed my bulky shoulders and arms suspiciously. 'You don't look like an ultra-runner. What do you do?'

'I row.'

'So why are you here today?'

'I just wanted the challenge. What about you?'

She seemed better already. The conversation had fired a hormonal reaction and given her a lift. Emotional, chemical and physiological states all combine on the road. You learn that too.

'Oh I'm obsessive,' she said. 'I do all of these I can. I competed in the world championships at Mont Blanc six weeks ago. My legs still haven't recovered. That's why I'm not having a great race.'

'Wow,' I thought. What a privilege to run with an elite competitor.

The best ultra-runners are usually anonymous. It's not about glory for them. Spectators are sparse and prize money scant. They have other reasons. A light rain fell.

'I started seven years ago,' she went on. 'I was diagnosed with stage two breast cancer and had to have a double mastectomy. After the operation I felt so low, so useless. I lay in hospital, thinking, "What have I done with my life?" I hadn't done anything, you know, nothing worth doing. I realised I'd never properly lived, never used my body to its fullest. I owed it to myself to do that.'

I felt like hugging her. If we had not been running, maybe I would have. Her words resonated with my own situation so deeply.

'So I entered a 5k,' she continued. 'Then a 10k, then a half-marathon, then a marathon. Every time I upped the distance, I found I needed something new to inspire me, a greater challenge. That was six years ago. Now here I am!'

Our resolve deepened as the rain grew harder. We pounded the fields, then the streets, side by side. For those last two hours, 76 and I were kindred spirits.

On the edge of town, we caught and passed the woman in first. She had her chin on her chest and moved in stuttering, staccato strides. Her breath wheezed. She looked ghoulish, half dead. A few hundred metres on, I shot a glance over my shoulder and saw her motionless, face contorted, gazing after us with her hands on her hips. Her eyes said, 'Why now? I came all this way and you pass me now?'

I don't know if she ever got to the end.

We almost sprinted the last 3km – 76 had won! I congratulated her as we breasted the line on Brighton beach, squeezing her hand before we parted. For me it had been perfect. I established heartfelt communication with another human being.

My wrist monitor told me I completed the course in just over 12 hours and burned 11,500 calories. I would need something sweet and something salty as soon as possible.

With the sun setting on the water I hauled myself off the pebbles, towards town to find a taxi. The change from running to walking, on the pavement, brought home the full physical reality of what I had done. My body seized up, back like an ironing board, buttocks like boulders. I felt sick. My hands shook.

Fashionably dressed people stared as they passed by, on their way out to bars and restaurants. To them I must have looked like a junkie.

The cabbie was a chatty one. We had an hour together in the car, on the M23 all the way back. He rattled on about how expensive football tickets and pints are these days and how London was being ruined by gentrification. I smiled and listened. None of it meant much to me. He asked what I had been up to, so I told him.

'You've just run all this way?' he cried, incredulous. 'I can't believe what you're telling me!'

After parking he had to help me out of the back seat and up to the house.

My joints had set solid. My calves had cramped into cricket balls, making my toes curl.

My quadriceps were like marble slabs. Feet and ankles had swollen inside my shoes, while pus oozed from spectacular blisters on to my socks. Standing under my own strength was impossible.

'I don't want to take your money, mate,' he said. 'Not after what you've done.'

It was a £90 fare, so I insisted.

Mum opened the door, horrified at my dishevelled state. She threw her arm around my shoulders and led me into the lounge, where I flopped on the sofa.

'I don't know why you do this to yourself,' she said, as sleep overcame me.

The next day, they took me back to prison.

Part One
Arrested Development

'Although protection racketeers such as the Kray and Richardson brothers had certainly been more feared in their day than the lower-profile robbery gangs, they were not so much admired by the next generation of aspiring criminals. They had held sway over their fiefdoms in east and south London by muscle and intimidation, but it was a tawdry business. They were capricious and vain, and ultimately brought down by their own hubris and stupidity.

'Successful armed robbers, by contrast, were seen through the underworld prism as wily, audacious and buccaneering – men who used brains and planning rather than psychopathic violence and who carried off huge one-off jobs rather than having to engage in the burdensome and monotonous business of extortion. The risks of epic robbery were high but quick, and the payday was potentially enormous. As early as 1963, the Great Train Robbers made more in 24 hours than any of the old racketeers made in a lifetime.

'As the Krays and Richardsons, Mad Frankie and the rest took their inevitable fall at the end of the 1960s, a new breed of mainly white, working-class armed robber was emerging from the pubs, drinking clubs and coffee bars of Walworth and Bermondsey, Hackney and Islington, Stepney and Bethnal Green.

'Their names – George Davis, Bertie Smalls, Billy Tobin, Ronnie Knight, Freddie Foreman, Mehmet Arif, Micky McAvoy – were barely known to the wider public, but they were ambitious and some would soon become notorious. They were also prolific. In 1972, the annual total of armed robberies in the Metropolitan district was 380. By 1978, it had risen to 734 and by 1982 it more than doubled to 1,772 – a 366 per cent increase in a decade.'

Neil Darbyshire, *The Telegraph*, 19 May 2004

1

Brinks-Mat and
How It All Began

IDENTITY? That's a tricky one. I'll try to make sense of it as far as possible. Can we really change and start again? Are we not always *who we are*?

In all the time I spent alone – way too much time – these questions stayed with me, turning over and over. They still follow me now.

Maybe they're what I'm running away from.

People like to believe in a common thread woven throughout your life, to tie up your sense of self, to make it neat and easy to understand. Everyone likes talking about their *journey*, don't they? 'Think of your childhood,' they might say. 'Pick a moment when you saw how things would be.'

A footballer might go misty-eyed and describe a goal he scored for the school team. A boxer may tell of a black eye or a dust-up with a bully, a Formula One driver his first spin in a kart. Not me.

I'm an Ironman, competing in the toughest test of one-day, all-round sporting endurance imaginable – a 2.4-mile swim, 112 miles on the bike followed by running a marathon.

Beyond extreme physical fitness it requires utter single-mindedness. Self-belief is not enough, although it helps. You have to belong on the road. If you are not prepared to die there, you can't win. I don't do things I can't win at.

Ironmen go through hell every time they race, maybe even every time they train. Ironmen like hell, they learn to thrive in it. Maybe that's what it is, my common thread, my link to before. Maybe I always liked hell.

The defining moment of my early years wasn't on the saddle of a bike, in a pool or on a track, but in the car park of a pub called The Plough, in Dulwich, south-east London. It was early summer 1999, a warmish day, about an hour before lunchtime opening. Ozcan, the Turkish lag I was due to meet, pulled up in an old Volvo, dark blue with a silver bonnet.

The wheel-arches were corroded. It was a proper shabby ride, a real third-class banger.

I sat perched on the edge of a picnic table and watched him park. As he got out and walked towards me, my excitement gave way to impatience. One of my associates had set up the deal and I had expected a *player*, but Ozcan was scruffy, twitchy and a mess of nerves. He looked as wrecked as the car.

'Have you got it then?' I asked him.

'Yes,' he nodded.

'Well, go on then.'

He gave me a bad feeling, bags under his eyes, dirty teeth, greasy hair. Rather than meet my eye and speak, he hissed in a conspiratorial whisper. This was supposed to be the *game*. Front mattered. His nervousness bothered the shit out of me. My instinct for jeopardy, stranger-danger, went into overdrive.

Should I back out? A helicopter flew across a corner of the sky and he froze. Mug.

He adjusted himself when he saw my concern then shook my hand gently.

'Okay, okay,' he said.

I followed him over to the rear of the Volvo. He popped the boot and there it was, a sawn-off shotgun in good, clean condition just lying there, like a baby in a crib, on top of a holdall in the wide space of the hatchback.

'You got any food for it?' I asked.

He nodded and fumbled around, pulling out a blue carrier bag. I peered inside. Sunlight glinted off a heap of golden cartridges.

'Here,' he said. 'How many?'

I shrugged.

'Twenty?'

At last he cracked a little smile. 'Six hundred pounds.'

He put the cartridges in with the gun and passed it all over. I slid a roll of notes from my jeans and pressed it into his hand. He put a fag-stained finger to his forehead in a mini salute, got back in his rust-bucket and drove off.

My eyes stayed on him for as long as humanly possible. His Volvo intermingled with the everyday traffic on the road, circled the roundabout and disappeared in the direction of Forest Hill.

Being alone felt good and I savoured the knowledge of what was in that bag. Pride swelled inside me.

South London looked somehow different. Everything was bright, everything was alive; the pavements glittered with opportunity.

I was 16.

* * *

People often ask how I came to be in the line of work that I was. It's not a regular thing, organised crime, not like working in Tesco or selling life insurance, but then regular people don't grow up as a McAvoy. They don't understand what that means.

My grandad came over from Ireland just before World War Two and fought for King and Crown on the Italian campaign. The IRA was yet to exist, but back in the old country his brothers were mixed up with the Irish Volunteers fighting against British rule. There was a fair bit of bloodshed involved – 'Protect your own, *chuckie-ar-la*, our day will come.' Maybe it all started there, I don't know. We're good Catholics, us McAvoys. Family honour always counted.

Grandad had 12 kids in London, seven of them boys and pretty much all of them ended up in various forms of villainy. Mostly it was armed robbery, but there's no sense restricting your options so some dabbled with the drugs trade, money laundering, dealing in stolen cars, any opportunistic way to make a bit of money. Theorists can come up with all sorts of reasons to explain why but I think it's pretty straightforward. They grew up on sink estates with few options. Back in the 1960s, first and second generation Irish immigrants didn't tend to get white collar jobs. That wasn't how the world worked. It was still the era of 'no blacks, no dogs, no Irish'.

Each part of London had its own group of emerald-isle hard-cases. The East End had the fighting O'Sullivans. Kilburn and Cricklewood in the West had the Sunshine Boys. Around Bermondsey and Southwark everybody knew the McAvoys. A family that size was bound to create an impression and nearly all of them got their hands dirty. The only one who didn't take that road was my Dad, but he suffered a massive heart attack and passed away just before I was born.

Apparently Dad used to say the family business was for mugs, that you could make a better and safer living legally. He ran nightclubs, betting shops, he even owned a construction firm. I don't know where he got his seed money from and I suppose it's possible some of it came from his brothers' activities, but his day-to-day interests were legitimate. Mum always said if he'd stayed alive he would have kept me out of it all, but I'm not so sure. I think there was something inside me, something that made me susceptible. And the game has a way of sucking you in if you grow up within its reach.

After Dad died we stayed close as a family, meeting around at my grandparents' house every Sunday, all the uncles, aunties and cousins. My uncle Micky kept an eye on Mum and made sure she was okay. He would pop to see her and give her regular money to cover bills and expenses. Unfortunately, before I was a year old, Micky disappeared as well, sent on a nice, long holiday at her majesty's pleasure. He masterminded the Brinks-Mat robbery, a legendary event in British criminal folklore and the biggest gold heist in UK history.

One of Micky's mates, a guy called Anthony Black, had managed to blag his way into a job as a guard at Heathrow Airport. He often watched over the high security vault, guarding huge amounts of cash. The idea was that Micky and his crew would turn up, their inside man would let them in, they would overpower the other guards, crack the vault and drive off in their transit van with about £3m of paper money. In and out in ten minutes – quick, easy and lucrative.

On the day the first part went off as expected. Anthony was ready and did his bit. Uncle Micky and his five masked mates stormed in, caught the other staff unaware, tied them up and covered them in petrol. It's amazing how amenable a captive drenched in flammable liquid can be if you're holding a lit match.

Unfortunately for Uncle Micky the security company had been clever. The supervisor spilled his guts and told the combination numbers for the vault doors, but his information wasn't enough on its own. His numbers had to be combined with two other codes to open the vault, but the men who knew those codes weren't there. With the cash inside and no way to get it, things got a little frantic before Micky and his mates realised there had been a delivery that morning that was still waiting to be secured.

Next to where they had tied up the hostages, stacked up on crates under plastic sheeting at the side of the depot, they found three tons of gold bullion bars. It was worth £26m, an unbelievable sum for 1983. In today's terms it would be valued at ten times that.

In the end it took two hours to load it all and the poor van's suspension could barely cope. They made their getaway with the chassis virtually scraping along the road surface, but in those precarious minutes, Uncle Micky's reputation was made forever. Inspired by headlines and TV news reports whispers spread about the daring raid and the incredible amount of loot. People still talk about it now.

Uncle Micky had a major problem though. While it's fairly easy to launder cash money, shifting that amount of raw gold presented a logistical nightmare. It would have to be melted down, combined with other gold to make it untraceable then sold off. That required specialist input.

Micky sought help from a powerful underworld figure known only as 'The Fox' who agreed to use his network of associates to shift it. Through him, Brinks-Mat turned from being a robbery committed by a small, tight-knit group, to a caper that involved half the criminal community of the UK. Tons of people got mixed up in it. Some of the original gang left the country. John Rowley ending up living in Colombia, for example, but after a few shenanigans Micky got collared. They gave him 25 years.

Police immediately searched every address with a McAvoy connection, trying to find the missing bullion. I was still just a baby and when they raided Mum's house a uniformed constable actually lifted me out of the cot to see if there was gold stashed under my mattress. That was my first brush with the law, at about a year old. After that they hung around for a couple of days, digging up the garden, but Mum wasn't hiding anything. She never got involved in all that stuff. She didn't like it.

Even today the Brinks-Mat investigation continues, with a string of murders and spin-offs related to it. All the side-deals led to double-crosses and a poisonous atmosphere of mistrust. I once heard it said that if you bought a piece of gold jewellery anywhere in Britain during the late 1980s or 90s, the chances are it came from Brinks-Mat. Uncle Micky touched a lot of lives.

Yet strange as it may seem, without Dad or Micky around, for most of my early childhood I lived what would be called a normal life. The same kind of life as everyone else, I guess. My Mum, Margaret, worked as a florist and we had a spacious house near Crystal Palace that Dad had left for her. One of Mum's best friends, Jacqui, was the stepmum of Kenny Sansom, the England footballer and Kenny's Dad, George, used to take me to Arsenal games. I loved it. He would bring me down to the changing rooms after matches to meet the players.

George must have been a lovely man, making lots of effort with me because he knew I had no father. Unfortunately, he also died of a heart attack when I was five. Perhaps if he stayed alive he might have encouraged me to get involved in sport as a youngster. Who knows?

In reality I wasn't an active kid, at all. Chubby and heavily-set, I preferred things I could do sitting down. A Greek guy called Edis, who lived next door to us, taught me chess when I was still a toddler. We used to sit in the garden and play for hours. I enjoyed the challenge, thinking forwards, planning, three, four, five moves ahead. Later I joined the chess club at primary school and thrashed everyone, a nice feeling. I liked winning.

We lived a life of ordinariness and the only signs we were slightly different were few. At the time I didn't dwell on them. You don't at that age. Sometimes uncles or friends would come over, stay for a drink and give Mum little cash gifts.

'They're just looking after us,' she would say. 'They're making sure we're okay. That's what we're like in our family. We look after each other.'

Good Catholics.

It was all I knew and I thought nothing of it. I was a typical kid. Primary school went fine, although I hated PE. I was rubbish at football and detested athletics. When they asked me to run the 200m I would get to halfway, pretend I'd pulled a muscle then walk. I was slower than most of my classmates and couldn't be bothered with it.

It didn't upset me. I just assumed nature hadn't blessed me with those abilities. I was perfectly happy eating crisps, playing Nintendo or watching TV. That was much more my scene.

All that changed when I was eight years old.

2

Good Stuff

MY Mum, my half-sister Donna and I were eating dinner in the kitchen, summer of 1991. I had the radio on in the corner playing 'Ice, Ice Baby' by Vanilla Ice.

Mum looked up from her chicken kiev and asked me to turn it down. I got up, lowered the volume and took a can of fizzy drink from the fridge. As I returned to the table she spoke again.

'Billy gets out tomorrow.'

Billy Tobin was Mum's first husband, Donna's Dad. They had grown up together on a council estate in Peckham and married at 16. In those early days Billy had been scraping a living as a builder and they had Donna when they were both just 18. Mum always used to say that Billy would have stayed out of crime but for the fact he witnessed his Dad get murdered. Three men set about him with knives during a pub fight in Nunhead. Billy was powerless to stop it.

'After that, he changed,' Mum used to say. 'He never wanted anyone to take advantage of him and end up a victim like his old man.'

Billy's new self-image blossomed quickly. In no time he became a major face on the London scene, a millionaire by the age of 20, driving around in a Rolls-Royce at 21. He and Mum divorced just before his first sentence, but by then he was on borrowed time anyway, having already had five acquittals at the Old Bailey. An informer on his last job tipped off the Flying Squad who intercepted their car and shot him three times.

By the time of his release he had served eight of a 16-year stretch for armed robbery and been granted parole.

'He'll probably come over,' she went on. 'He's been away for quite a while so give him a bit of space, okay?'

We both nodded.

When Billy arrived the next day, he didn't look anything like my expectation of someone just released from jail. He was tall, strong and dressed like a movie star; £400 loafers, a Rolex watch, designer clothes. He settled into a chair in the lounge and smiled so warmly you couldn't help but fall for him a bit. He called me over.

'You must be John,' he said. 'Do me a favour. Go make me a cup of tea?'

When I came back from the kitchen with the drink, he patted me on the head.

'Nice work,' he grinned. 'I'd like to shake your hand.'

The generosity in his manner overrode my wariness and I reached up. He held on for a few seconds, just long enough for me to feel the strength of his grip. When he released, a £20 note was stuck to my palm. No one had ever given me folding money before.

'Thanks Billy!' I said.

He laughed and ruffled my hair.

'Good stuff.'

A few days later, he took me and my sister out shopping together. Donna was 18 and keen on getting a car, so he bought her a brand new MG convertible, just like that.

'You haven't seen me for a long time,' he told her as she signed off on the papers. 'And I missed you in prison. This is my way of making it up to you.'

Here was a man just days out of jail. Yet he spent money freely and had an aura. He was so confident, so charismatic.

From then on, Billy became a regular fixture at our house. He didn't stay over, but he and Mum had a close bond that went right back to early childhood. They believed in supporting each other. Whenever he was there I'd rush to get him a drink and he always gave me money. He would tell little stories and make jokes. They were happy times and I suppose there was quite a deep emotional need behind it all. We stepped into a sort of mutual void – I didn't have a father and he didn't have a son. We became close.

By the time I was ten, Billy and I were hanging out regularly. He would take me out for the day or on little trips in the evening. Sometimes we would go to lunch or dinner at expensive restaurants. He taught me which fork to use for fish and the right glasses for water or wine. To begin with I didn't realise, but I was meeting and interacting with infamous members of the criminal fraternity. I didn't think of them like that, they were just Billy's mates. Guys like Mehmet Arif, Georgie Davis, Ronnie Knight. Every time it would work the same way.

'Who's the kid, Billy?'

'It's all right, he's Micky's nephew. He's good stuff.'

And with those words I'd be welcomed with open arms.

For Christmas of 1993 we went to an Italian restaurant, the Don Amici. It was full of families having get-togethers for the festive period and we had a big table reserved in the middle for Billy, us and some of Billy's friends. The manager met us at the door.

'What a pleasure to see you Mr Tobin, we have our best table for you, any special requests please let us know, we can put everything on your tab.'

It was always like that with him, anywhere he went. You couldn't help but be swept along by it. Our crowd stood to greet us and each handshake that came my way carried notes, sometimes lots of them. One after the other pressed my palm and leaned into my ear.

'Here's a little something for Christmas, John. Nice to see you. Give my regards to your Uncle Micky. Your Dad was a good man.'

I took home nearly a grand in cash that night, not bad going when you're ten. Nobody said it in so many words, they had no reason to, but an inkling was forming in my mind. Without understanding any specifics, I realised that all this money and respect didn't come from the normal world. Not the world the other kids at school and their parents came from. This wasn't how most people lived.

Billy and his mates were from working class backgrounds. Most of them had grown up on estates. They were sharp, but they weren't book-clever. None of them were employed, but they were wealthy and larger-than-life. In my young head a little light went on in the darkness.

Early in the New Year a movie called *Fool's Gold* premiered on TV and I sat to watch it in the lounge. It starred Sean Bean, who was one of the UK's biggest stars at the time. Within the first few seconds it became clear that Bean was playing my Uncle Micky and the film was about Brinks-Mat.

Sitting at home, viewing that movie by myself was a surreal experience. Other than Uncle Micky, the characters – John Palmer, my Auntie Jackie, Brian Robinson – these were all people I knew in real life. Most of them had visited my house. The film was a load of sensationalised nonsense, but as I watched I started to get a sense of scale, to understand the magnitude of my family's name.

A few months after that Grandad died and after the funeral I went to his house with Mum and a couple of aunties to clear out his stuff. We found a box in a kitchen cupboard full of newspaper clippings about Billy, Uncle Micky and the rest of them. They were taken from *The Sun*, *The Mirror* and various other national newspapers.

The red-tops had dubbed Billy as 'Billy the Liar' while they called Uncle Micky 'Mad Micky McAvoy'. Grandad had kept them all, like you might keep your kids' football trophies. A strange feeling came over me as I looked through them.

I was a McAvoy. And the McAvoys were so notorious they made films and wrote front page articles about us. More lights went on.

So this is who I am?

It was unsettling, but exciting at the same time. There was glamour and danger in it. That's a potent mixture for a kid.

By then I was attending Kelsey Park secondary school in Beckenham, which was a real pain to get to, about eight miles from my house. Perhaps that's why I started bunking off so much. I think too that I subconsciously understood I had another path to follow. The family business, whatever it was, could provide me with a very decent living without having to listen to crap from teachers.

I began to develop the disdain for authority that I'd absorbed from Billy and his mates. Anyone who was part of the system was on the wrong side. We were free men, making our own way, living off our wits, like cowboys. We existed in the moment and didn't appreciate interference.

I would spend my days loafing about the shops or the park, or even just kicking around at home. Mum half knew, I think, but turned a blind eye. On one occasion when I was 13, as I sat in the lounge playing computer games, I heard the front door go. It was the middle of the day and Mum wasn't due back yet. Had she forgotten something?

Instinctively I turned off the TV and dived behind the sofa. Peering out from between the cushions I saw that it wasn't her, but Billy, carrying a bulging bin liner tied in a knot. I watched as he walked into the kitchen, sat down at the table, opened the bag and shook out its contents. Feeling silly, I crept out from my hiding place.

'Billy!' I said.

He spun around.

'Jesus, John!' he laughed. 'I didn't know you were in!'

The tabletop behind him was covered in banknotes.

'How much is that?' I asked.

'Dunno, haven't counted it yet, should be about £250,000.'

I felt like asking where it came from, but stopped myself. Instinct told me he would not welcome the question.

Not long after that I was picked up by police for the first time. I had been in a local park with some friends and a bag of beers. There had been a scuffle and I got gobby with someone, not a big deal really. A passer-by must have heard the disturbance and dialled 999 because the cops appeared out of nowhere. They questioned us, found my bag with all the booze and made an issue out of it because we were underage. Rather than take me to the station, one copper decided to drive me home. He seemed a nice enough bloke and we had a little chat in the car. He asked who I had been with and I gave him a few names.

When he knocked on the front door Mum came out, hovering on the step like a thundercloud, grey-faced with fear. Her prior experiences of opening doors to policemen were not happy memories. He explained the relatively trivial situation and she settled down.

'Thank you officer,' Mum said. 'It was very kind of you to bring John home safely.'

'Not at all madam. I'm just happy to be of help.' The copper whistled through his teeth and turned to me.

'What on earth are you doing young man?' he said. 'You've got a lovely home and a mother worrying about you. Half the places I go into around here I have to wipe my feet on the way out. You've got a nice life, son, you're very lucky, but if you carry on the way you're going, you'll end up in Feltham young offenders' institution. Mark my words. I see this all the time, believe me. It's up to you. Don't make the wrong choices.'

Choices? He didn't know the half of it.

When Billy found out he was absolutely furious. Not because I had behaved badly or got myself in trouble, but because I communicated with the law.

'You never speak to them, do you understand!' he shouted. 'It doesn't matter if they take you in and stick you in a cell. It doesn't matter if they get rough! When Old Bill ask questions, you say nothing. Don't tell them your name. Don't tell them where you live, not a thing!'

I nodded, accepting the lesson. Then like the kid I was, I blurted out, 'What was it like in prison?'

Billy's face changed. The sneer left his lips. His eyes went flat. 'I don't want to talk about it. It'll jinx me.'

For me, that was how everything started to come together. Bit by bit, I learned how it works. Don't speak to police and don't talk about prison. That's bad karma. I soaked up everything Billy told me, absorbing all his hard-earned wisdom. If I put it all together, it would go something like this:

Police are scum. They'll try and be your mate because they admire what we do. They see we've got balls, but they're still scum. Politicians, judges, solicitors too, except the bent ones. Banks, insurance companies, big corporations or financial institutions, they're all fair game, they don't deserve respect. You can do what you like to them and it's victimless. Don't let anyone tell you otherwise, but the average working man? That's another story.

You never take from working people, that's what little dickheads do. Burglary, street crime, mugging, all that stuff is for spotty herberts in Nike trainers who watch too many rap videos. For us, robbing a bank or turning over a security van is a job, but we won't so much as steal a bar of chocolate from a corner shop. In fact, we do the opposite. Any local restaurants or bars we go to, any local businesses we use, we pay extra. We tip everyone. A tenner here, a score there – this is our way.

To thrive in our world, you have to get on with anyone. You can be in a boozer with a bunch of thugs one day or the Pont de la Tour on Tower Bridge with barristers and brokers the next. The most important thing of all is loyalty, respect. Your name, your reputation is everything. If your name is shit, then so are you. And you never hurt women or children. If you have an issue with someone you deal with them. You never touch their family. People think its old-fashioned, but this is our code and it's set in fucking stone.

Billy and his mates used to spit with anger when they heard news stories about gangs who killed someone's kid in a reprisal. That disgusted them. It really was a case of honour among thieves. We had our morals.

We were good stuff.

Some of the other lads at school got involved in petty crime, selling £10 bags of weed, vandalism, street nonsense. I was above all that. I knew where I was going and had bigger goals. By the time exams rolled around when I was 16, I never attended. School didn't interest me. It held no relevance to my life. Who cares why Henry VIII dissolved the monasteries?

Billy turned up one day with a brand new, silver, Porsche 911 turbo. The thing was a real work of art, special edition; leather seats, top-end stereo, fully kitted out. He had it super-chipped so it could do 0-60 in about two and a half seconds with a top speed of nearly 200mph. He asked if I wanted to go out for lunch. I jumped in.

For the first few minutes we sat in silence as he drove through Bromley, then he wound the window down and pointed at the street. There were a few everyday types walking the pavements, folks in their standard euro-box cars on the road.

'You see all them?' he said. 'All them with their mortgages and direct debits and problems at the office? They're all mugs, the lot of 'em. They're slaves to the system. And the system doesn't give a fuck about them. They go to work, they pay their taxes and then they die. They all get fucked and they bend over and take it. You only get one shot at life John. If you want something, you go out and get it. End of.'

I sat in that gorgeous Porsche and thought about all the kids in my year, in their revision classes, feeling pressured to achieve grades. Billy was right. Who needed that? That wasn't for people like us.

By the time summer term got underway, I had not been to school in weeks and GCSEs loomed. Mum banged on about it every day, repetitive and pleading.

'You should go in for your exams John. Please, love. It might give you some options.'

In her heart I think she knew where I was going, but still had that slice of hope, of mother's desperation. I had a go for her sake.

I didn't want her to be upset. I hadn't completed any coursework or preparation but tried to do the exams. What a headache!

One particular morning we were having breakfast about eight o'clock and I had an English paper I was supposed to sit. I was tired, it was raining and I really could not be bothered. Billy had popped in for coffee and heard me whining.

'I'm not doing this one, Mum.'

'But it's English, John. It's one of the important ones.' She was nearly in tears.

'I can't be arsed getting the bus. It's a massive ball-ache and it's pointless. I'm staying here today.'

Billy found it funny.

'Why are you talking to your Mum like that, John?'

'I ain't getting the fucking bus, Billy. It takes ages and I don't want to go anyway.'

He looked at me, straight.

'You're a big man are you?'

'What do you mean?'

'You're a big man, yes or no?'

'Yeah!' I was indignant.

'Then take my car.'

'What, the Porsche?'

He nodded. 'Yeah, take it. If you've got the bottle, take the car.'

I shrugged, trying to play it cool.

'All right.'

He passed me the keys and I went out to the driveway, climbed in and revved the engine. It roared like a jet plane. I kept expecting him to come out smiling, saying it was all a big joke. He never did.

Obviously I didn't have a licence, I was too young, but Billy had taught me to drive around some local back streets. I had even had a go in a few lorries on an industrial estate in Millwall, but I wasn't fully competent yet. I kept stalling it because the clutch was so twitchy and got plenty of funny looks from pedestrians, but arrived without incident and had the sense to park around the corner from school. If teachers had seen me they would probably have phoned the law.

I walked in, head in the clouds, grinned all the way through my literature exam surrounded by anxious classmates, then drove back feeling like the king of the world. Sixteen years old and cruising around south London in a brand-new, special edition Porsche 911. There were only about 20 of them in the whole country. *That* was what it meant to be a McAvoy.

Billy was waiting for me with a big smile.

'You haven't scratched it have you?'

'No.'

'Course you haven't!' I gave him the keys. 'You're one of us. You're good stuff.'

How I loved him.

I don't believe in fate, but by then my future was set. Billy never made me do anything I didn't want to do. But he taught me a way of looking at things, a way of being that was just a fantasy to most people.

Billy was my bridge to the underworld.

3

Brains

BY the time the whole school charade was over and exams were finished, getting a job or going to college were the furthest things from my mind. Billy and I were inseparable and I drove him around, like some sort of unofficial chauffeur. It was a way for him to support me financially until I found my feet.

The summer of 1999 became a hectic one, with lots of meet-ups in bars and restaurants and lots of parties. I found out very early on that the criminal fraternity like to load up on booze and drugs in their downtime. When you always have to look over your shoulder, wondering when your end will come, it can be a stressful existence. You need to blow off steam. The parties were raucous and you would see the same faces – the villains and all their kids. We were like our own social sub-set.

Billy had a particular Spanish restaurant in Blackheath, El Pirata, that he used a lot. He knew the proprietor and paid him well, so we would just take the place over. On our nights everyone in there was a player. We would help ourselves at the bar, order any food we felt like and it was all paid for. The owner loved it. There would be 150 of us, drinking crates of Dom Perignon and eating steak and lobster. On a typical night with us he could make

£50,000. The actor Tamer Hassan worked in there before he was famous. He would bring us our drinks.

Next door to the restaurant was a high-end clothes shop called Raffles and we all had accounts there too. Sometimes you would be in the restaurant, get a bit of food on yourself, then go straight into Raffles and spend a grand on some new gear before hitting a club. Why bother with A Levels or an apprenticeship when you can do that? What a life!

In August of that year a friend of mine turned 16. The occasion was marked with a big get-together at his Dad's house in Chislehurst, an enormous villa complete with tennis courts and a swimming pool. Above a grandiose bar in the garden hung a Scales of Justice sign, a replica of the one from the Old Bailey. Criminals love a bit of irony.

Players and faces packed the place and everyone was drunk or using drugs. Billy, in particular, was getting right on one and there was more powder knocking around that house than a launderette. Among all the mayhem and merriment, I noticed a new kid bouncing around, someone I didn't recognise, blond haired, with a well-fed, open face. He looked like a nice-boy, rugby-player type. He was not one of us.

Suspicious, I went over and started a conversation. Was he Old Bill? He seemed very open, very confident. He was funny too. The girls were all over him.

He told me his name was Aaron Wild and he went to school with the host. As we spoke he kept looking up at the surroundings, open mouthed.

'I've never been to a party like this before,' he said. 'It's like some sort of reality TV show.'

I grinned. The kid was a good laugh. And you could see the wonder in his eyes.

Blending in with that crowd is not easy if you're an outsider, so I made a bit of effort to keep the conversation going and made him feel at home. I gave him a drink and he soon loosened up. We hit it off straight away and kept in touch from then on. Soon we were great mates.

Aaron went to Colfe's, a private school in Greenwich with fees of four grand a term, which was full of the children of criminals. Billy and his mates always sat around bemoaning the failings of state education and a lot of them paid for their children's schooling. People find it surprising, but at many of the most expensive private schools you can find the children of top bankers sitting next to the children of top bank-robbers. The two groups have more in common than they realise.

Aaron wasn't like that though. His Dad was a black cab driver and his Mum ran a beautician's. They were lovely people and worked incredibly hard to send him there.

Aaron's academic abilities saw him achieve well at school, following a carefully laid plan that led into the world of high finance. When we met he was serving an apprenticeship at one of the big firms in the city, trading equities packages, private investments, forex markets and all that sort of thing. In his downtime he continued mixing with us. We accepted him into our circle, but his goals were different. He enjoyed the lifestyle and was jealous of our cars and clothes, but was determined to get them through legitimate means. We all respected that. I liked Aaron and enjoyed his company. What he chose to do didn't matter as much as what he was like.

From my point of view, after I bought the gun from Ozcan in Dulwich, I was ready to get started. I stashed it at a friend's house, following another of Billy's lessons – never keep anything under your own roof. That way, if the door ever comes through (and one day it will, it always does) they can't find anything to incriminate you. My education was still ongoing.

At the time I had a girlfriend called Katrina, a lovely girl, from a good family. Her parents had done a bit of research and were not too keen on me but we had a nice connection and saw each other often. Unfortunately, a local chancer called Chris kept harassing her and asking her out. I shrugged it off, but he was slimy and persistent. She told him repeatedly that she was with me, but he continued. After one failed approach he asked her, 'Why are you going out with that fucking idiot anyway?'

Unluckily for Chris, my mate Nick overheard the conversation and reported back. I felt belittled and disrespected, in my own area too. Didn't he know who I was? I put feelers out and found the pub he usually drank in, then cooked up a half-arsed plan involving bundling him into the back of a van, roughing him up a bit and teaching him some manners.

On the night I waited outside the pub, in the back of the van, with my mean face on and a bat. Nick went to coax Chris out and initially he came, but when he saw the van waiting, he sensed danger and ran. He ended up phoning us a couple of hours later, in tears, pleading with me to leave him alone, saying he had misunderstood the situation and would not bother Katrina again. Friends of his made desperate phone calls to whoever they could. They didn't want Chris on the wrong side of the McAvoys.

I was happy, having got exactly the result I wanted, but when Billy heard he was incensed. He closed the kitchen door and stood over me.

'You're behaving like an idiot,' he said. 'Like a fucking thug. You should know better than that. Was there any money involved? Was there?'

'No.'

'So why are you hanging yourself out there for no reward? If you'd bashed this kid up you could have been pinched. You could even end up going away! For what, for a fucking bird? That's what mugs do. Are you a mug?'

'No.'

'Now listen, this is important.' He said these words slowly, staring straight into my eyes. 'YOU AREN'T A GANGSTER. We aren't gangsters. Gangsters are filth. We call them "thieves' ponces". All they do is steal using bullying and intimidation. There's no brains in it. What we are, are money getters. Do you understand?'

'Yes Bill.'

'Let the little prick try his luck, who gives a toss? This Katrina might be a nice girl but she's not your wife, she's not going to be around in three years' time if you get sent down. Don't ever get yourself in trouble over a woman. Do you hear me? And never trust women, neither. It happens all the time, guys are loose lipped when it comes to pillow talk, then years later their ex-girlfriend is the main witness for the prosecution. It's not worth it.'

Just to reinforce the point, a few days later we took a drive up the M4 towards Heathrow. I had an idea for a big robbery and wanted to show him the target and the basic plan. My phone rang in my pocket. It was Katrina, so I answered.

'Hello babe.'

Billy looked sideways at me with an expression of absolute horror. 'What in the name of blue fuck do you think you're doing?' he said.

'What? It's my girlfriend…'

'Give me the phone.' He snatched it off me and threw it out of the window.

'You never bring phones on work, never, ever, ever. And you definitely don't use them to make calls.'

I nodded.

'You don't help those bastards by giving them evidence. They can use a phone to cell-site you. And if the signal's picked up near a job, you're as good as gone.'

Without him I probably wouldn't have lasted five minutes. At that stage I still only had ideas I was developing, but had been out of school a few months and was eager to start.

I got a new phone sorted the following morning and Aaron was the first to call me on it. It was about 11am and I was getting ready to meet Billy for lunch.

'I can't do it,' Aaron said, as soon as I picked up.

'What are you on about, mate?'

'I can't keep going like this. It's doing my head in. Years and years of this? It's not worth it.'

'Eh, you've lost me. Are you all right?'

'This job, all the bullshit, I can't do it.'

He had been moaning about work for a while, which I had written off as needless whining.

'What do you mean? Are you going to quit?'

'I already have.'

Aaron had got within a few weeks of the end of his apprenticeship, but our world and way of life, with all its excitement and fast rewards got inside his head. He wanted what we had. The game had sucked him in, too.

Later I found out the full story. He had been on his way to work that morning on a typically crowded tube train. Aaron spent the whole 30-minute journey pressed against an Australian's armpit, with an enormous African sandwiching him from behind. He had disembarked feeling angry and sick, only to plod up to the escalators in a funereal procession of silent, slate-faced office drones. When he finally emerged from the station on to the street, with suits hurrying this way and that, fighting for every second, every inch of space, he paused, breathed in and had a moment.

It struck him, hard. No one looked happy. Words lit up in his head like a neon sign.

I can't live like this.

Aaron took his tie off, headed straight in to the boss's office and told him he was leaving. Then he bought a beer, sat in a nearby park and laughed at all the superficiality. As he observed the suits and the tramps and the mums with buggies buzzing here and there, he had a chat with himself. He knew it. He had decided. Unlike all of them, he would exist outside the system from then on, *the fucking system*.

He still had the same goal – to make a lot of money – but he couldn't accept the means he was supposed to use to get it. He would have to be an innovator, earn from unconventional sources, as we did. From that day on, Aaron became one of us.

I spoke to a friend called Paul who left school with nothing like me. He was known as a loose cannon, always in fights and situations, which I thought would be useful. I knew I would need someone headstrong, so asked him if he fancied starting work. His Dad had been involved in a few bits and pieces in the past. He had been in and out of prison. Paul agreed straight away.

Pretty quickly Aaron used his own contacts to get involved in the drugs trade, shifting decent-sized packets of gear in no time. Meanwhile Paul and I started going out in the day, driving around, following security vans. I would map their routes, note delivery times and could not believe how easy it seemed.

All the big security firms used the same vans with the same crews on the same days, making the same trips. After a few weeks of watching them, I got to know the routines of the staff and even what they looked like – *at ten past ten the one with the moustache will handcuff the case to his arm and walk into the bank.* I even developed a sense of how much money they were carrying at different points on the route.

At the end of each day I would pick one van and follow it back to base, then go home and catch a bit of sleep. At three in the morning I would get up and drive back to the security depot and sit outside with a video camera, filming the vans coming in and out.

In this way I got to know all the depots around the M25 motorway. One in Croydon, one at Swanley Roundabout, one in Tunbridge Wells, one at Dartford, I cased every single one of them. My personal favourite was Tunbridge Wells. It was a sitting duck for surveillance. You could get up at the back, on to a little hill where there was a small wood. You could set up under the trees knowing you were shielded from security cameras. I would sit there for hours, with binoculars under a khaki net, like I was on a military operation. I had such plans for that place, but never got to see them through. While I was inside it got taken for £53m.

The vans would leave at 5.30am and I learned where they went for their first drop on different days. On a Monday it would be Abbey National, Tuesday they would head to Barclays, Wednesday morning was NatWest. I thought of those pre-dawn jobs as my golden ticket. A normal cash machine would need £125,000 to fill it up and each of those vehicles would be carrying at least that. Hit a couple in a month and you can lie low for a while.

Once a target was identified, my focus shifted to the best possible place to smack it. There were different things to look out for, fewer CCTV cameras, less police activity. Of absolute importance were escape routes.

Ideally you wanted an ambush point away from built-up areas, or if not, somewhere with lots of alleys, so you could get out of one car and into another quickly and easily. A little foible of mine was to find one next to a flyover. I always liked that. You can do the job, run over the bridge and have a car waiting on the other side. You would be in a completely different postcode. You would be away.

Just before my first independent job and still not long out of school, I found myself in a bar in Beckenham called BlueEye, owned by Mehmet Arif. As usual it was full of London criminals. Bottles of champagne were being sent to the table and there was enough coke in the place to fill a garage. We were having a ball.

There is a certain kind of woman attracted to that crowd, well dressed, great looking, but vain and shallow. That night there were more than a few of them in BlueEye. Lots of gorgeous, sexily dressed dolly-birds in their early 20s, out of their heads and throwing themselves at anyone they thought was a player. We had the time of our lives. How many 16- or 17-year-olds have that kind of experience?

Aaron was already making a few quid by then and told us how it was going. He was mostly selling shipments of cannabis that came in from Holland, but was looking to diversify his interests in the near future. He had some very interesting ideas.

'It's our time now,' I said to Paul, as we stumbled out of the bar, sniffing and grinding our teeth at five in the morning. 'Our time now mate.'

My approach was meticulous and I obsessed over details. Someone could say, 'Have you got anything lined up?' casually, in conversation and I could tell them straight off, how and where the job would be done, how the getaway would work and what the likely score was. I never even had to write anything down.

I may not have got GCSEs, but within the criminal fraternity I became known as 'Brains'. Men two or three times my age could not believe what I put together so young. 'He's hot,' they would say. 'He's real good stuff.'

In my mind I made a resolution to become the best. I wouldn't just be an armed robber. I would be *the* armed robber. If I achieved all the ambitions that formed in my mind, my accomplishments would outshine those of Billy and even Uncle Micky. John McAvoy would be a name known by the world.

4

Busy, Busy, Busy

WHEN Uncle Micky got out on parole in 2000 he came over to Mum's, looking well for a man who had just served 17 years.

'I've been hearing things about you, John,' he said, over a cup of tea. 'Sounds like you know what you're doing.'

'Thanks Micky,' I replied. 'Starting as I mean to go on. What are your plans now?'

'I'll get off abroad I think, somewhere sunny. This country's had enough of my time.'

By then I was already flying high and the game was treating me well. Job followed job. It's amazing how quickly one thing can lead to another.

Paul and I did well for ourselves for the first year and a half and our success brought added motivation, like a snowball effect.

My goal was to be a millionaire by 21, the same as Billy. It never happened. Our golden spell only lasted until a few months before my 18th birthday.

In early summer 2001 I found myself questioned regarding six counts of armed robbery I was alleged to have committed with Billy. According to the law we were a proper father-and-son crimewave. They also charged me with three others they said I did on my own. That's what a name can do for you in that world. The label 'McAvoy' went before me like a banner. At 17 and while my former schoolmates were studying or starting work, I was up for nine counts of armed robbery.

The chain of events that led to my arrest had more to do with Billy than me and began when he and a close associate of his called Kevin Barnes, along with several others, were collared for a series of alleged heists around Kent and Sussex. Barnes was eventually found not guilty, but Billy's case stuck. Some of the stories were pretty mental. Lorries cut open on motorways, hand grenades, all kinds of crazy stuff. As security firms got used to robbers' methods, it created a need to come up with something new. The element of surprise is crucial.

More than any of that, anything you did on a job had to be well judged. It was important not to over-scare people. You needed to make them fearful to ensure co-operation, but if you take it too far they freeze and you get nothing out of them. Your actions and manner have to be pitched at just the right level, aggressive, menacing, believable, but not Tarantino-style psychotic.

Unluckily for us all, Billy's last job, an attempted smack on a Post Office lorry containing £2m, went wrong. He managed to cut it open but it got pushed down into a ditch during the hit, making removal of the loot problematic. In panic one of the guards threw £30,000 out in £5 notes, so Billy and his crew cut their losses, took the bag and scarpered.

There was no real comeback to begin with but problems arose about a week later when one of the suspects went out *kiting* (buying goods with a fake cheque guarantee card). She ended up getting pinched for it. In the police station the custody sergeant went through her purse and found £500 in fivers. Realising that it was brand new money he ran a check and found the serial numbers of the notes were sequential. That triggered an investigation and within half an hour they sussed the money had come from the botched robbery in Kent.

A massive operation was quickly put into place by Kent Serious Crime Squad. They raided Kevin's house and searched a farmhouse he was alleged to have been sighted at, where they found five handguns and a pump action 12-gauge shotgun, along with £60,000 in cash. Kevin was arrested that day on the M25 courtesy of a tracking device that had been attached to his car. While they apprehended him, a heated discussion between Kent SCS and the London Flying Squad took place regarding who would lead the arrest. In the end Kent hung on to it, claiming they had weightier evidence.

Four other arrests were made within hours and it was all over the news. Things did not look promising. I spoke to Billy that night on the phone.

'You've got to go, Billy,' I said. 'Just leave, get out of the country. Everyone's getting nicked. Doors are being kicked in all over the place.'

'Nah, it'll be fine,' he said.

'At least sort yourself a new car. Don't drive around in yours.'

'It's okay, John,' he kept saying. 'It's okay.' He didn't sound right to me.

Billy had holed himself up in the Clarendon Hotel in Blackheath, under an assumed identity. I went up there the next morning to visit him and he was completely off his head, boozing and snorting tons of cocaine. He didn't have a clue what he was doing.

'Mate, look at you, you're fucked,' I said.

'It's fine John, its fine,' he replied. 'I haven't been connected to this case. No one has grassed me. It'll all blow over.'

'But they're on you!'

'Nah…' He wasn't dealing with reality, at all.

At the time he was sleeping with a girl called Kelly who was in the hotel with him. I tried to make them both see sense. She needed to disappear and he needed to go abroad, but he would not have it. His attitude was off-hand and blasé.

After I gave up and left, he got in his Range Rover with Kelly and drove along the Old Kent Road, looking for somewhere to have lunch. Fate conspired and that very day the Serious Crime Squad had come to the area to interview Kevin's family in Bermondsey.

As Billy pootled along weighing up the culinary choices on offer, the cops ended up driving right behind him, recognised the car, put his number plate through the system and that was it. They could not believe their luck.

As if he didn't have a care in the world, while under suspicion for armed robberies several of his associates had already been nicked for, Billy was driving his own car around London in broad daylight. He virtually bumped into the team investigating his case and had literally served himself up on a plate. All the booze and gear had wrecked his judgement.

When police checked the hotel register they discovered the false name, which added to Billy's problems. Some expensive emergency tools known as the 'jaws of life', commonly used by fire and ambulance services to extract survivors from car accidents, had been bought using that name earlier in the year. The very same tools had been found, discarded, near the lorry that had been run into the ditch. Billy, quite simply, was screwed.

The next day Mum phoned, saying police had been around to her place and kicked the door in, demanding to know where I was. Arrests were ongoing. A number of our crowd were nabbed. A friend of mine suggested I buy myself a plane ticket to Australia.

'They can't have anything on me,' I told him. It wasn't possible. I had only been in the game a year and was not even known to the police as far as I was aware.

Regardless, Billy's demise bothered me. He had been a big part of my life for such a long time and I still thought the world of him. In a funny way I felt I owed it to him to carry on, to get one over on the bastards.

Strangely enough, the next job I had planned was also going to be a Post Office van, on a delivery to the main sorting office in Dartford. Paul and I discussed it and agreed there was no point pulling out. We needed funds if we were to disappear for a while and did not see how we could be implicated in the Kent SCS case.

'Screw it,' we said, over a beer. 'Keep rolling!'

Unknown to us, it was not Kent we needed to worry about. Billy's arrest had triggered a huge surveillance operation on my activities by the London Flying Squad who were still keen to make arrests. My links to Billy and Uncle Micky had put my name firmly on their radar and it transpired later, that on one job, a witness described Billy talking to an accomplice 'as if they were father and son'. At 17 I became the Sweeney's number one target.

They pinpointed my address and monitored my movements, while I remained blissfully unaware and carried on as normal. Paul and I drove to Dartford to case the job and decided to do it. All the while, they were watching. I thought if I made a few quid in one hit I could leave the country, maybe head out to Marbella and visit Uncle Micky.

We decided to smack the van on a Wednesday morning early in June, which turned out to be a lovely day, bright and hot. We had parked our getaway vehicle there the night before, down a back alley and had crash helmets and uniforms in the primary car, so we would look like guards when we hit them. It was a camouflage-through-confusion approach. Witnesses would not know who was security and who was a robber.

I had running shorts and a vest on under my clothes too, with a £20 note in my sock, a little back-up plan I had come up with myself. To complete the package, there was a .38 revolver on the back seat.

The Flying Squad had understood from observing us that we were planning something and were covering a variety of possibilities. Among them was a stretch of dual carriageway we intended to use for part of the journey. On that particular day the DVLA (Driver and Vehicle Licensing Agency) were there conducting random roadside stops, ensuring car registrations and paperwork were in order. We were in a brand new Toyota Avensis, a stolen car, of course, with false plates.

As we drove toward the zone where the DVLA were conducting their checks, an official holding up a clipboard saw us approach. Police stood dotted behind him. He put his whistle to his mouth and held up his hand, as a signal to halt. Coldness came over me, the excitement of the imminent robbery replaced by concern.

'I'm not fucking stopping,' I said to Paul.

Split-seconds ticked by. We got nearer. The official blew his whistle again, louder and more insistent, causing the police behind him to turn and look.

'Shall I let some shots off out the window?' Paul asked. 'Just to put the shits up 'em?'

He meant it, too, the maniac.

'Fuck that, mate!' I said. The situation could still come to nothing. The last thing we needed was a stray bullet in someone's brain.

I began to manoeuvre the Toyota towards the demarcated area so as not to arouse suspicion until the last second. Just as it appeared we were going to comply with their request and stop, I threw the car into first and slammed my foot down. Tyres squealed, cones flew all over the place and we screamed past the checkpoint.

A police motorbike waited right at the end, positioned there to pursue anyone who took off. If I had stayed on the same course I would have ploughed through him, but fortunately kept a cool head. When you start hurting or killing coppers, you know you are in for a hell of a time. Instinctive reactions meant I missed him by a couple of feet and we tore off, down the road, zig-zagging through the traffic.

My mind raced. We needed somewhere to ditch the Toyota and escape. Before long they would send a helicopter up and when it got to that stage we were finished.

Half a mile on from the checkpoint we came to a roundabout, so I flew around it and started hammering back down the A-road in the opposite direction from where we had just come. A glance in the rear-view mirror confirmed what I feared.

The motorbike was right up my arse. I couldn't shake him off. We had to get off that dual carriageway.

Within seconds I came to a turning for a little slip road, which I took as late as possible, jumping on the brakes and making the tyres screech again. The outrider was wise to it and kept on our tail. It led us off into a quiet residential area and I found myself blasting around little back streets penned in by terraced houses, taking random, sharp turns left and right. I managed to put a bit of distance between us and the bike. Not enough to be comfortable though.

'Listen Paul,' I said. 'It's just a traffic cop. He won't even be armed. He's gonna come after me because I'm the driver. I'm gonna pull over. You run one way, I'll run the other. We've got a decent chance. I'll call you tonight.'

'If the worst happens we could be charged with a traffic incident,' I thought, still having no idea that the Flying Squad were involved.

I stopped the car at the end of a little side road and Paul immediately jumped out of the passenger door and sprinted off. I did the same on my side, hopped over about 12 garden fences and found myself in a field. As I ran I began pulling my clothes off, stripping down to my vest and shorts, throwing everything into a stream that trickled along by the side of the grass. I was miles away from home but as far as anyone asking questions would be concerned, I was just out for a run in the countryside. There's no law against that is there?

Hot and heavy-legged, getting more and more out of breath, I lumbered along and ended up re-entering civilisation near Sidcup. I must have run five or six miles, which for me at the time was a hell of a distance. Right on the edge of the town I found a phone box opposite a café and remembered that one of Billy's mates, a guy called Keith, owned a car hire firm in the area. I thought I would stop, make a couple of calls and sort a plan to get home.

I bought a drink from the café to get change, went over to the phone box and dialled the number. 'Come on, pick up,' I urged, listening impatiently to the ringer, until a sudden roar of engines drew my attention from outside. From the corner of my eye I became aware that two cars had skidded to a standstill on the road by the payphone.

I swivelled to see what was happening and dropped the receiver in shock. It bounced around on its cord. A heavy-set, bald guy in an open neck shirt was running at me, red-faced, pointing a gun, a posse of other men following closely behind.

Flashes of fear jolted my body. In the milliseconds in which the brain works in those moments, I still hadn't twigged the reality and thought he was someone from the game, someone with a grudge who wanted me gone.

'I'm dead,' I thought to myself. 'He's gonna iron me out.'

Before I had time to react seven of them surrounded the phone box.

'Put your hands up!' the bald man screamed, as they dragged me out and threw me on the ground.

'He's not armed!' one of them cried.

At that point I understood and relief flooded my system like a drug. It wasn't a crew of assassins. It was just the police.

5

Category A

THE bald man handcuffed me and pulled me up to my feet. Another stepped in front and looked straight in my eyes, nose-to-nose, giving it all the macho bad-cop posturing he could muster. He had black curly hair and wore a lumberjack shirt over his bullet-proof vest. His breath smelled of Trebor Extra Strong Mints.

'Where are the guns John?' he asked, matter-of-factly.

'I don't know what you're talking about.'

His voice remained even and confident. 'Listen you little cunt. You've had a good run, had a decent score, but now you're fucked. We know all about you and who you are. We know all about your stepdad and Kevin Barnes, so don't mess me about, just tell us where the guns are and admit to what you've done.'

I grinned. 'Oh please fuck off!'

He sighed, with measured melodrama. 'So what have you been up to today then?'

'I'm just out getting fit, doing a bit of jogging.'

He pursed his lips, looked up and then back down. 'Okay,' he said. 'Have it your way.'

They threw me in one of the cars and we hurtled over to Orpington police station, where they dragged me out and shoved me through the doors. The custody sergeant checked me in and asked if I wanted to call my solicitor.

'Yeah.'

'Who is it, Milner?'

I nodded. They didn't even need to ask. Henry Milner had represented Billy and several of my other relatives, a trusted man within our world and a funny, quirky guy. I guess he had to be to defend the sort of cases he worked on.

He had an old-fashioned BBC accent and an upright manner, but really knew the law and would do whatever was best for his clients. He once told me, 'It is not for the lawyer to decide a case on his opinion. My opinion is not the issue. A court case is a contest and I do not sit in moral judgement of my clients. I deal in legal justice, not moral justice.'

Whether you agreed with him or not, the man talked a lot of sense. After the phonecall they dragged me into an interview room where the interrogating officer, the macho idiot from my arrest, introduced himself as DCI Currie.

'Name?'

Silence.

'Name?'

I looked down at my lap.

'Name?'

He gave up after that and they ushered me back to my cell. On the way a smarmy little bobby got in my ear.

'You're doing well then John,' he said. 'Taking over the family business I see. Tell your uncle I said hello won't you? He's a right character isn't he, old Micky? He's got a real creative side.'

A couple of years before Uncle Micky had tried to organise an escape from prison by helicopter. He had a dry run which went okay, but on the day was ratted out by someone on the inside and it all fell through. Even then, nearly 20 years after Brinks-Mat, he was still on the minds of Old Bill. The bobby wanted a reaction from me, so I blanked him and looked straight ahead.

Late that afternoon Henry sent a young barrister called Sutherland down and we went through as many of the details as I knew, without appreciating what the police had up their sleeve.

'How fucked am I?' I asked him.

'If they don't find any guns, the worst they can do you for is nicking the car.'

'All right.' I was happy with that.

'Don't tell them anything,' he said. 'Don't wind them up, there's no point, but don't say a word.' He was called out for a moment and when he returned looked a little less sure of himself, which worried me. 'They want to interview you again,' he said.

I was taken back to the interview room where Currie waited with his arms folded, like a man who had just ordered the bill at a restaurant.

'We've had a turn-up,' he said when I sat down. I could tell by the sound of his voice he was enjoying himself. 'It's all right, you don't need to reply John. I know how much of an emotional strain it is for you to speak. The last thing we want to do is upset you. So for now, you can just listen. Are you listening?'

I looked down at the floor.

'Here's the thing. About two miles from the checkpoint you jumped, literally only about 20 metres from the car you abandoned, an old man was watering his rosebushes. Nice old fella. Now you're not going to believe this, but do you know what he found John? He was most surprised.'

I shook my head despite knowing what was coming.

'He found a .38 revolver, in his flowerbed, imagine that!'

I winced inwardly but hid it, looking down at the table.

'So where does that leave us? Are you going to admit the gun is yours? Or have we got to drag this pantomime out any further?'

I remained expressionless. Currie shook his head theatrically, tutted and sent me back to my cell. I still thought everything would blow over, until that evening a screw came to my door and told me I had a legal call. My concern only deepened after I spoke to Milner.

'I'm sorry I can't be there in person John,' he said, 'but I thought I should let you know that Special Branch are coming to see you.'

'Eh? Special Branch? They deal with terrorism don't they? Why?'

'It seems you were seen, in your BMW, casing a security depot in Ainsford a few months ago. The witness thought it looked suspicious and wrote the number plate down. Don't say anything please John, but a week later a gang of robbers front and backed a lorry carrying about £8m in that location. They were armed with shotguns and one of them, get this, one of them ran up to the front windscreen and held up a landmine. He shouted to the driver what he was doing, then threw it under the wheel.

'The police take that sort of thing very seriously, John. Landmines are weapons of war. Anyway, in the meantime a van turned up with a spike mounted on it and started ramming the lorry, trying to get the back doors open. Unfortunately for them, it didn't work. The spike came off the bracket and ended up useless. The robbers had to leave with nothing. There was a canal nearby and they made their escape on speedboats. It was a really well planned operation, very high level stuff and because your car was seen there, you have been implicated. The police have discussed it and believe you and Billy led the job.'

'Right,' I said.

'Forewarned is forearmed John. Sutherland will be back in the morning.'

The next morning, when Sutherland came back, he looked a touch stressed.

'They want to interview you about other crimes,' he said. 'Now don't say anything out loud.'

He held out a piece of paper with a list of robberies on it. 'This is called a police disclosure. These are all the things they think you've been a part of.'

I looked through the list.

'Hmm...' I said. Sutherland's face dropped.

'Okay. I see. Don't say anything other than your name and no comment.'

Before long I was taken back to the interview room to spend more quality time with Currie.

'So it's quite an impressive-looking CV we've got here John,' he said. 'Let's pick out a few highlights shall we? There was an attack on a Securicor van where the guard was threatened but wouldn't throw the money out. As a result shots were fired in the high street at midday. That's a nice one isn't it? You're turning our country into a battle-zone, aren't you John?'

'No comment,' I replied. He made a big show of perusing the list with wide eyes.

'It seems the biggest earner was a raid outside an Abbey National cash machine at night time, when £150,000 was nicked. You know altogether we're looking at half a million pounds' worth of armed robberies here?'

'No comment.'

He turned to Sutherland. 'How old is he?'

'He was born in February 1983.'

'Seventeen!' Currie cried. 'Seventeen and he's got this sort of form! I've never seen anything like it.' My feeling that we were in trouble grew. Old Bill seemed too confident.

'Do you know what's funny about all this, John?'

'No comment.'

'If you were out the other morning getting fit, as you said and you know, fair play, you had your gym kit on, we all saw that. Why is it that you've been in this police station for three days and you've never once protested your innocence?'

'No comment.'

'If you were an innocent man, you'd be screaming the walls down at the injustice of being kept here. But I'm not seeing that. You're only a kid but you've stayed cool. You've avoided all our questions. You've given us as little as possible, it's textbook, John, absolute textbook. You're not behaving like an innocent youngster, you're behaving like someone who knows the ropes and will be fabricating evidence to get an acquittal. That's what it looks like to me.'

I met his eye for a second. There was victory in it.

'No comment.'

He was right though, that was exactly the strategy, to wait for all their evidence, or more specifically the holes in it and then build a case around that. For then, it was enough that they believed there was a strong case against me. They took me out and I soon found myself on the back seat of another car, on my way to Bromley Magistrates' Court.

The magistrates took no time in remanding me to Feltham young offenders' institution, in west London, where the policeman had told me all those years earlier, on Mum's doorstep, that I would end up. Initially I was placed on the reception wing, with a bunch of nervous, sinewy little guttersnipes. It was like being back at school.

To begin with I thought I might stay there until my case went to trial, but on my second day some officers arrived and said I would have to go to the segregation unit, while they waited for information on my future. It was bleak down there and lonely. I sat on my own all day until about six in the evening, when the door opened up. A tall, blond man introduced himself as the governor.

'John McAvoy,' he said simply. 'You've been made category A.'

There are four classifications of inmate in the British prison system, beginning with D which refers to those who are considered of no risk and can be kept in open prisons then heading upwards from there. My family connections, access to firearms and the incredible list of crimes they were preparing to charge me with, meant that I was given the highest classification, reserved for those whose escape would be highly dangerous to the public or national security. It was very unusual for someone of my age, on their first offence to be inducted into the prison system like this, but that was how it worked as a McAvoy, straight in at the top.

The problem was that the only category A prisons were in the adult system, but people under the age of 21 were not supposed to be housed in adult prisons. With my case they were therefore faced with an anomaly and at just 17 years old, after two short days in Feltham, I was transferred to HMP Woodhill, near Milton Keynes, a maximum security prison that had a young offenders' wing attached to it. It was serious place. The so-called 'most violent inmate in Britain', Charles Bronson, was a resident, among others. They hoped the administrators there could somehow sort through the muddle.

I arrived in my yellow and green cat A jumpsuit and walked on to the spur. The fact that I wore that marked me out to begin with and I got a lot of looks. I had to be in for something serious and was probably not a guy to be trifled with. Unsure of what to do with me, in the first instance the staff again placed me in the block, the segregation unit usually reserved for those who had committed a contravention of prison rules.

I had a cardboard desk, a cardboard chair and the bed was a little bit of concrete on the floor. Once a day they took me outside to a small, caged area where I was allowed to walk around in circles, for exercise. Category A, adult institution and in the block, welcome to the prison system, John McAvoy!

At Woodhill they operated a seven-stage model which was claimed to be for rehabilitation but in reality was designed to try and break you. You go in at stage one with no privileges at all. You cannot wear your own clothes, your cell is bare and it's a really bleak existence. If they think you are showing progress and your behaviour is improving they will move you to stage two. You could be at stage two for a year, maybe allowed your own trainers to wear and eventually moved up to stage three. Again you could be at stage three for ages, be given a couple of minor perks, have one bad day, say the wrong thing to one of the screws and be bumped all the way back down to stage one. You would lose everything and have to start all over again. The guys that go through the whole process and come out at the end of stage seven are cabbages. All the repetition and monotony fries their brains.

After a week of complete solitude in the block, the governor came down to see me.

'Look John,' he said. He seemed all right. 'This is a very unique set of circumstances and we can't put you into the wider prison population with adults.'

'Can you star me up?' I asked.

That meant officially re-categorising me as an adult prisoner because I was considered such a risk. I hadn't presented any problems in prison yet, but I thought if it would get me out of segregation, it was worth it.

'We can't do it,' he said. 'You've done nothing to warrant that. How about if we put you on the young offenders' wing, but as a category A prisoner? How would that be? Are you going to start playing up?'

'No.'

'You won't use your reputation to start bullying people and throwing your weight around?'

'No.'

'Okay. We can work on trust.'

So they took me down to the young offenders' section in my yellow and green cat A suit, which drew admiring attention immediately. In my first day there I must have been asked about 20 times what I had done. There was only one other inmate on the wing in the same category and he was a murderer.

'You must be proper serious, bruv!' kids were saying, shaking my hand, touching fists with me. It probably made life a little easier. Sometimes, when I had legal visits from Sutherland or Milner, I would have to go over into the adult wing to use the meeting room. Whenever I was taken through there everyone was eager to speak to me too.

'Are you Micky McAvoy's nephew?' they'd say. 'He's a top man, Micky. If you have any problems just let me know.'

Within the first week I began receiving special treatment. Screws came over from the adult wing to visit me on the young offenders' side, bringing extra newspapers, books, food and other privileges. It was being organised by some of the most influential inmates in the jail.

My name might have helped create my predicament, but had its advantages too.

The scenario was similar when I went to the prison gym. Because of my status I could not exercise with the other juveniles and had to go in a small group with the category A guys. I would be in there with all these hardened jailbirds, men who had committed very serious offences and done loads of time. They saw the way I refused to kowtow to the screws and liked it. There was no way I would let myself be bullied.

'You're game aren't ya?' they would say.

All the respect bolstered my ego and as I grew used to the internal dynamics of prison life, I used it in my psychological battle with the staff. I took no shit off them and made it very clear there was nothing they could do to intimidate me. I was not bothered about visits, like most prisoners, so I did not need to stay in the area. It was important they had nothing over me. For a lot of inmates, the screws used that as a bartering tool.

'Look, if you keep playing up, we'll move you up north and no one will come to visit you anymore.'

'You can send me anywhere you like in the country,' I would tell them. 'I don't give a toss.'

Uncle Micky had told me how he coped with his time inside by reminding himself that it wasn't his life. 'It was just an interval,' he used to say. He would read a broadsheet newspaper every day, front to back, to keep up to date with world affairs. He would involve himself with as little prison routine as possible. It's important to make your own decisions.

I took that attitude on board and knew I was mentally strong enough to get through whatever sentence they gave me. In my head, they had kidnapped me. I would get up every morning and say, 'I am not here out of choice.' It was like a mantra. 'They choose to come here and I don't. This is their life, not mine.' I refused to become institutionalised, to be one of those people where prison becomes their whole existence as a human. There was still so much I wanted to do.

As a result of that way of thinking, I would not interact with prison officers on any level besides 'I want to go to the gym' or 'I want to use the phone'. I would never make small talk with them. If they tried, I ignored them. One or two tried to chat about my case.

'I'm innocent,' I would say and walk away.

Plans began forming in my mind. I was not 100 per cent convinced that armed robbery was the right game to stay in. It can be very lucrative but so risky. Once the authorities know you are a player, they will always keep tabs on you. Maybe Aaron had the right idea? I thought perhaps as soon as they let me out, whether that be in two, five, ten years, whenever, I would break parole, skip the country and make a fresh start in a new business. But before any of that, one thing loomed large in my future. Soon I would have to face the judge.

6

A Shit and a Shave!

MY first ever case was due to be heard in courtroom number one at the Old Bailey. That's a bit like being a tennis player and having your first professional match on Wimbledon's Centre Court. They took me up there in handcuffs in the back of a van, surrounded by screws, as if I was some sort of serial killer. Once there I was placed in a maximum security cell in the basement, beneath the courtroom. None of it seemed real, as if I was acting in a costume drama. The building looked so distinguished, all oak panels and marble, while everyone exuded purpose and seriousness.

My accomplice Paul pleaded guilty to all offences and they asked him to turn Queen's Evidence against me, meaning they made him an offer of a reduced sentence and a favourable location for his time, in return for ratting me out. Fortunately for me and for him, long term, he told them where to stick their offer.

We were surprised to discover that the police evidence was quite circumstantial and weak, centring around one of Paul's fingerprints found on the rear-view mirror of a Range Rover that had been used for one of the jobs. There was a crash helmet found in Paul's house too, that they said looked similar to a crash helmet used for one of the more extreme robberies. If the police had got their way and convinced Paul to implicate me in everything they wanted, I would likely have been convicted of all nine counts. It would have been the end of me for a very long time.

Milner was upbeat when he heard about the offer and Paul's response.

'It sounds rather like they're desperate,' he said. 'Their case must be very poor to depend on that sort of manoeuvre.'

Before long news came back that they had offered a plea bargain. Milner met with the prosecution who accepted that without Paul's testimony there was a 50/50 chance the whole case would crumble, meaning I would be free. At that point I had no previous convictions and although the police suspected my involvement in Billy's alleged activities, they could not prove it.

As a way of salvaging something, they suggested I plead guilty to conspiracy to rob only for the day when they were watching me. If I did that, they would drop all other charges. The pendulum had swung back in my direction and I waited with a strange, steely calmness.

When the time came for the trial they opened my cell door, put a guard on each arm and walked me up. We ascended a very claustrophobic, narrow stairway and when we reached the top, one of the guards reached up and rapped on the door. As it was opened from the inside by the clerk I heard the chatter of the public gallery and squinted up into the lights. It was how I imagine it must be for an actor to wait in the wings then walk on stage.

'Here we go,' I thought. 'Show time!'

As I climbed the last few steep steps, I emerged, head first, straight into the dock, to be confronted by all my scowling accusers and the po-faced judge and barristers in their robes and wigs. A sense of absurdity took hold and for a moment I felt like laughing, but a glance up at my mother and the anguish on her features changed my mood. I was 18 by then. I had my birthday at Woodhill and was caught up in a surreal theatre performance that could have seen me behind bars until middle age.

We had a female judge called Goddard, a petite, church-fete-looking lady with pearl earrings. She peered at us imperiously over her glasses. Paul entered his guilty plea and was given nine years.

The judge accepted news of my plea bargain with stoicism and gave me a total of nine years too, divided into two sentences. There was one of five and one of four, but due to run concurrently, which meant full-term was actually five. It's one of those bits of legal nonsense that makes no sense to outsiders. It suited me though.

By that point I had already served a year and a half and as she spoke I worked things out in my head. On a five-year sentence the most I would do would be three, meaning I only had another 18 months, maybe a year if I was lucky, while the list of serious crimes I had been accused of was brushed under the carpet. It was a real result.

The police sat in a line beside the dock looking sheepish. Currie was there. There was no victory on his face then. I turned to face them all, grinning broadly, looking from one to the other.

'It's nothing boys,' I said, enjoying my moment, 'just a shit and a shave!'

Most of them looked away. Currie tried to stare me down. My prison officers escorted me back to the cells, crying with laughter.

'I can't believe you said that to them!' one remarked. 'Did you see their faces? That's the funniest thing I've ever seen!'

Buoyed by my *coup de grace*, the journey back to Woodhill was a happy one. I had survived my trip to the Old Bailey and come off better than my accomplice who had pleaded guilty. Better even than that, I had given the police almost nothing and still came out on top.

After about a month back on the wing, the governor came to see me again.

'Bearing in mind the sentence you've been given we can't justify keeping you category A anymore,' he said.

'Okay.'

'You're going to be downgraded and go to a regular young offenders' institution for the rest of your time.'

I shrugged. In truth I wasn't bothered. One cell is much the same as another.

'Aylesbury,' he said. 'It's a high security young offenders' prison.'

And that was it, the next day I was gone, not realising what I headed towards. The journey was not long, only about 45 minutes in the back of the van as it sheeted with rain outside. We pulled up in a courtyard in front of an austere, red-brick building with a high, crimson, steel door, set in an archway more than two stories high. First impressions were that Aylesbury nick was an imposing place.

7

My Time, My Way

THE officers from Woodhill handed me over while the new screws tried to assert their authority.

'Come with us McAvoy,' one said, grabbing my arm. 'We'll show you the ropes.' At Woodhill, they called me John.

They took me through reception and checked me in. The prison itself was laid out around a quadrangle that doubled up as the exercise yard with some basic outdoor gym equipment. There were four rectangular buildings knocked up from the same brick as the front entrance along each side.

'We have some right characters in here,' the screw said. 'Some of the most serious young offenders in the country, you'll soon find out McAvoy, some of the things these toe-rags have done are absolutely appalling.'

It was unclear if he was trying to warn me or intimidate me, but I didn't give him the satisfaction of a reaction. They led me through and showed me my cell.

I soon discovered the officer was right. By and large, the other inmates in that place were low-end scumbags. There were 16- and 17-year-olds in there, starting 20-year sentences for murder, but they were like kids, just petulant children. They didn't know how to behave and I used to feel embarrassed to be around them. They carried on like toddlers, whining, shouting and threatening, mouthing off left, right and centre. They had no control over themselves and I didn't want to listen to their nonsense.

Even the crimes they had committed were ridiculous. One had murdered his sister. Another had killed someone over a £20 bag of weed.

Dickheads and lowlifes. I refused to waste my time with them and kept my own counsel. I didn't bother them and they didn't bother me.

I had been there for a few days, just settling myself in, figuring out the best way to get through my remaining time, when the screws came bursting through my door in the morning.

'Where's all your kit McAvoy?' one shouted.

'What kit?'

'Where's your prison issue shoes and tracksuit?'

'It's all there,' I said, pointing to the pile of bright yellow clothing next to my bed.

They pulled out a big HMP plastic bin liner.

'Take off the clothes you've got on,' they said.

'Bollocks.'

After a few minutes of arguing, the senior officer turned up.

'Look John,' he said. 'We need you to wear the special kit. As you were formerly a category A prisoner in an adult institution you're regarded as high risk of escape.'

'I'm not putting it on. I'll look like an idiot.'

He sighed. 'If you won't comply we'll do you for refusing a lawful order and sling you in the block.'

'Go on then.'

As far as I was concerned, a bit of segregation would be a relief. I could get away from the demented chatter of all the little herberts on the wing.

'Okay then,' he said. 'You're placed under adjudication.'

I let them take me down to the segregation unit and the next morning the SO brought the governor to see me. He had a thin, miserable, civil-servant's face.

'This is McAvoy, J., 5859,' the SO said. 'He's been placed in adjudication for refusing a lawful order as a result of his escape classification.'

The governor looked me up and down.

'So what are you refusing?' he asked.

I wouldn't answer.

'He's refusing to take his clothes off and put the kit on,' the SO said.

The governor nodded and turned back to me.

'Is this true?'

'Yes.'

'Yes, *sir*,' the SO chided. I tutted at him.

'Why did you refuse?' asked the governor.

'Listen, you're taking the piss. I've got a year and a half left, if that. There are guys in here doing 20 years and you've classified me as high escape risk. It's a joke.'

'That's not the issue here. The issue is you've refused that order.'

'I don't care.'

'So are you going to continue to refuse this order?'

'Yes I am.'

The governor sighed. 'Okay then,' he said. 'Put him back in seg.'

I remained in segregation for a couple of days before the SO came to see me again.

'OK McAvoy,' he recited, 'your case has been through adjudication and we've decided that you've lost the right to association for seven days. We'll take you back to the wing now.'

'Whatever,' I smiled.

After they returned me to my cell he resumed speaking, a little cautiously. 'By the way, you've been allotted work.'

I started laughing.

'You're now the wing cleaner.'

I literally doubled over at the hilarity of it. I couldn't believe what I was hearing.

'Do you honestly think I'm going to clean your shit up every day? Get fucked.'

You could almost see the clockwork going inside his head. Eventually he coughed the words out.

'So are you refusing a lawful order?'

'Yes.'

'In that case I'll have to take you to the block.'

'Brilliant!'

They marched me back downstairs while I dabbed tears from my eyes. Within minutes the governor arrived again.

'I hear you're refusing to work now.'

'Yes I am.'

'You're not being very co-operative, are you?'

'No.'

'Is there anything you are prepared to do?'

I paused for effect. 'I tell you what I am going to do. I am going to refuse every single order and every request to work, every single day I am in this place. Is that clear enough for you?'

'Well then you're going to get nicked every day.'

'Fine. I don't care. I'm doing a fixed sentence. I'll be out in a year and a bit. Keep me down here. It doesn't bother me.'

He turned to the SO. 'Let's change his loss of association to seven days confined to cell,' he said. 'Maybe that will change his mind.'

I spent the next seven days completely alone. I slept, had my meals and spent all my waking hours in my tiny cell. I read newspapers every day, sometimes more than once. I started exercising, doing step-ups, squats and burpees, thousands of them to kill the time, press-ups too. They thought I would crack but I wasn't giving them that. When the seven days were up the SO came back.

'We're taking you back to the wing,' he said.

'No you're not.'

He was flummoxed. 'What do you mean?'

'I'm not going. I'm staying here. I refuse to comply with any orders whatsoever, nothing. Just bring me my meals and fuck off.'

No matter what they said or what they did, I dug my heels in and refused to budge. They even came to take me out to exercise in the yard and I wouldn't go. The way I looked at it, this was the worst they had to offer. This was supposed to be the big punishment that all the prisoners were scared of. If it didn't bother me, they had nothing over me and there was nothing they could do. I would be free to do my time in my own way. They didn't understand it, but that was important.

On Christmas Day one of them came to see me.

'Do you want to phone your Mum?' he asked. 'It's Christmas.'

'No,' I shook my head. 'Fuck off.'

Prison rules meant you had to be given access to books and you had to be allowed a radio. I read avidly, developing an interest in history and politics. I was genuinely fascinated to discover that Henry VIII dissolved the monasteries because he angered the pope after divorcing his first wife.

For the next year I devoured books, listened to sports, music or news programmes and exercised in my cell. I became obsessive about it, counting my repetitions in hundreds and marking them off on the notepad I used to write letters to Mum. Each day I would do a few more, I saw it as a challenge, something I had to get through to prove I had the mental strength to survive. I never had a moment of doubt I would persevere.

The food was shocking. Stodgy muck, white rice, goulash, fish and chips, puddings with custard, all of it the lowest quality you could imagine. It was like eating cardboard, absolute filth, but despite my poor diet, the weight fell off me. I became firm and lean from all the exercise. Not only would they be unable to break me, but I would come out stronger and smarter than before. It was me against them.

I would watch them sometimes from the peephole on the door and every fibre of my being would hum with hate. Going about their pathetic routine, their uniforms, their lame jokes. They represented the system, the establishment, everything Billy had taught me to despise.

'I am going to make you pay for this,' I would think. 'You watch. When I get out of here I'm taking it all back. You took my freedom. You stole three years of my life. I want £5m for that. And I'm going to get it, every fucking penny.'

Before the *system* had been an imaginary thing, something that tried to control your life and pull invisible strings. In prison, the mystery was gone. The system was in front of you and all around you every day. It was ubiquitous. There is no better place for fostering anger, alienation and resentment than jail.

Two weeks before I was due to be freed I phoned Mum, asking her to send some money and arrange for someone to pick me up. I longed for that moment, to walk out of that gate, but stubbornly kept my routine going despite my eagerness. Finally one of the screws came up to the cell door and opened it.

'You're being released,' he said.

They took me down to the reception area and returned my belongings, which amounted to the suit I had worn at the Old Bailey, £200 my mate Johnny had organised for me and some change I had when I was arrested.

I signed several forms for my licence. Release was dependent on me reporting to parole officers and keeping out of trouble for nine months.

'You've been allocated a discharge grant,' the screw said.

'What's that?'

'Fifty pounds to help you get started.'

'Do you know what you can do with that?' I sneered. 'You can shove it up your fucking arse. Take me to the gate.'

He stood there staring at me, rocking backwards and forwards, biting his lip. There was nothing he could do.

'Come on,' I said. 'Chop, chop, I want to go.'

He nodded slowly. 'All right, McAvoy, I'll be seeing you again in a couple of years, no doubt.'

'Of course you will mate.'

They took me out to the front and the screw opened up the big, crimson steel door. I took a step forwards and he closed it behind me – *clang*.

It was a cold, clear January day. The sky seemed so huge. I looked left then right. It was a feeling of…not much. If anything it was a bit of an anti-climax. For so long I yearned for that moment, although I hadn't shown it, but as soon as I was out, my mind started ticking over with what I needed to do.

My friend Mehmet had come to pick me up. He hugged me and asked how I was. We jumped in his car and soon were speeding down the motorway.

'Can you pull over at the next services?' I asked.

'Sure,' he replied, 'are you okay?'

'I'm fine. I just want to go into a shop and buy something. I want to remember what it feels like.'

I bought a newspaper and a carton of Ribena. When I pierced the little foil circle with the straw and had that first drink, I closed my eyes and smiled. It tasted of freedom.

8

On Road

MEHMET dropped me off at Mum's. Predictably, she was in tears for hours and wouldn't let go of me. All my aunts were there.

I knew Mum felt guilty about the way things had gone, which was upsetting. She had been the one person in my life who tried to keep me on the straight path from the beginning. The choices I made weren't her fault and she did all she could. I was an adult and responsible for myself, but it's natural for a mother to think like that.

We went out for a Chinese with the family to celebrate. Mum cheered up and we all enjoyed ourselves. The food was average, but after eating HMP goulash for three years, any old plate of slop can seem like a royal banquet. No one asked what I was going to do from then, which was nice. It would have been a shame to spoil the party mood by lying.

Before we went to bed that night, Mum grabbed me, sobbing and shaking.

'Promise me you won't ever go to prison again,' she said.

I looked into her eyes. 'I promise Mum.' I meant it too. I had no intention of returning to jail. I would be too smart for that.

The following day I went around to visit Auntie Kathy, Uncle Micky's wife, at their house in Keston. They were doing nicely in Spain and building a good life for themselves. Auntie Kathy had popped back to sort out some things and by coincidence he phoned up while I was there.

'Jonathon's here,' she said before passing the phone to me.

'What you doing John?' he asked.

'What do you mean?'

'Long term? You coming out here?'

'Maybe, yeah.'

'Do it. Just book a flight. Come.'

'I can't Micky, not now. I'm on licence for nine months.'

'Okay, listen, the day the licence is finished, get over here. You won't do yourself any favours hanging about in England. They're on you now. I'll get Kathy to give you some money so you're okay for a while.'

As I was leaving Auntie Kathy gave me an envelope with five grand inside.

'Listen to Micky,' she said, as she kissed me goodbye. 'Keep your head down, okay?'

I knew that Micky was talking sense, so started making plans. I thought it best to stay away from armed robbery for a while and my thoughts were to ride out the nine months, head to Europe and get involved in the drugs trade. Aaron had really pushed on during my time inside, bringing hundred-kilo shipments of cannabis into the country, distributing it and making a nice living. Through him I had high-profile contacts, ready to use. It could be very lucrative.

My only concern was the scum you had to deal with in that line of work. Armed robbers tend to be tight, small groups with a code of honour, but the drugs world sucked in every two-bob wanker who had watched a couple of Guy Ritchie films. We used to laugh about it, the weekend criminals, as we called them. They weren't proper villains, like us. A lot of them had jobs and worked for the system. They were people from outside our world who didn't really understand it, had stumbled into drugs, often by being users and then found they could make a few quid out of it.

A lot of those sorts of people got carried away and started thinking they were hard-men, but most of them were fake as a copper's promise. The real trouble with them is they are unlikely to hold their nerve when needed. You do business with them but when police threaten them or offer incentives for information, they won't think twice about singing their hearts out to save themselves.

Nice house and family you've got, must be expensive maintaining all that? If you don't give us names, we'll go public with this. I'm sure your boss would like to know what you're up to.

I would need to manage my associates very carefully.

Life kicked back in at a million miles an hour as I rushed around to meetings and chased up leads. I wanted to have everything ready so that when the time came, I could hop on a plane and go. Yet the more I made my arrangements, the more I began to get an uneasy feeling. I often saw the same cars around me, sometimes the same drivers. For a time, I wrote it off as paranoia but the suspicion persisted, so I took my Golf GTi to a mechanic for reassurance.

Aaron picked me up from the garage and within five minutes my phone went.

'Do you mind coming back quickly, John?' the mechanic said. 'There's some important work needs doing on your car and I want to run it by you.'

When we returned the Golf was up on a hydraulic lift. The mechanic put his finger to his lips.

'Listen mate,' he said. 'There's a bit of a problem. Do you mind coming into the office to talk it over?'

I followed him into his office, a classic grease monkey's gaff, Pirelli calendars, mess everywhere.

He shut the door, turned to me and started to speak so quietly I could barely hear it.

'They're fucking on you mate,' he whispered.

'What do you mean?'

'I found a GPS tracker and a radar device on the underside of your chassis.'

I followed him back out to the workshop and he showed me what he had found. He had removed them and placed them on a stool next to the car.

Immediately my mind was a blur. Where had I been? Who had I seen? Was there anything in my movements that could incriminate me, or anyone else?

I had a think and told him to put them back on. At least I knew they were tracking me. It made more sense to leave the devices intact so they wouldn't suspect I had second-guessed their ploy.

Later that day I rang up my friend Brendan, who ran a small construction company.

'I'm bang in trouble, mate,' I told him. 'I've only been out three weeks and I've got them all over me. I'm on licence. If they suspect I'm organising anything they'll recall me. I'll be back inside.'

'So how can I help?'

'Can I come to your office during the day, so it looks like I've got a job? If they think I've found work they might believe I've gone straight.'

'Not a problem, mate!'

The next morning, about half past five, I turned up at Brendan's house. He answered the door with the smile of someone who was used to being up at that time and we jumped in his car to head down to the site. No more than a minute into the journey the air filled with the roar of high-powered engines and five unmarked police cars with little blue lights flew past us back towards his house.

'What the hell?' Brendan asked.

'They were on standby,' I told him. 'They've followed me down here. Because the car's stopped they think I'm doing a job. That's how it works. They track the vehicle and when it's not moving is their time to come steaming in. If you're driving, you're not robbing!'

To maintain the pretence, I continued going to work with Brendan for a few weeks. I did no actual work, I just sat in his office, but it meant they had a log of me being there. I thought about them, analysing the readings from their devices, wondering what I was up to. It gave me a little kick. Soon I started coming up with other ways to mess with their heads.

'Okay,' I thought. 'You're going to follow me around? In that case I'll make your lives as tedious as possible.'

Some days I would just go on random drives up the M1, pull in at a junction for a bit, give it a few minutes, then go around a roundabout and start coming back the other way. Other days I would drive into central London and spend the whole day crawling around in nose-to-nose traffic. I knew they were probably only 100 metres behind me and just wanted to tire them out.

Sometimes I would come out of my house with a holdall and chuck it in the back seat, to make it look like I was up to something. If they were watching me I knew they would be extra hot on me that day. Then I would just spend the afternoon pottering around Hyde Park, doing about 15mph.

After a couple of months of living like that, the novelty wore off. I still had six months of my licence to serve and couldn't keep it up for the duration. That level of constant paranoia can get to you.

I went down to the car, removed the trackers, took pictures of them and threw them in a carrier bag. Then I phoned Henry Milner, who told me to go and see him at his office in Hatton Garden.

'Hello John!' he beamed, when I arrived. 'Come in.'

I sat down and looked at him. He could tell something was up from my face.

'What's wrong?'

'They're all over me.'

I emptied the carrier bag out on to the table and his eyes widened in shock.

'Good God man!' he cried. 'Don't bring those into the office. They're probably listening to everything we're saying.'

He called his secretary and asked her to take the trackers back out to reception. After the door closed behind her he said, 'John, listen to me. Whatever you're doing, stop. Stop now.'

I had not committed any actual crime as such since getting out, but I had been to a few meetings, rubbed shoulders with a few faces. 'Is there anything we can do?' I asked. 'I've only just got out and they're not giving me room to breathe.'

'Look John, you know how it works. If I write to the Met and tell them they're harassing you, all they will do is write back and say, "We neither confirm nor deny that we placed tracking devices on your client's car." It's nonsense, but it gets them off the hook. Obviously they haven't got a warrant for this, but we can't press the issue.'

Henry took a couple of photographs then wrote a legal statement verifying he had seen them. I thanked him, put them back in the bag and drove down to the Thames by Surrey Quays. There were a few joggers and dog walkers wandering about, but I didn't let that bother me.

'Have that you cunts,' I said. I pulled the batteries out and chucked them both into the river. The devices sank into the dirty water without a trace and a misplaced feeling of liberty rose in my chest.

The truth was, all it meant was from then on the game changed. They knew that I knew. I still had to be careful, maybe even more so than before, but the police would have to back off a little bit.

There was no doubt in my mind that it was the Flying Squad. They hadn't forgiven me for beating those nine charges at the Old Bailey and what I said to them in the dock. Currie and his boys were desperate to put me away.

Fortunately, among my many associates were a few involved in buying, letting and developing properties, whom I used to organise temporary accommodation. No one was to know where I lived so I would move from one set of digs to another, every four to five weeks. They were nice places, fully furnished, but I couldn't risk staying at one address.

My paranoia was such that if anything slipped out about where I was living, I would move immediately. On one occasion in a bar, Johnny forgot himself. A girl asked where I lived and I lied, but Johnny was a few drinks into the evening, chimed in and said, 'That's not right John, you're living on Bluethorne Road.' I had a real go at him later, slept somewhere else that night, then the next morning cleared my stuff out and left.

Whenever I moved I would go to WH Smith and buy packs of small coloured stickers, so I could put them over the screw fittings on my plug sockets and light fittings. If I went out, the first thing I would do on getting home would be to check all the stickers for disruption. That way, if my flat was entered while I was out and listening devices were installed, I would know about it. Bugs are usually fitted behind electrical points.

For the same reason I would put tiny strips of sellotape around the doorframe so I could see if anyone had been in. To alleviate the stress, I treated it all like a game, like the chess matches I enjoyed as a child. I had to think several moves ahead of any surveillance that could be taking place.

Whenever I was in a car with another player, we would have pointless, false conversations, never, ever about crime, just in case they were listening. We would try to sound as normal as possible.

'So how's things at the office John?'

'Yeah, not bad, got a big report to do for Thursday though.'

'Looking forward to the big match at the weekend?'

'Oh yeah, can't wait.'

I had a kid who went out and nicked cars for me. He would take them off garage forecourts and places like that. If anyone left their keys in the ignition, even if only for a few seconds, he would jump in and be away. Once he stole it we would *ring it up*.

We would find a hire car of the same model and get false plates made with that registration number then put the fake plates on to the stolen car. One of us would hire the rental car and nick the tax disc. That way you could drive around in the stolen vehicle and know that if police run a check it will come up as a legitimate car with tax and insurance. You can only do that for a month or so, then dump it and get another one.

Generally, I would only drive ringers and any cars I had, I would not park them near my house. When driving I wore gloves so as not to leave fingerprints. I would go to the Oxfam shop and buy second-hand clothes then leave them in the back seat. That way, if it ever got found, it would have other people's DNA in there as well as mine.

I continued to get a buzz out of it, enjoying the feeling that I was smarter than them. I joined a gym, a posh David Lloyd place where I used to lift a few weights and jump in the sauna, just for reasons of vanity. It was absolutely crawling with police. I got a little thrill from talking to them and passing myself off as someone else. I would sit in the Jacuzzi and ask, 'What do you do for a living then?'

'I'm in the police. You?'

'I've got my own internet business. We do website design and graphics.'

'Oh, interesting.'

'So what department do you work for?'

'I'm on the safer neighbourhoods team.'

'Oh, I bet that's hard work, isn't it? Dealing with all those little scallywags? Rather you than me.'

Despite the fun I invented for myself, I was also under pressure. I began to sense that their observations were becoming more overt. They knew I was playing games and didn't like it.

There was a blonde woman with a fringe who I knew was connected to the Flying Squad and I kept seeing her around. If I parked my car, she would drive past. I would come out of a shop and see her walking away on the other side of the road. She kept popping up everywhere.

While I waited for the last couple of months of my licence to play itself out, I decided to start up a legitimate business interest with Aaron. We found a wholesaler who sold us cheap sex products, dildos, lubricants, porn, anything sleazy. The idea was to get a couple of girls we knew in an office with a few phones and a computer. They could run it for us and it would bring in a few quid until I started working properly.

As a result, we booked an appointment at HSBC in Bromley to discuss setting up a business account. It went well enough, although they asked a few awkward questions. As we left the branch a friend of ours called Tim drove past and beeped his horn at us. Moments later my phone rang.

'John, it's Tim.'

'All right Tim?'

'I'm good mate, what are you doing outside the bank?'

'Just had a meeting, why?'

'There's a plain car on the corner of Charleston Road, with a man and a woman in it. The woman had a camera with a long lens. She was taking pictures of you.'

'What did she look like?'

'She had blonde hair with a fringe.'

'Cheers mate.'

Anger swelled in my chest. I was not even planning any robberies, but the bastards were really limiting my freedom. I could barely go out and buy a pint of milk without them following me. It helped to clarify things in my mind. My only option was to wait for my licence to expire and go abroad. They were giving me no choice.

9

Dutch Masters

I STILL had about a month left to run when I was offered a very lucrative bit of work stealing high-end electrical goods from a warehouse.

I had to turn it down despite the fact there was half a million on the table. It was an attractive job, but committing a robbery would have been tantamount to suicide under that sort of surveillance.

By then I had begun putting things in place for my planned foreign adventure. Where would I live? How would I make money?

I met up with a Scottish guy called Craig, who was known to our circle as a decent bloke and had just completed a ten-year sentence for major drugs offences. We had breakfast together in a local café and talked a few things over.

'I can definitely put some ideas your way,' he said. 'I know a few fellas out in Holland.'

'Oh yeah?'

'Good contacts, they're quite high up in the food chain. If you want to meet them I can set it up.'

Gary's contact, Dimitar, was not Dutch, as it turned out, but Serbian, although he spent most of his time in Holland. I met him in a bar in Eltham. He seemed pleasant enough but had very steady, dark eyes which rarely blinked.

'We can do business,' he said. 'But first you have to come to Holland. Come to my friend's house. This is important to us. We don't do business with men we don't know.'

I explained the situation with my licence conditions, and that I would be happy to come in a couple of months, but he was adamant. If I wanted to start the ball rolling, either myself or one of my associates had to travel over in the next few weeks.

I spoke to Aaron as he had bags of experience in this sort of work. He agreed without hesitation. Before he left for Rotterdam we made a list of payphone numbers around the Bromley area. Each payphone had a letter – A, B, C and so on, the idea being that we would communicate only using a different payphone each evening, making it virtually impossible for police to trace or tap our calls. For the first night we arranged to speak on payphone C at 8pm.

'What have you done to me?' Aaron yelled after I picked up the phone. 'These guys are fucking nuts!'

'What do you mean?'

'They picked me up from the Hook of Holland, four of them in a Mercedes Sport and bombed down the motorway doing about 150mph with all this Bosnian rap music playing. They're fucking loopy. I thought I'd be staying in hotels as well, but they've given me a bed at their place.'

'Yeah, maybe I should have mentioned that. Is everything all right though?'

'Mate, they are on it, believe me.'

Aaron came home three days later and explained in detail the operation the Serbs had going. They had large farms where they grew cannabis plants, a few factories to process and package it and a very efficient distribution network. They were ideal partners for us and it promised to be a profitable arrangement.

The one issue still left to iron out was how to transport the packets from Holland to the UK. Getting them through coastguards would not be easy, but we had a few leads on that and found a viable solution. By the time arrangements had been made, my licence period had nearly expired and I had my final probation appointment to look forward to. I told the officer some nonsense about my internet business and how I would be focusing on that from now on. I suspect she didn't believe me, but all the necessary boxes were ticked. We signed the document and I almost skipped out of the building. At last I was free to leave the UK.

Within two days myself and Aaron were in a hired BMW, heading down to Dover, on to a ferry and then the continent. We threw a bunch of fishing rods and nets in the boot, so if anyone asked we could say we were going for an angling holiday.

On arrival, we tried to find an apartment in one of the nicer parts of Rotterdam, which was a bit like looking for an earring in a skip. Rotterdam had been bombed to all hell in World War Two and rebuilt in monotonous, grey concrete. Eventually we found a decent corner, picturesque and traditional.

A meet was arranged with the Serbians' top guy at a Chinese restaurant near the Feyenoord football ground. This, we were told, was the boss man, one of Europe's main drugs kingpins. After five minutes sitting by the window, we both clocked him before we even knew who he was. The guy was like something out of a comic book. If you asked your average 14-year-old to imagine an eastern European drug baron, he would likely picture someone pretty similar to Eddie.

We could barely stifle our laughter as a gaudy, red, open top sports car pulled up on the road outside. Its driver had black, slicked back hair and wore sunglasses. A stocky guy, about as broad as he was tall, sharply dressed in an Armani suit, dripping in jewellery, he saw us straight away and smiled. He had several gold teeth.

'He's having a laugh, isn't he?' Aaron said.

Eddie, as he called himself, seemed surprised by our youth. We were both still only 21 and he was not used to doing business with men of that age.

'I hear you're a good man,' he said. 'You come from good people. This is important for me.'

'Good,' I replied. 'I've heard the same about you.'

He smiled and had a sip of wine.

'I am wanted in my own country,' he began. 'They want to put me on trial at Den Haag, so I have to be very careful who I deal with.'

I had no idea who this guy was, but I knew that Den Haag (The Hague) was the international court used for war crimes. The Bosnian conflict had finished nine years earlier, in 1995, and he seemed to be hinting that he had been involved in some kind of atrocity. It was impossible for me to know whether or not it was just bluster, so I ignored him and steered the conversation back to business.

What he suggested was a tidy arrangement that increased our chances for high profit. The Serbs had a fixed sum in mind for their part of the shipment. Any mark-up we made on that, we could keep.

We debated numbers for a while before reaching an agreement and by the end of the meeting I felt satisfied. I had not particularly liked Eddie or enjoyed his company, but he struck me as pretty straight down the line. If no one fucked anyone else around, it would all work well.

With the foundations laid, Aaron travelled back to England because he was buying a house in Chelsfield. I had no desire to return and stayed, quickly learning the relaxed Dutch way of doing things, which was so different to the British.

Over there you would get a maximum 12-month sentence for possession of a handgun, of which you would only serve ten to 14 weeks. If you got caught with 20kg of cannabis, they would confiscate it, write it up and let you go, the same way police in England would if you had a tiny amount for personal use. Their whole culture was far more permissive.

I buzzed around for a while, enjoying myself, making living arrangements, meeting some of the British criminals who lived over there. Knowing that UK police were not watching my every move gave me a feeling of complete freedom and for the first time since leaving jail I began to feel genuinely happy.

I moved out of Rotterdam and found a new place at The Hague. It was idyllic, almost stereotypically so. My flat was beautiful and it backed on to a tulip field. Each morning I would wake up and go for breakfast at a lovely café with paintings by Dutch masters on the walls and classical music playing. Every now and then I would meet up with Eddie, to discuss business, but other than that it was a life of leisure.

I spent lots of time on my own and was able to reflect. England clearly was not the place for me anymore. I had great connections there but it was crowded and busy. More than anything I was too well known to the authorities. In the short time I had been abroad, the continental lifestyle had proven far more amenable.

I met a girl in a club called Hooters, a half-Spanish cutie named Elodi. She twigged fairly quickly what I was up to but wasn't particularly bothered. A lot of English guys pass through Holland setting up cannabis-related business and the national attitude to it is so relaxed, most of them don't care.

After a month and a half of easy living in The Hague, some players I knew came up to visit from Spain. The drug trade tends to work like that, it's very seasonal. In the winter everyone's in Holland, stocking up and shipping to the UK. Then in the summer they all head down to Spain. Weed (the leaves and buds of the marijuana plant) tends to come from Holland, while cannabis resin generally comes up from Morocco. The players follow the sun, follow the money and head down to the Costa del Sol for four or five months of partying.

When the lads from Spain arrived we went out to a cocktail bar in Amsterdam where they introduced me to a Colombian known as Bubba. He had been recently released after serving 15 years in the USA for trafficking cocaine. We got absolutely smashed on MaiTais and Capiroskas, while everyone made fun of Bubba because he had a leather man bag over his shoulder. He took it all in good humour. Once he had got drunk enough to lose his inhibitions, he opened the bag, pulled out a pistol and started waving it around. The guy was a proper lunatic.

I liked Bubba. He was a laugh and didn't give a shit about anything. We swapped numbers and started meeting up for the occasional night out. We would get smashed together, destroy ourselves on ecstasy and cocaine, then hit some nightspots. One night at a club called Zoo, a proper, heavy Dutch, techno-trance night, he got out of his head on Es and started jumping around on the dance floor waving his gun in time to the music. The bouncers knew who he was and left him alone.

Bubba frequently asked me to get involved in work with him, but I always turned him down. He was funny but way too much of a cowboy. Guys who live like that don't tend to last too long in open society.

Altogether I stayed over in Holland for about four months then popped back to England to see Mum and tie up loose ends. She was worried about me. I told her I was fine, that I was setting myself up abroad. She didn't ask too many questions, there was not really any point, and that was the way I liked it.

10

Sun, Sex and Sangria

WITH the groundwork prepared in Holland the next step was to head out to the Costa del Sol and follow up on my contacts out there. Aaron had sorted out his house, a nice place on a leafy avenue, with five bedrooms and a big garden. He was ready too.

We booked a flight together and flew into Marbella, having a couple of drinks and a catch-up on the plane. Everything was ticking over with Eddie and we could examine other possibilities. The future looked bright.

The heat hit us like a wall as we stepped off on to the runway. We found accommodation quickly and settled in. One of the first things I did was meet up with Uncle Micky for dinner. He looked great, sun-tanned and really well.

'You were right,' I told him. 'Old Bill made my life untenable back home.'

He nodded. 'So stay out here. You're done in England. Don't bother with that anymore.'

'I know.'

'You still have to be careful though John. Interpol are getting hot on all the Brits out here. They send spotters into nightclubs, to pick out groups of English. If there's a few of you together, they swoop in with mobile fingerprint scanners. Anyone who's wanted back in the UK, they're gone, straight away, so don't get silly out here and think you can mess around. You've still got to be smart.

'The other thing to look out for is the Russians. They've turned up in the last few years and they're ruthless as fuck. They'll end you quicker than the law will. If you have any problems with Russians, you've got to have it with them. It's probably best to get in first. The crazy bastards will iron you out and iron all your family out too, if they feel like it. They went after a bloke recently who was getting a haircut, burst into the hairdressers with a Kalashnikov, opened up and killed everyone in the shop, just to make sure. They don't give a shit. Half of them have grown up in war zones and their value of life is completely different. My advice is not to fuck about with them.'

At the time I had little to worry about, though. I was not wanted back in the UK, meaning Interpol would not interfere, while my business arrangement with Eddie and his boys meant I was fixed up for the near future. I wasn't desperate for new work, Russian or otherwise. With that untroubled attitude, I soon realised why the Costa is such a popular place for the criminal fraternity.

In Marbella and its surrounding areas, there are incredible amounts of exciting ways for rich, young men to spend money. At times I was staying up for days, going from a bar, to a club, to a restaurant for breakfast. Then off to a clothes shop for some fresh togs, throwing the previous night's clothes in a bin, buying some toothpaste and brushing my teeth in the sea, before going back to another bar and so the cycle would continue. I could quite easily spend 20 or 30,000 euros without stopping.

Cocaine was my drug of choice, although I was knocking back the booze and doing handfuls of Es as well. We got top quality gear through our network and as much of it as we wanted, whenever we wanted it. Five o'clock in the morning and you need an ounce of coke and 20 pills? No problem Mr McAvoy!

A favourite of ours was the pool party on Nikki beach, a tantalising slice of pure hedonism. There were podiums with half-naked dancers and everyone in the place was off their head on drugs. You could bounce about chatting to film stars, then Saudi princes, then top international businessmen. Me and Aaron would go down there, spend money like there was no tomorrow and think, 'Yes! We've cracked it!'

One time I shared a spoon of coke with a well-known American businessman at the bar and he told me he had just sold one of his companies for nearly £100m. He bought ten crates of champagne and asked for it to be distributed around the club. Another time we shared a table with Antonio Banderas. None of it seemed unnatural.

The truth was that whole period was one in which I was incredibly happy. I was a young man, living life to the full and enjoying everything. I could look back on my time in prison with a smile. It seemed a lifetime away and I was surrounded by like-minded people.

We were mixing with multi-millionaires and royalty and the funny thing was that they were trying to get around us. We weren't living in their shadow. They admired who we were as people, the self-earned lifestyle we had at such a young age. Their attention and companionship brought all sorts of new opportunities.

There was a day in the middle of the summer that myself and Aaron were sitting on Plaza beach. It was nearly lunchtime and we wondered which bar to hit before getting some food. I looked over the ocean and all the sun-seekers moored in the shallow waters. A DJ was playing tuneful house music in the bar behind us. We were just coming up on some lovely, floaty Es. Everything seemed so right.

'Do you know what, mate?' he said. 'I always knew we would make it. I felt it in my guts.'

I reached over and slapped him on the shoulder.

'I've been thinking the same thing. We're gonna smash it.'

'Listen though,' he said, taking my hand. 'If anything ever goes wrong, if you go down, I'll come for you, alright? That's the way it has to be. I'm always there if you need me.'

I squeezed his hand back.

'Of course mate. Me too.'

It wasn't just the drugs talking. Both of us meant it. The criminal life can get you like that.

In the normal world you might say you 'trust someone with your life' but it's just empty talk, a cliché. In our world it was literal, word for word, breath for breath. I had Aaron's back and he had mine. The contacts we made over the holiday period, coupled with the drug smuggling operation meant that we were poised to ascend to the next level, the level everyone aims for, where the lines between criminality and legitimate business get blurred by the sheer amount of money involved. At that level, the police no longer come near you. We both knew it. We were in our early 20s and about to hit the big league.

Girls came and went, like Imogen, a hostess I hooked up with. She worked at a bar called the Panius Lounge where we got chatting over a bottle of Moet. You couldn't help but fall for her a little bit, lovely looking, classy, with long legs and silky brown hair. She was wearing tight white hot-pants when we met and we started seeing each other regularly. I would pick her up from the bar when she finished work and take her out clubbing. On one occasion we were in a nightclub called Dreamers, one of my favourites. We danced for a few hours, did a fair bit of MDMA then headed back to hers for a spot of chemically induced lovemaking. In the morning I got up for a glass of water and bumped into her housemate Jodie in the kitchen. She was an unbelievable sort as well, with lighter hair than Imogen, but an amazing body. Marbella is like that. It attracts beautiful young women from around Europe who are looking for rich boyfriends. For any man with a few quid, it's a great place to go!

I got Jodie's number as well and a couple of nights later took her to a party. We shared a couple of grams of coke and boogied for a while then she started giving me her come-to-bed eyes. I was never one to say no in those sorts of circumstances, so we went back to hers and got it on for an hour or two. She looked unbelievable without her clothes.

About 2am we heard the front door go. Imogen had finished work early and rather than go out to a club, as she usually did, had come home. To make matters worse, she knocked on the door of Jodie's room and walked in on the two of us in bed. I pretended to be asleep while they launched into a vicious argument. Imogen went bonkers.

'You slut, you fucking slag, what are you doing with him?'

'We've just got together you bitch, you don't own him!'

'I fucking saw him first!'

'So what, you shag anything in trousers, you can't say I'm in the wrong.'

I buried my head under the duvet and cracked up laughing, waiting for the to-and-fro to end. Eventually Imogen stormed out, threw her clothes in a case and left. I gave it ten minutes to make sure the coast was clear then turned to Jodie.

'Sorry babe, that was a lovely night until the end, but I've got to get going. I need to sort some stuff out.'

I padded into the lounge and found my clothes scattered over the coffee table and sofa in shreds. Even the £400 Gucci loafers I had been wearing had been cut into crude triangles. Imogen had taken revenge with scissors.

Jodie went to a neighbour's flat and banged on the door to ask if I could borrow a pair of swimming shorts to go home in. After all that I sacked both of them off, they were more trouble than they were worth.

Not long after that, I hooked up with Annalise, a tall, blonde girl with huge fake tits. She looked like a glamour model and you would spot her a mile off if you were on the beach. She was a lovely person really, quite down to earth, with a strong Scouse accent. She also happened to be good friends with a guy known as 'Mouse' who supplied drugs to all the British holidaymakers in the town, so she was useful to know.

I found myself on Nikki beach at about one o'clock in the afternoon, at a bit of a loose end, with a hankering for some Es. Unfortunately, Mouse wasn't answering his phone. A lot of the Marbella crowd don't get out of bed until the middle of the afternoon. I scanned the beach and saw Annalise lying on a sun-lounger with no one next to her, so bought her a drink and sat down.

'Fucking hell, I'm dying for some Es,' I told her. 'Do you know where I can get hold of some?'

She turned around and gave me the biggest smile I had ever seen. I could tell from her eyes over her sunglasses that she was completely off her face.

'Don't worry, la',' she said. 'I've got some.'

I watched in disbelief and she put her hand inside her bikini bottoms, fumbled around then made a little face as she pulled something out. Grinning, she held up a plastic bag full of tablets.

'Old school white doves,' she said. 'I always think it's wise to keep them hidden.'

She started feeding me pills on the beach and by early afternoon I was quite spectacularly spannered. We stayed there all day, drinking, popping pills, getting higher and higher. They came to close the bar at 6pm so I gave the barman 100 euros and told him to leave us there.

They cleared out the other customers and we laid there just the two of us, buzzing our blocks off and watching the sunset. We were so euphoric and starting hugging. As the last rim of sun boiled into the sea I planted a massive kiss on her.

'I've fallen in love with you, Annalise,' I told her. 'I want to be with you forever.' We kissed passionately until it was too cold to stay.

With our bond formed through chemical romance, we headed out for the evening and bumped into Aaron having dinner at a seafood restaurant, with a friend of ours called Harry. They both cracked up laughing when we walked in. I had sunglasses on, my jaw was all over the place, I was grinding my teeth and had a six-foot-tall page three girl on my arm. We sat at the table with them for about a minute.

'What the fuck have you been up to?' Aaron asked.

'There's no way I can eat anything lads,' I told them and went off with Annalise to continue our one-night love affair elsewhere.

Towards the end of the summer, Elodi came down to Spain with a couple of friends of hers, Lucia from Switzerland and Faye from Dubai. Lucia was an incredible-looking, dark-haired, willowy girl who spoke five languages. She was easily the most impressive woman I had ever met, while Faye looked like an Arabian princess. For a while they became my night-time companions and we went out 24/7 for the best part of a month.

One night we found ourselves in Dreamers and were there until it closed at five in the morning. We'd all done so much gear there was no chance of sleep, so we went back to my place, then went straight to the beach. We were only there for about five minutes when I jumped up.

My heart raced and my face poured with sweat, as I suffered the onset of what coke users call the 'horrors'. A feeling of paranoia washed over me, my vision blurred and my legs shook.

We got back in the car, drove back to my flat and as I laid there naked on the bed, with Elodi beside me, I genuinely thought I would have a heart attack. I stared up at the ceiling, unable to sleep for hours, heart thundering, breath short, waiting for the drugs to wear off. Gripped with fear, I promised myself to stop overdoing it. I was pushing my luck, sometimes getting through hundreds of pounds of drugs in a week. It was great fun, but seriously unhealthy. I knew if I kept going like that I could have major problems.

By then, the middle of August 2005, I was still in the process of moving my life to the continent permanently and paid a couple of friends to hire a van, load it up with furniture and belongings in London then drive it out to Spain. I organised a few hundred quid and quarter of an ounce of top-notch cocaine for them, so they could keep themselves awake and do the whole journey in one hit. Unfortunately, the air conditioning broke and they arrived on the Costa after 24 hours of solid driving in a terrible state. High as planets, but dehydrated and suffering with heat exhaustion, it took them a few days to recover.

Still, with the last of my possessions with me in Marbella, I felt truly settled. I had no reason to return to the UK and no intention of doing so, until I got a phone call reminding me that Paul, my crazy friend who had been with me for my arrest, was celebrating his 25th birthday in early September back in London. A big party was planned and Paul had especially requested that I receive an invitation. We had been through a lot together. He hadn't cracked when the police applied pressure before the trial and I felt I owed it to him to be there.

Aaron and I booked ourselves a flight back to the UK and Elodi drove us to the airport.

'Why are you going back?' she asked as she dropped us off.

'Just a party I need to go to.'

'I don't get it, why not stay out here?'

'Its fine babe, I'll be back next week.'

'I've got a bad feeling.'

I laughed.

'Bad feeling about what, you silly cow?'

I gave her a kiss goodbye and headed into the terminal with Aaron. On the plane I told him I was quitting drugs. The risk to reward ratio wasn't working for me anymore and I had to think of the future. He didn't believe me, but I was determined.

We landed at Gatwick and I went straight into a phone shop in arrivals to buy a pay-as-you-go. I didn't want to give out my Spanish number to anyone while I was back.

Johnny came to pick us up and as we were heading up the M23 back to London, I wrote the new mobile number down on a strip of paper and gave it to him.

'Where do you want to go?' Johnny asked.

'Drop me round my Mum's please mate.'

'Okay. I'll come and pick you up again later. We can go out.'

Mum was delighted to see me and kept talking about how well I looked. It was nice to see her happy. I had put on some weight and developed a lovely tan.

In early evening Johnny phoned and said something had come up. He would not be picking me up after all. In some ways it was a welcome relief. All summer in Spain I had burned the candle at both ends and an early night was sensible. By 11pm I was asleep in my old bedroom at home. First thing in the morning, at about seven, my new phone rang. I answered it, assuming it was Johnny as he was the only one I had given the number to.

'Hello mate.'

'Hello?' The voice was unfamiliar. 'Who's this?'

'It's Kevin.'

I had not heard from Billy's associate Kevin Barnes for years. He had been acquitted when their case had come up, but by the time of his release I had already been put away, meaning there had been no opportunity for our paths to cross.

'How'd you get my number?'

'I was out with Johnny last night. He told me you were back.'

'Well it's great to hear from you Kevin. How are you?'

We exchanged a few pleasantries and chit-chat.

'So as you're back for a few days, how about a meeting?' he asked.

There was no reason to rebuff an old friend and we arranged to meet for breakfast at a local café that morning. I had no idea at the time and sadly neither did he, but Kevin was subject to an enormous, combined surveillance operation by the Met and the Flying Squad. I met him outside the café, shook his hand, then went inside and ordered a bacon roll and a coffee. All the while I was being videoed and photographed.

It only cost about £4, but in many ways it would end up being the most expensive breakfast imaginable.

11

Déjà Vu

W E HAD a casual conversation at the corner table of the café, just talking about life and what we were up to. Kevin seemed a bit down, as if he was struggling, so I held back on telling him how well things were going in Spain. It wasn't really his business and could have sounded like I was boasting.

The conversation drifted on until he asked if I was interested in some work. I shook my head.

'Nah, don't need to mate.'

'But I've got a few bits. Good earners too.'

'Nah, I'm fine.'

He looked really downcast.

'What's wrong with you, Kev?'

His words came in a rush, like someone had pulled the stopper out. 'I've done all my money. I'm on my arse and I really need to go to work. I had this wingman lined up, but had to let him go. He was a clown, an attention seeker. I need someone who knows what they're doing.'

I felt for him. It's never nice to see an old mate in need, but I really didn't want to get involved. I had the party in two days and then a flight back to Spain booked for the following week. That was that, as far as I was concerned. I reached into the inside pocket of my jacket and pulled out a roll of notes.

'You can have this,' I said. 'Not 100 per cent sure but I think there's five or six hundred quid there. That'll keep you going for today at least. It's all I've got on me, but give me a while and I'll find you some money. Just pay me back whenever you can.'

'I don't want handouts. I'm a grafter John, you know that. And I'm not talking about pocket money anyway. You know what I mean. Are you sure you don't want to come to work?'

'Definitely not mate. That's not why I'm here.'

'Okay,' he sighed. 'Fair enough, I won't keep asking. Can you do me one favour then?'

'Of course mate, what?'

'You know that security depot down in Dartford? Can you take me down there and give me a run-down on it? I've got a couple of ideas but I don't remember exactly where it is.'

Dartford had been one of my favourites in the old days, located just under the Queen Elizabeth II Bridge, next to the Hilton Hotel. I had calculated that most weeks it was holding about £3.5m.

'Okay,' I said, a little reluctantly. 'I'll take you there, but nothing else.'

As far as the police tracking our every move were concerned, with those words I had already committed conspiracy to rob. I had no idea about any of that, but something tingled in the back of my brain. As we walked to his car I turned to Kevin.

'Are they on you?' I asked.

'No,' he replied.

'Are you sure?'

'Absolutely mate. I wouldn't ask if they were.'

Kevin had a reputation as wily and very hard to catch. He had beaten more counts than anyone else on the scene. I took him at his word.

We drove down to Dartford. I showed him the depot then we headed back to London. Kevin dropped me off at the end of my Mum's road and asked if I wanted to meet for breakfast again the following morning. I didn't want him to think I was brushing him off.

'Of course mate. See you tomorrow.'

Neither of us were aware, but police had followed us all day. After I got out of Kevin's car they watched to see which house I went into. Once they ran an address check and the intelligence was shared, their operation absolutely exploded. Now that two convicted armed robbers had been seen casing a job, the green light was lit.

A team of more than 100 officers were called to a meeting overnight and allocated roles geared toward observing and ultimately intercepting our activities. Of course I went to bed in blissful ignorance.

It had been nice seeing Kevin. He'd always been a good guy, but the haunted look on his face bothered me. He seemed like he was having a tougher time than he was letting on. Could I have done more to help him? Billy would have wanted me to – *look after your own*. The following morning we met at the same café.

'Look,' Kevin said. 'I know you said no yesterday, but I think I've got something quick and easy for £300,000. Are you interested?'

He pleaded me with his eyes. Maybe a quick one wouldn't hurt, just to help him out.

'What is it?' I asked.

'There's a cash delivery in Sydenham, next to a Sainsbury's. There are four cash machines there and they take in ten to 12 boxes every time.'

It was good money and I didn't have much on for a couple of days. There was no harm in earning a few quid while I was home, was there?

'All right.'

For the second day running I drove down to a potential robbery site with Kevin. He showed me what his idea was and I got drawn in. It looked so easy.

We checked possible escape routes and decided the best option would be a motorbike parked up in an alleyway on the other side of the car park. About a mile of riding would bring you to the Pool river, where the bike could be dumped. There was a bridge there and a car waiting on the other side would take you off towards Beckenham and away.

'It looks good,' I told him. 'But I wanna watch it.'

The next delivery was due for the following day. Again I travelled there with Kevin and we scrutinised the security team delivering boxes of money for the cashpoints. My curiosity was satisfied, but that afternoon, as we went to double check on part of the escape plan, I started to get a bad sense. Something was awry. As we scoped the area a Vauxhall Omega drove past with four blokes in it. The one in the passenger seat eyeballed us then looked away when I returned his gaze.

'I'm telling you mate, that was Old Bill,' I told Kevin.

'You're paranoid,' he replied. 'You're thinking like them! We'll never get anywhere like that.'

Later on the same day Kevin wanted to show me another potential job. We parked up opposite a different supermarket with four cashpoints. I noticed a transit van sitting on the other side of the road.

'That's sore mate,' I said, pointing. 'Look at it. It just looks wrong sitting there.'

'Fucking hell, John, it's just a van!'

In the past, whenever my instincts had told me to back away from a job I always had, but Kevin was a big name and one of Billy's most trusted associates. His certainty and need for assistance kept me from bailing out altogether.

'Honestly Kev, I'm not waiting around for this,' I told him. 'I'm going back to Spain.'

'Okay,' he pleaded. 'I've got something else, a van job. Its super easy and we could do it tomorrow.'

I nodded slowly. He was a mate and mates should support each other, but it was still the worst mistake I ever made.

The idea was a petrol station cash delivery where the van would have to pull up on the forecourt. It was the first drop after leaving the depot, so it should have been well loaded with cash. It was simple. Kevin would jump in the van and drive it off. I'd be waiting on the other side of the fence in a car parked at the end of a cul-de-sac. When Kevin took the van, I'd follow. We would take it to a nearby rugby ground, cut it open, dump it and disappear. With an expected haul of £250,000 it was not as good as the other job but looked a doddle.

Something else I could not know at the time was that in the two months they had been monitoring Kevin, he had come very close to committing robberies on several occasions. They had literally watched him pull on a balaclava and prepare himself to smack a van five or six times, only to duck out at the last minute. By the time of my arrival they were champing at the bit.

Having invested so much manpower in the operation since I got involved, the Sweeney had to get a result soon, so they decided to act, no matter what. The minute we tried anything they would jump, filing a charge of conspiracy to rob if necessary, rather than wait and wait in case we did nothing.

On the morning, the van pulled up. It was warm and I wiped some sweat from my forehead as the guard got out. I zoned in, focused on what I had to do, not afraid, but aware of the danger, calm, prepared and ready. A loaded pistol rested on my lap.

Nothing happened.

I radioed Kevin on the walkie-talkie, trying to find out what was going on. Nothing came back. I fumed. What was he up to? I had put myself on offer and he was letting me down.

Cautiously I drove out of the cul-de-sac to get a view of the rest of the petrol station. There didn't appear to be much taking place. The van was still there, while the guard was inside the forecourt shop. Suddenly, from out of nowhere, three cars roared around the corner and tore down the cul-de-sac I had just left.

Knowing it was Old Bill I put the car into gear and drove away from the robbery site, all the while trying to get Kevin on the walkie-talkie, with no success. I found a quiet street, out of view from the petrol station and parked.

'What do I do?' I thought. I could get out of the car and run, jump over some fences and try to put as much distance between myself and them as possible. That made the most sense. By the time the police found the car I would have been gone for ten minutes. I would find someone to hide me, then smuggle myself back out to Spain somehow.

I switched the engine off, opened the door, stepped out and broke into a jog. My conscience pulled me back. Before I had taken five strides from the car I stopped. An overpowering feeling of guilt overcame me. I had been on the job with Kevin. Now I was effectively abandoning him. Anything could be happening back there. He had guns on him and if he was unaware the police were on us, things could get serious very quickly. He could even be killed.

With every cell in my brain screaming at me to do the opposite, I walked back to the car, climbed in, did a U-turn and drove back to the petrol station. As I turned on to the road where we intended to carry out the robbery, a car spun out from the side of the kerb, came tearing forwards and swung behind me, trying to box me in. Two other cars joined in from nowhere, one on the side and one in front. On the back seat of the car in front of me, one of the coppers twisted himself around and raised a gun. They had caged me in like an animal. I had no choice.

'Fuck this,' I thought.

I threw the car into first and put my foot down, smashing into the rear corner of the car in front, pushing it to one side. I mounted the pavement, grazed a lamppost and sped off down the road, managing to squeeze between the other two police cars. All three realigned themselves and came after me.

'I'm not going back to prison,' I thought. 'I'm not going back to prison.'

A feeling of déjà vu came over me as I tore through the back streets of Eltham. There were so many similarities to that day back in 2001 with Paul. Again, I knew that before long they would call out a helicopter. Again I knew that sooner or later I would have to bail.

I could not shake them off, so I drove into a large housing estate full of walls and gardens. It was as good a chance as I was likely to get. They would come after me but at least there was the possibility of outrunning them or hiding.

Acting on sheer adrenaline, I burst out of the door, but as I emerged, one of the police vehicles smashed into the back of my car. My seatbelt looped around my arm and the impact pulled me back into the driver's seat, smashing my elbow on the window. It exploded with pain but I ignored it, released the seatbelt and ran.

Expecting to hear gunshots that never came, somehow I got away. I sprinted off through the alleyways between the blocks, turning this way and that. After a minute of frantic helter-skeltering I allowed myself to look back and was amazed to see there was no one directly behind me. Out of sight, even if only temporarily, I had some sort of chance. I just had to find a way out of the estate, or somewhere to hide.

I was hemmed in by two tall tower blocks and as I emerged from between them, out of breath and sweaty, into the courtyard beyond, my heart sank. A dead-end confronted me, full of high-doored garages, with trellis fencing on top. The only way out was to do an about-face and return from where I had come.

I turned to go back and stopped. Between the two buildings, a heaving pile of police charged towards me through the narrow passage, some with guns up, scrambling over each other in their eagerness like the Keystone Cops.

'Get down on the floor, get down on the floor!' one screamed.

I did not comply, but had a last look up at the sky, which was very blue, with small wisps of cloud like cigarette smoke. I stood there and waited for the wave of law enforcement to crash upon me. And crash it did.

The first officer rugby-tackled me to the ground and the rest pounced like hounds on a fox. They absolutely battered me. Boots flew in from all angles and I lay, pinned to the concrete, absorbing the pain. As I did, I kept seeing a brown shoe swinging backwards and forwards into my face.

At last a voice said, 'Stop, there's a window cleaner up there. He's watching.'

'You lucky little cunt,' said another.

They handcuffed me and pulled me up. Through my swollen eyes I saw that the owner of the brown shoes was a woman. She had a blonde fringe.

'You fucking slag,' I hissed.

She smiled. 'You shouldn't go out robbing, should you?'

They bundled me into the back of the closest police car as my mind worked overtime, coming up with possible solutions to this mess. They had given me a hell of a beating and if I pretended to be concussed they would have to take me to hospital. It would be far easier to escape from a ward than a cell.

I began lolling my head around, closing my eyes and pretending I was drifting in and out of consciousness.

'Are you all right?' one copper asked.

'No, I'm nauseous and I'm seeing things floating in front of my eyes.'

All the while I listened to everything going on. It came through their radios that Kevin had not yet been arrested. I looked up and through slitted eyes, saw them go to the boot of my car and open it. The copper pulled a carrier bag out and all the others crowded around to see what he had found. He opened the bag and pulled out a towel. Then he pulled out a pair of gym shorts.

A few of the police gave each other worried looks. After that he took out a pair of trainers and a vest.

One of them put his head in his hands. Another visibly said 'shit'. They had been expecting guns.

The conversation on the radios resumed.

'Have you nicked Barnes?' one said.

'No,' came the reply. 'He's in Sidcup high street.'

'What the fuck?' I thought. 'What's he doing there?'

Minutes dragged by. I prayed that Kevin understood the gravity of the situation and had the sense to dispose of the weapons. Without firearms, there wouldn't be much of a case. The worst they could do me for would be theft. I maintained my act of losing consciousness for a while.

Then one of the police received an update.

'He's screaming "fit-up",' he shouted.

Kevin had been caught and in desperation was claiming police harassment. The jig was up.

I felt someone climb into the driver's seat of the car. I had my head down, eyes drooping.

'John,' a voice said.

I ignored it.

'John!' Rougher now, more insistent, it sounded familiar and I opened my eyes a crack. Sitting in the front, craning his neck around, grinning from ear to ear, was none other than DCI Currie. I sat up a little.

'So, we meet again! You haven't learned your lesson have you, John?' He allowed himself a little chuckle. 'I don't think Kevin's going to get you out of this like Paul did. Nah, I just can't see it. You're going to have to answer for this one.'

I mumbled something, still trying to feign concussion.

'Listen me old mate and listen well. You are fucked. Well and truly. You do know that, don't you?'

With every gloating word he sucked a bit more life out of me. I sank into the seat, knowing he was right. Soon all three cars formed a convoy, taking me to Bromley police station. Currie drove my car, while I sat sandwiched between two meathead coppers in the back. My brain churned and churned, scrambling for possibilities.

'I'm not going back to prison. Got to do something. I'm not going back to prison.'

Currie broke my trance.

'Look out the window John,' he said, fixing my eyes in the rear-view mirror.

I looked. We were passing through Bromley town centre at 10am on a Wednesday. There were supermarkets, buses and a few gap-toothed old drunks smoking outside Wetherspoons. One of them was on a mobility scooter. Never had it all looked so beautiful.

'You won't be seeing this for a very long time.'

A lump rose in my throat. I looked down, attention suddenly drawn by the gearstick and handbrake.

'If I time it right and kick those,' I thought, 'when we're going at speed, there's a chance the car might flip. If the car flips, maybe I can get out.'

The copper next to me seemed to sense what I was thinking, sidled closer and locked his leg over mine. I had to accept it. There was no point struggling. It would just make it worse.

My elbow throbbed but I tried to ignore it, to relax and let the tension out of my body. I thought of Elodi, waiting for me back in Spain, of Aaron and our grand plans, the shining Mediterranean, the parties. Had it all just been an illusion? I looked down at my knees and waited.

Part Two

A Process of Adaptation

'Britain's most dangerous prisoners are being held in Belmarsh jail in a bleak and oppressive "prison within a prison" with a highly restrictive regime, official prison inspectors have found.

'Nick Hardwick, the chief inspector of prisons, says that the "depth of custody" at the specialist high-security facility at Belmarsh is greater than anywhere else in the country.

'He says that the south-east London jail is the only one in the country to hold "exceptional risk category A prisoners" and they are held in "dark and oppressive" conditions. A segregation unit within the special secure unit is described as "austere and sterile" while the outside exercise area is referred to as "claustrophobic" and "caged in with no seating".

'Michael Spurr, the chief executive officer of the National Offender Management Service, said he accepted that more work needed to be done to get the balance right between security and providing effective rehabilitative opportunities for the majority of prisoners.'

Alan Travis, *The Guardian*, 21 March 2014

12

'Top of the Tree of Armed Robbers'

THEY bundled me out of the car at Bromley nick and there was no need to fake it anymore. I felt genuinely nauseous.

Eighteen months since my release from Aylesbury and they had me again. How had I been so silly to get involved with Kevin's plans? Why had I even left Spain? All for a birthday party which I would never get to attend. What a kick in the nuts.

Currie and his colleagues placed me *incommunicado* to begin with, meaning I was neither allowed access to phones nor any other contact with the outside world. No one was to know where I was, until they gathered their initial evidence. The level of precaution showed their resolve – they wanted nothing to impede their task.

Nearly a full day passed before I was allowed to make a call and the police used the time to raid every address with an attachment to myself or Kevin. They were looking for hard evidence to prop up their case, exhibits for the courtroom – guns, crash helmets or any paraphernalia associated with armed robbery. I lay on my bunk and thought of them turning up at Mum's, how distraught she would be. It was heart-breaking.

When they eventually allowed me two phonecalls I spoke to Milner first, as was customary.

'Don't worry, John,' he said. 'I'm already aware of your situation. Someone's coming down in the morning. We'll do the very best we can.'

Dreading the next conversation, I dialled Mum's number warily. She would be beside herself. How could I put a positive spin on this?

'Mum, I'm sorry…' I began.

'You promised me,' she interrupted. 'You promised you'd never go back.'

'They haven't got anything,' I tried to argue. 'It'll be fine. The charges won't stick. I've done nothing.'

She paused. I knew she wanted to believe me and could almost hear her mulling it over down the line. 'Okay,' she said at last. 'Don't worry love. Everything will be all right. I'll come down later and drop your stuff off.'

When the duty officer came in that night he was holding the sports bag I had brought home from Spain. Opening it was demoralising beyond belief. Pastel shirts, beach shorts, flip-flops, all the stuff I had thrown in there hurriedly before leaving my apartment in Marbella. None of it appropriate to where I found myself. As I didn't have any other clothes available I put them on.

Old Bill must have wondered what I was up to when they returned to take me down for interview. I was sitting in my cell dressed as if I were sipping cocktails by a pool.

Milner sent a junior brief from his office down to see me, a guy called Dentif.

'How bad do you think this will be?' I asked. He puffed out his cheeks.

'We have to wait and see. The two semi-automatic pistols and the stun-gun are a big negative. It depends what else they've got. Obviously if you're found guilty, your previous conviction will be considered in sentencing. Let's hope it doesn't get to that stage, though.'

Just as I had the first time, I sat with police for three days in that police station and refused to answer a question, not even to confirm my name. I made no eye contact. I gave them nothing.

Messages were mixed and they kept telling me I would be taken to different magistrates' courts. One copper said Bromley, another said Westminster. At other times I was told Bexley, or City of London. They were confusing me, deliberately. The only thing I knew was that my hearing was due on Saturday morning.

I woke on the Saturday and asked to be taken to the showers, so that I could wash and brush my teeth before court. Repeatedly they said I had to wait, which made no sense. Feeling ignored, I became enraged. I shouted and swore, kicking at the door of my cell. Eventually the custody sergeant came back down.

'Calm down, John,' he said. 'You'll get to have a shower and a change of clothes, don't worry, but I've been asked to hold on for a bit. When your arresting officers arrive they'll come and open up your cell, okay?'

'My arresting officers?'

'Yes.'

'You mean the Flying Squad?'

'Yes.'

'For my shower?'

'Yes.'

They had to be up to something but I couldn't fathom what. About ten minutes later Currie arrived with DCI Foreman and two other suits, all the top brass from the Sweeney. Currie smiled, arousing my suspicion straight away. I had never seen anything on his face other than disdain. When he spoke his voice was unusually friendly.

'Hi John,' he said. 'Do you want a shower then mate?'

'Yeah.'

'Can I get you anything else at all, a newspaper or magazine perhaps, a snack or something?'

I narrowed my eyes. 'No, just a wash.'

'Okey dokey!'

He let me out and all four of them escorted me down to the bathroom, waited outside while I washed, then led me back to my cell. I put my suit on, a nice charcoal grey, tailored Savile Row number and tried to figure out their intentions.

'Are you ready then John?' Currie asked after a few minutes, still doing his best 'nice guy' impression.

'Yeah, course I am. I can't wait to get out of here. There are junkies and piss-heads next door and I've had virtually no sleep for three days. The food tastes like dog shit. Let's go.'

'Come on then mate,' he said. His voice remained low and calm. 'Let's get the handcuffs on you.'

'Mind the watch,' I told him. I was wearing a 15 grand Rolex Daytona.

They restrained my wrists and cuffed me to Foreman, all of which was unusual procedure for a magistrate's hearing. As we began walking along the corridor, I decided just to be direct and asked as nonchalantly as I could.

'What's going on? Why are you lot here?'

Currie gave another little smile. 'We're not taking any chances with you John,' he said, leading me down the corridor. 'We need to be absolutely sure.'

Squinting into the sun, as we emerged from the back doors of the station into the car park, I understood. A bombproof lorry was parked up with the back doors open and its engine running.

The thing was the size of a standard heavy goods vehicle, white, with an orange police stripe around it like a belt. Five tiny windows sat just below the roof.

The whirring of blades alerted me to a helicopter hovering in the sky directly above while 20 armed officers holding semi-automatic carbines formed a guard of honour down to the waiting transport. Foreman took me ceremonially through the middle of them, like some kind of military parade, slowly walking the gauntlet of their expressionless faces and cold eyes. I turned my head to look at him.

'You have got to be having a laugh,' I said. 'This is fucking overkill ain't it?'

'Can't have any of your mates coming along to break you out, can we?' he replied.

He manoeuvred me inside and they strapped me on to a seat at the far end of the lorry, by the driver's cab. Two doors made of bulletproof Perspex were closed around me. I felt like Hannibal Lecter in his cage, while they busily taped over all the interior windows. Through the rear doors, which were still open, I watched a convoy of police cars and motorbikes surround the lorry in formation.

'You lot are on a jolly,' I said, concern mounting. 'Just get me to fucking prison. I want to go to sleep.'

'It's nice to know you're keen to get back where you belong,' Foreman replied.

'Piss off! I'll be out in a year. Bit of time on remand and I'm away.'

'We'll see about that.'

'We will fucking see.'

A while later the van ground to a halt, they opened up the cage and re-handcuffed me to Foreman. He led me out of the lorry and through the rectangular, concrete frontage of Camberwell magistrates' court. I was surprised to see Kevin in the waiting area, our first meeting since the aborted job.

He looked terrible. Black eyes, cuts and scrapes all over his face, they had obviously given him a proper going over. I sat on a chair next to him and he turned, looking at me out of the one eye he could open. There wasn't anger in his manner, but a kind of weariness, almost disappointment. He stared past me silently for a while then whispered, 'You fucking brought it on us.'

'No mate,' I replied. My head was clear. 'You've brought it on me. There's no way that activity was linked to me. I haven't even been in the country.'

'No, it's you. You, Billy and Micky, the McAvoy name and all that rubbish, you've been over there, meeting with Micky, they've clocked on and then you've come home and brought it on me.'

'No way mate, I couldn't have. What happened to you, anyway?'

'I clocked them early on, so I got out of there. Thought you'd done the same.'

I nodded.

'I just can't believe all this is happening,' he said, eyes down.

The hearing was brief. Agonisingly, Mum was there, her face white, mouth twitching. They remanded us into custody and she waved as they dragged me back out. Handcuffed, I tried to wave back with my eyebrows.

On the way down to the lorry, Currie spoke matter-of-factly, as if he was talking about a shopping list, or the weather.

'So, John, we've made a few arrangements and you're going to go to Belmarsh.'

I shrugged. 'Whatever.'

It was only a 30-minute drive across south London, not that I could see any of it. The brakes screeched and they dragged me out. I could smell the Thames.

Belmarsh doesn't look like much from the outside. The main entrance is a simple, standard doorway set into a wide, red brick building that resembles a sports hall.

I was led into a bright, white reception room and placed in a holding cell until they were ready to receive me. Kevin was already in there. He looked up and sniggered.

'What do you make of all this?' he asked.

'Mate, we're fucked,' I said. 'Look at all this shit. This is high-end. Are you sure they haven't been on you?'

'Course they haven't, I know what I'm doing.'

I believed him. He had been in so much trouble so many times and always seemed to pull his irons out of the fire. He even earned a nickname of 'Untouchable', a reputation he relished.

'Maybe they just drove past on the day and got lucky?' I offered, clutching at straws.

'Fuck knows.'

They pulled him out first. Left alone, I stewed on my dilemma. Even without details I knew it was his fault. It had to be.

They came for me 20 minutes later, took me to reception, strip-searched and checked me. Out of stubbornness I refused to confirm my name, address or anything. By that stage it was pointless but I still wanted to give them nothing, especially not the satisfaction of knowing they 'had me'. When the formalities were completed they placed me back in a holding cell and one of the senior officers came in.

'John McAvoy?' he said.

I nodded.

'You've provisionally been made category double A. Do you know what that means?'

I shook my head.

'An application was made to the Home Office and through that application, it has been deemed that you have the access to money, means, capability and of course the associates to stage an armed escape from prison. As a result, you've been assigned to the HSU.'

I thought it sounded like some sort of hospital.

'What's that?'

'You're going on to the High Security Unit.'

It meant very little to me so I accepted the news without comment.

He closed the door and I had another ten minutes to myself before five other officers appeared in a group.

'You all right?' the leader asked, casually.

'Yeah.'

'Great. We've been told you're coming with us to the HSU. You're not going to start causing trouble down there are you?'

'Nah.'

'It's not like a normal prison, it's much more relaxed and we like to keep it that way.'

'Okay.'

'Good. That's what we like to hear.'

Another stepped forward and handcuffed my wrist to his, while the rest formed a ring around me. Rather than walking me through corridors to the wing, as I expected, they took me back out of the front doors, on to the forecourt and into a waiting van. The HSU, I soon gathered, was housed in a completely separate building, in the south-west corner of the prison complex, away from all the other wings.

As they drove me past the brick and concrete strongholds toward my new home, outside on the streets of London, the *Evening Standard* was being sold on news-stands. 'Brinks-Mat robber's nephew among dangerous gang jailed' read the headline.

In a front-page article Kevin and I were called 'extremely dangerous' and 'the top of the tree of armed robbers'.

I hadn't made my name in the way I always hoped, but without even knowing it I was famous.

13

Welcome, Brother

THE high walls of Belmarsh echoed with voices. Prisoners shouted from barred windows to neighbours or friends in other wings. As we passed by, their cries carried around the courtyards, building into an eerie chorus, like animals in a rainforest.

The van soon pulled up in front of a tall electric gate, beyond which lay a vast, squat concrete structure, like a giant nuclear bunker. Several officers stood outside with wolf-like Alsatian dogs on leads.

A bubbling in the pit of my stomach acknowledged the seriousness of my situation. This place did not look like other prisons. It looked like science fiction.

As they pulled me up from my seat I glimpsed my handcuffed wrists, realised how tanned they looked and shook my head. I would have to banish those kinds of thoughts. Prison had taught me before to live purely in the future. Thinking too much about what you had lost or were missing out on was a shortcut to despair. I had to be strong, never let them get the better of me. *Good stuff* doesn't lose its cool.

The driver spoke into an intercom, the gate opened and we passed through.

Our van circled the foreboding building in front of us until we arrived at a loading bay at the rear. Again the driver leant out of the window and spoke into an intercom system. A huge steel door eased itself outward, until we were able to drive through the gap, then it slid closed behind.

The building had swallowed us. We were in the unseen catacombs of the UK criminal justice system, the belly of the whale. This was a new sort of underworld for me – a prison within a prison.

My eyes darted around. First impressions of the HSU were disconcerting. It was how I imagine the interior of a submarine would look, with claustrophobic, tube-like corridors and low ceilings. Everything was a kind of eggshell, off-white colour and strip-lit with fluorescent bulbs. It smelled strongly of bleach.

They began walking me through and it soon registered that none of the staff had keys. Every single heavy, steel door, of which there were many, opened only via intercom. A control centre sat in the bowels of the place where officers scrutinised CCTV monitors. They alone decided whether or not a door could open, a system devised to remove the incentive to attack officers for keys, or take hostages then demand keys be handed over.

As well as several leading members of the IRA and KGB, the HSU had previously housed Ian Huntley (the Soham murderer), Great Train Robber Ronnie Biggs and Charles Bronson, who has popped up in most places at the top end of the UK prison system. While there, Bronson famously took two Iraqi hijackers hostage in his cell, forcing them to tickle his feet and call him 'General'. Unhappy with their service, he beat one around the head with a metal tray, then felt guilty about it and told them to attack him with it. Growing tired of his own games, he then threatened to kill them.

Once he had everybody's attention Bronson issued a list of demands including a plane to Libya, two automatic rifles and some ice cream. Throughout my stay at Belmarsh, the officers talked about the incident with a strange mixture of humour and misty-eyed affection. Something my time in prisons showed me repeatedly was that the criminals perceived to be the most dangerous were also the ones afforded most respect by staff. They all want to get along with the top boys. Everything is topsy-turvy on the inside.

With this one building containing a selection of ultra-high-risk inmates, security was intense. No one had ever escaped from the HSU in its 25 years of operation. When first built they tested its impenetrability by locking the SAS in there, equipped with sledge hammers and crowbars, giving them specific orders to break out over the course of a weekend. In 48 hours and with specialist equipment at their disposal, the country's elite commandos got through one door.

On the reception area for my wing I was strip-searched again then made to squat over a mirror to ensure I wasn't concealing drugs in my anus. Still naked, they sent me through a metal detector to check for interred weapons.

The final indignity was an intimate frisk with a transmission sensor, to see if I had a mobile phone secreted in my bowel. Only in prison do you learn the numerous combinations of items that can be hidden up a man's arse.

With all the cavity searching out of the way, they walked me up. 'You're starting on spur three,' a screw told me.

Again I was genuinely surprised at the size of the place. It seemed so tiny compared to its external bulk. From the outside the HSU appeared a hulking citadel, from the inside, a few inter-connected tunnels. All the rooms and walkways were really compact. I surmised this had to be because the walls were so thick.

My half of the wing was empty because the inmates had been taken out to the yard. Two rows of eight cells each lined a central area with a pool table, two rowing machines, an exercise bike and a television. There were CCTV cameras everywhere and no sources of natural light.

'You've got two options,' a screw said. 'You can go straight to bang-up in your cell or you can take your exercise now with the others. If I was you, I'd take the exercise. You only get one hour a day.'

'Yeah, I'll do that.'

Our footsteps echoed as I followed him along a corridor, through another pair of air-locking doors and into what can only be described as an enormous cage. Looking up, I could see sky, but carved into little blue triangles. Criss-crossed metal barriers formed walls and roof around us, casting a geometric grid of shadow on the ground.

On closer inspection I realised there were actually two layers of fencing with a kind of steel mesh-netting between them – a helicopter-proof design.

Standing there stirred strange sensations. The air changed, so you knew you were outside, but the light was so disrupted your eyes weren't sure. It looked like something from a Mad Max movie.

Alongside us a guard sat in his own small, fenced-in area, detached from the inmates, observing. My officer showed me into the main yard and swung the gate shut. Just four days earlier I had been a free man, now I found myself in a metal enclosure with a bunch of top-end cons I didn't know.

I tried to stay detached from the artificiality and remain alert, looking for weak spots. *Is there any possible way I could get out of here?* Nothing leapt to mind.

Other prisoners meandered around, some alone, some in pairs or threes. I moved slowly towards them. One looked up, saw me and began striding purposefully in my direction. I tensed up. Who was this? Was he going to try something?

I was ready. You have to be. He had close-cropped blond hair and a heavy build, but as he neared I relaxed. He wore a broad, welcoming smile.

'Are you John?' he asked, extending his hand.

'Yeah.'

He hugged me. 'I'm Roger, a good friend of your Uncle Micky. I heard you were coming here on the radio.'

Roger Vincent was charged with a contract killing, the shooting of a bodybuilder called David King, outside a gym in Hertfordshire. King was a tough-nut himself, a minder with links to the drug trade. The word around the game was that he turned police informer and when the powers-that-be found out, a hit was ordered.

Roger allegedly cornered him in broad daylight and ripped into him with an AK-47, releasing 26 rounds in a two-second burst. It was the first time that gun had ever been used for a gangland killing in the UK.

'Are you all right?' he asked.

'I've been better, but yeah.'

'I know,' he said, smirking and looking around. 'This place is a bit of a trip, isn't it? Don't worry, you'll get used to it.'

We began to walk around the edge of the exercise area together.

'Where have you been before?'

'Just regular places, Woodhill, Aylesbury, that sort of thing.'

'Well here you'll find there isn't too much trouble. The screws won't bother you if you don't bother them and the other inmates… well they're an interesting bunch.'

For the first time I looked around at some of the others strolling the yard. A group of four dark-skinned men captured my attention immediately. I knew of them from the TV news.

'Fucking hell, I recognise them,' I said to Roger. 'Are they the guys that did 21/7?'

He nodded silently.

Ismail, Mukhtar, Yassin and Ramzy had attempted to set off a series of suicide bombs on the London Underground on 21 July 2005. There had been a problem with some of the detonators which had not all exploded, but they managed to create havoc nonetheless. After a manhunt they were apprehended and sentenced to 40 years for conspiracy to murder.

Walking just ahead of those four were two other men, one of them quite large, with his shirt sleeves flapping around his chest.

'Is that who I think it is?'

'The man himself,' Roger confirmed.

I instantly recognised Abu Hamza, the infamous, hook-handed imam of the Finsbury Park mosque in north London, who publicly declared his support for Bin Laden and Al Qaeda.

He wasn't allowed hooks in prison and his arms ended in stumps just below the elbow.

'Come on,' Roger said. 'I'll introduce you.'

We quickened our pace and soon were walking just behind him.

'Hamza,' Roger said. 'This is John. He's just come in today.'

Hamza stopped walking, turned around and smiled. He was missing his left eye and didn't look particularly well, but did his best to be friendly.

'Hello John,' he said. 'Welcome, brother. May you find strength here.'

'Thank you.'

'You'll find it is not as bad as it seems.'

We exchanged pleasantries, nothing more than greetings and small talk, but he couldn't have been more polite, which I found strange. He had barely been off the front pages of the tabloids for months and the media always portrayed him as a semi-hysterical psycho, frothing at the mouth and spewing bile.

The screws called time on the exercise period and we began walking back up to the spur.

'Do you need anything?' Hamza asked. 'Do you want some food?'

'No thanks.'

'Are you sure? I can offer you milk and Weetabix.'

I laughed. 'No, I'm all right.'

On arrival back at the spur, it emerged that he and I were neighbours. Hamza had the next cell to mine. I borrowed a towel from Roger and went for a shower.

When I returned, a little mound of Weetabix packs, some single portions of UHT milk and a copy of the Qur'an had appeared on my bunk. I assumed it was intended as an amicable gesture, but I had enough problems already. I figured it was important to avoid confusion, so picked up the book and went to his cell to return it.

'Mate, thanks but you can have that back,' I said.

He smiled, was even a little timid.

'No, no, please keep it, just something for you to read.'

I put it on the table in his cell. 'Really, I'm fine thanks.'

'Okay, brother, no problem.'

There was no menace, no venom. He sat down calmly and accepted my choice, which I soon learned was typical of his demeanour. In the time we spent together in the HSU, he never tried to push religion on me again. I actually ended up having quite a laugh with Hamza. Contrary to his public image, he had a good sense of humour.

'They say I'm a danger to society but everyone knows I'm "armless",' he would say, waving his stumps around. We used to make fun of him because he had a prison medic attending to him, who was the campest, most effeminate man you could imagine, a skinny mixed race guy with a stud earring and a high-pitched voice. Roger called him 'Michael Jackson'.

'The prison officers know what they are doing!' Hamza would say. 'They are taking the piss. You don't give a gay nurse to a Muslim!'

He had a real hang-up about that stuff which made for some great comedic moments. There was one officer we used to call 'Boyband', because he looked like he could have been in Take That. Tanned, blond hair, fashionable dragon tattoos on his arms. Hamza refused to be strip-searched by him because he claimed he was homosexual. Boyband denied the accusation vigorously. It caused lots of problems, which we found hilarious, giving us all plenty of ammunition to make fun of Boyband, which really wound him up.

'It's nothing to be ashamed of,' we'd say. 'Come on, it's the 21st century, just come out of the closet!' We would all crack up laughing. The look on his face was priceless.

At the back of my mind lingered the thought that if I committed an armed robbery in Saudi Arabia, Syria or Afghanistan, Sharia law would demand an execution and as devotees, Hamza and the others would probably support that. Yet in jail we were all the same. Muslim, Christian, black or white, it didn't matter, our common enemy was the system.

There were rare times when watching the news they would comment on something that touched their beliefs. But they never got agitated or insistent. On one occasion there was an item about the 9/11 enquiry.

'It's impossible,' Hamza said. 'The official version of this story is impossible. I was an engineer and I can tell you it cannot have happened like that. They are covering something up.'

The other Muslim inmates all agreed. Other than myself, Roger and Kevin, who arrived the day after me, most of the men on our side of the wing were in for terrorism related offences, but we mixed with them comfortably. I took it as a learning opportunity. I was unlikely to have another time when I could associate with Muslim extremists, so spoke to them whenever possible, not probingly, just general conversations about life. Their whole outlook and world view fascinated me.

'I don't understand why you pleaded not guilty at court,' I would say. 'Why don't you do what the IRA did? Just sit there and have complete disdain for the system? The IRA never bothered denying their guilt because they knew there was no point. So they'd go in with the sole intention of wasting as much public money as possible. You lot should do the same. If you're passionate about what you're doing and you believe in it so much, why don't you do the same thing?'

'But we're innocent,' they would say.

There was a culture clash only in the sense that I saw the law as a blunt instrument, a functional thing, an opponent to be overcome, rather than a value system. Those guys did believe in the rule of law and they believed in it absolutely. It was just a completely different one to westerners.

Over time I even formed friendships with some of them. Ramzy was more or less my age and used to come and exercise with me on the bike and the rowing machines. We would set up circuits in the yard of sprints, burpees and press-ups. Sometimes Roger and Yassin would join in too.

Soon I started to really look forward to those sessions. The charge of adrenaline was intoxicating, even a little freeing. As I had on my first sentence, I felt my fitness improve and physical exertion helped relieve the boredom of captivity.

In this way we formed a kind of community and with such a large Muslim contingent, the annual festival of Ramadan, which occurred shortly after my arrival, was a big deal in there. It culminated in Hamza and the others having their Eid celebration, with special food delivered on to the spur and a table set up for all the biscuits and sweets.

'Come brothers, come,' they said. We joined them and shared their goodies.

I sat there and marvelled at the scene. Around that table, making small talk over jaffa cakes and plastic cups of orange juice, were armed robbers, a contract killer, a drug trafficker, four attempted suicide bombers and one of the world's most infamous Al Qaeda activists.

'Can you pass the Swiss roll please?'

That was life inside the bubble of the Belmarsh HSU.

14

Further Charges

TIME dragged unendingly. It always does in prison, but in that place with no natural light and its cramped sterility you really felt a pause button had been pressed on your existence. We used to call it the bat-cave.

Every night, after lock-up, I would lie there, look at the ceiling and repeat the mantras that worked for me before. *This is not your life. You do not choose to be here. Don't let this define who you are.*

Altogether we had 90 minutes a day out of our cells. An hour's exercise in the yard and 30 minutes' association, when you could grab a shower, wash your clothes and maybe play a game of pool if you had time. The rest of it, you were alone.

The routine was broken at intervals by other formalities, which for someone in there long enough formed their own, overarching routine. This created a routine beyond the routine, for the prison within a prison. Every 28 days we had to move cell, in case we were digging tunnels, despite the fact we only had plastic cutlery. How the hell they thought we could burrow out of there with a Spork when the SAS only managed one door with sledgehammers, God knows.

Screws were moved between wings every three months and moved off the HSU altogether every six months. They did not want lasting relationships developing between officers and inmates. Top criminals can be charismatic and could conceivably turn staff into conspirators. I rarely spoke to them anyway so that didn't bother me.

One of the hardest things to get used to was the night-time checks. Officers would observe inmates sleeping in their cells every 15 minutes throughout the night. You could hear them shuffling around, before a little red light would come on while they watched what you were doing. To begin with it woke me up every time.

If you had a serious problem with something, you had to go to Governor Arden, the top man in the HSU who only appeared on the wing occasionally. A tall, ginger, very slender character, he always struck me as a typical civil servant. Marks and Spencer suit, short back and sides haircut, with a clipped voice. When anyone spoke to him, especially Hamza, he would reply with a nervous stammer. Even minor, vocal confrontation made him uncomfortable.

For two months I lingered in there on remand, before my pleas and directions hearing, at which I went not guilty on solicitor's advice. Dentif came in for regular meetings. The first time he smiled, shook my hand, then scribbled down six words on a piece of paper and passed it.

How much money have you got?

He wanted to know what legal costs I was able to pay for before we began. Not the best starting point, but at least we understood each other.

At that stage we were yet to understand the sheer depth of evidence but he spoke candidly about realities, explaining that my stay in the HSU was costing the taxpayer £5,000 a week. I talked to Roger about it, who laughed knowingly.

'That's right,' he said. 'Five grand per man. And they are not going to invest all that money for us to walk scot-free, are they?'

Prisoners on the HSU had a 98 per cent conviction rate when their cases went to court, which was not especially encouraging. Whether they were guilty or not, many of the reasons for that were environmental.

All of us were aware that legal visits were bugged. No one had laid it out in so many words, but with men involved in international terrorist conspiracies on the wing, there was no chance to speak to your legal advisor, or any other visitor, freely and unmolested. As far as the authorities were concerned it was a matter of national security and they were entitled to infringe civil liberties.

In one sense you could understand that, but it meant that any evidence, alibis or strategies you discussed with your solicitor would become known to the prosecution before the trial. On the other hand, they were able to prepare their evidence without your knowledge. To my eyes, that compromised the principles of a fair hearing and the basic tenet of 'innocent until proven guilty', but when you are in that situation, there is nothing you can do about it.

Visits took place in special block. After being notified of the visit a screw would handcuff you and walk you off the wing, through the self-opening and locking set of security doors and out as if you were going to the exercise yard. You would have to strip, be searched and given a fresh set of sterile clothing to wear. After the visit you were searched again, the clothing was taken off you and bagged, before you were given your old clothes back.

During any non-legal visit, a prison officer would sit in the booth with you. There were cameras trained on both your face and that of your visitor, checking for non-verbal communication. If you covered up your mouth with your hands, the visit was stopped. If you used any sort of code, the visit was stopped. If you conversed in any language other than English, the visit was stopped.

All visits had to be pre-approved by the police, meaning prior to the day they would meet your visitor at their home to satisfy security measures. Unfortunately, when my mother first visited, during my initial fortnight on the wing, she had not been approved yet. The governor allowed her a discretionary pass, but because security protocol was not satisfied, she had to sit behind a screen. To make matters worse, there was a problem with the internal prison transport and guards escorted her, on foot, through the whole length of the grounds, past the various cell blocks, all the way to the HSU. By the time she arrived she was crying and snivelling. Seeing Abu Hamza sitting in the next booth with his lawyer didn't help calm her down either.

'Are you all right, are you all right?' she kept asking, looking at the scabs I had on my face from when I'd been arrested.

I tried to make her feel better. 'Don't worry Mum, the case is terrible. They've got no evidence. I'll be out of here in no time.'

'I love you John,' she wailed, 'I love you so much.'

When the visit was done I told the screws I didn't want her to come back. It was better for both of us if she stayed away. Being in there was hard enough as it was and from then on, I kept in touch with Mum by the prison phone, speaking to her regularly. I hope she understood my reasons.

In addition to the costs of keeping a prisoner in the rarefied environment of the HSU, the specialist bombproof lorry escorts to and from court cost £20,000 a day. Originally mine and Kevin's trial was scheduled for the Old Bailey, but they knew it had the potential to be a lengthy procedure and would therefore be highly expensive.

When Belmarsh had first been built, the designs included a secret tunnel which ran underneath the road directly to Woolwich Crown Court. Like everything else about the place it had been constructed with the movement of high-profile IRA operatives in mind and reduced costs considerably. All they would have to pay for was a squad of armed officers to escort prisoners through the tunnel. Our trial was duly switched to there.

All these details fed into the near-impossibility of being found innocent. For most of the prisoners on the HSU, whose faces had been splashed all over newspapers and TV news, trial conditions were different to the norm. When Roger had his trial in Luton, they constructed a scaffold around the courthouse with armed police all over it. Helicopters hovered in the sky above. Imagine the psychological impact on jury members as they arrived!

Equally, you can foresee a jury confronting someone like Abu Hamza and being totally jaundiced. If someone has been built up into a figure of hate by the media, objectivity is impossible. Regardless of any mitigating circumstances, high-security status was a shortcut to a guilty verdict and we all knew it.

The only one who struggled to accept this grim reality was Kevin, which worried me as he was my co-defendant. In the visits I had with Dentif, over time it had become clear to me that our case was hopeless and that as I suspected, they had been monitoring him.

The police had occupied a flat opposite Kevin's house since early summer and watched his every move for two months. They had 45 surveillance videotapes and in several of them he was blatantly casing jobs. I was only in the last three.

By the time I arrived from Spain they knew he was red hot and were on him like fleas. He could not go to the toilet without them knowing about it. The thing that really stuck in my craw was that my sixth sense had been right. The van and car I had seen had both been full of police, as I suspected. It played on my mind. I should have got myself out of there. I should have known better. The bottom line was that Kevin had been really sloppy.

His cars were radar-tracked and bugged. They had films of him waiting for security vans, films of his meetings with me and others. They had literally every kind of evidence you could possibly have and their case was watertight. It was hard not to feel angry. Maybe because he needed the money so much, Kevin had put himself on offer, but as a result he had dragged me down with him.

I tried speaking to him on association, or in the exercise yard.

'You're completely fucked mate. We need to work something out.'

'What are you on about?'

'Mate, the evidence is overwhelming. You need to start thinking straight.'

'They can't get me. No chance.'

'If we don't plan something here, we're both getting stitched up.'

'Leave off, John. You're thinking like them.'

All that 'Untouchable' rubbish had gone to his head. He was delusional.

By the time I had been on the HSU for three months, Abdi, another Muslim kid, a convicted murderer, was transferred in from the main prison for fighting. I got on quite well with him. Roger did too. We were out on association one day and he came and sat next to me, holding a bag of chip sticks.

'Do you want some crisps?' he said.

'No, you're all right mate.'

'No really, have some crisps.'

'I don't want any!'

He fixed me in the eye.

'I think you do. Just try them. They're nice crisps.'

Sensing that there was something going on, I took the bag. It was heavy. A quick glimpse revealed a Nokia cellphone covered in crumbs and salt. I have no idea how he got it past all the security measures, but there it was.

That mobile phone was like a rare diamond to us. We looked after it collectively and passed it around. When night fell and the lights were off, whoever had the phone could send texts or make whispered phone calls. The first night with the phone in my possession, I called Aaron. He was back in Holland at the time.

'What the fuck's happening?' he asked.

'Mate, I'm fucked. You've got to come and get me.'

'What about Kevin? Isn't he going to get you off?'

'Nah, he thinks he's going to beat it.'

'Is there any way you can get out?'

'There's nothing mate. This place is like Alcatraz. Just make sure you're ready. If an opportunity comes, I'm going to need you. It might be difficult, might involve some aggro. You know what I'm talking about, don't you?'

'Of course mate, no problem, whatever it takes. All you have to do is give me a call, you know that.'

I was determined not to become desperate, but at the same time it was tough to contemplate spending too long in the HSU. The sheer deprivation would fry your brains and the food was appalling. Dinner was cooked in the prison kitchen at 3pm and served to most of the prisoners by four, but because it had to be wheeled all the way through the grounds and pass through security checks before it got to us, we would not receive it until nearly five.

It was poor-quality prison muck anyway, but it was also cold and congealed by the time it reached us. After three solid months of putting up with it, I could take no more. I looked at my plate one day, then at the other boys and said, 'Fuck this. Do you know what? We should refuse to eat it. Maybe they'll have to do something about it then.'

My idea was met with instant agreement and word spread quickly. Messages were passed on exercise sessions and prayer meetings. Within a couple of days, all four wings of the HSU had agreed to unite on hunger strike.

That Friday afternoon, when they wheeled the hot plate over from the main prison, no one ate. No dinner became no breakfast and then no lunch the following day. Twenty-four hours in, Governor Arden came to see us.

'L-l-look I just want to know why you're n-n-not eating. W-w-what do you hope to ach-ch-chieve?'

We explained our reasons. That night after bang-up, I watched the news on TV in my cell. There were a couple of items about the economy and wars in the Middle East and then it came.

'Inmates in the high security unit at Belmarsh jail have gone on a hunger strike, led by notorious imam, Abu Hamza,' they said.

I could not believe what I was seeing and rushed to my door, shouting through the bars.

'Rog, Rog we're on the fucking news!'

'No way!' he shouted back.

'And guess what Hamza, they've pegged you as the ringleader!'

'Bloody hell,' Hamza's voice came back. 'I was only following you lot!'

It seemed his fate to get the blame for everything. In the end we lasted three days and every national newspaper carried the story, causing enough embarrassment to prison authorities for them to address our concerns. Arden came back and promised improvements. We started eating and from then on, they never served us two-hour-old meals again.

As our trial date approached, Kevin and I received regular police visits and we both noticed that the conversations began taking on a different character, broadening out, which concerned me. My fears were confirmed by Milner, who called me one evening.

'John, they've got some very serious bits and pieces they want to attach to your case. Yet another armed robbery and a multiple shooting. They'll be taking you out of Belmarsh to interview you sometime in the next few days.'

The chance to nail Kevin once and for all was too much to pass up, so they were taking the approach of throwing as much mud at him as possible and hoping some would stick. By being seen as his accomplice I was in danger of guilt purely by association.

These were crimes committed while I had been in Spain and the police knew that, but it's all part of their game. Once they have you in a place like the HSU they can stick extras on you because your circumstances make you vulnerable. It gives them the opportunity to tidy up their backlog of unsolved crimes. Serious Crime and Flying Squad officers have targets to meet, like all the rest of them. Nonetheless I was excited by the news and spoke to Roger in the exercise yard.

'They're taking me out,' I told him. 'I can't wait. I tell you what, if I see a chink of light, any sliver of a chance, I'm gone, no bother.'

Every day from that phonecall onwards I woke up sharply at six in the morning, listening for any sounds of a police van turning up. Psychologically, I prepped myself and worked out how it could happen.

'They're going to get you out,' I thought, 'and put you in a car. You've got to do something to stop that car, whatever you need to do. Aaron can be there waiting. It's your fucking chance.'

Three days after I spoke to Milner, the door crashed open at about 8.30am.

'This is it,' I thought.

'You've got a police visit,' the screw said.

As usual we went through all the standard rigmarole, doors locked and unlocked, changes of clothes, strip-searching. Once the procedures were done they took me down to HSU reception, the first time I had been there since my arrival. The familiar faces of DCI Foreman, DCI Currie and their various acolytes stood around by the door.

'Hello John,' Currie said. 'Long time, no see.'

They handcuffed me to Foreman and took me out. My heart sank when I saw they had brought a lorry. Foreman walked me over, put me in the Perspex box and took the cuffs off. About ten minutes later they brought Kevin in and locked him into a separate box next to mine.

As soon as the lorry had driven out of the prison grounds, Foreman took a seat near my box.

'Jonathon Michael McAvoy,' he said, 'we're going to arrest you for further offences this morning. You're being charged with a series of conspiracies to commit armed robbery between July and September of last year and the fatal shootings of Paul Anthony Lewis and Nicholas Wellington.'

He then turned to Kevin and said exactly the same thing. While he reeled off his little speech again the lorry screamed off and did not stop for 20 minutes. As with the last time, the windows were taped up and it was impossible to see where we were headed.

When it did eventually pull up we emerged into the rear car park of Walworth Road police station, which absolutely crawled with armed officers. I took a few breaths and accepted my fate. There would be no chance of escape that day.

I was taken in, placed in a cell and within minutes Dentif was at my door.

'I have been a solicitor for 20 years,' he said. 'And I have never seen security like this. They've set up an armed perimeter and are preventing anyone from entering while you're here. It's crazy.'

Once the interviews began, two things became clear. Firstly, the shootings were nonsense and they knew it. I had nothing to do with them and hadn't even been in the UK. I had never even heard of the victims.

The further conspiracy charges were also a stretch, to say the least. Although I had only met up with Kevin for the final six days of the two months they had watched him, they decided to charge me for all of Kevin's illegal activities during the whole period. Their reasoning was that he had been planning robberies and waiting for me to return from Spain to commit them with him, in some pre-arranged set-up, which was pure fantasy. As I learned though, the law relating to conspiracy is a slippery and malleable thing.

Dentif explained it to me as being like a bus journey. The bus might start at one end of a town and finish at another. You may have only ridden the bus for a couple of stops, but the fact you were a passenger at all made you responsible for anything that happened during the whole trip.

Currie laid out all the crimes for which I could be deemed culpable, with a sense of satisfaction. Dentif was largely quiet, but I could tell from his manner that we were hamstrung. He had a downcast expression.

Once he had achieved the desired effect, Currie stopped and paused. He stood up, stretched, took a couple of steps towards the back of the room then turned around.

'Do you know what we're going to do, John?' he said. 'We're going to give you an opportunity.'

Dentif looked my way and raised his eyebrows.

'Myself and DCI Foreman will leave the room, we'll switch all the recording equipment off and you and your solicitor can have a discussion in complete privacy. We'll let you prepare a statement now and we'll seal it in an evidence bag and leave it unopened until the day of your trial. If you've got a real defence, it won't change between now and the trial and that will stand you in good stead. But obviously if you change your story between now and then, it won't look good. What do you say?'

Dentif burst out laughing. 'That's a good one!' he said. 'There's no chance on God's earth my client will limit his defence in that way and you know it! I really have heard it all now!'

Despite the bravado, that meeting brought home to us the scale of the case they were planning. Being sentenced for my second armed robbery would be bad enough and would ensure a hefty sentence, but with the add-ons literally anything was possible. They were aiming to hang us out to dry.

That evening they took us back to Belmarsh. I knew there was no hope of getting away while I remained in the HSU. I would have to come up with something else.

15

Untouchable

IN the weeks leading up to our date at Woolwich Crown Court, Dentif became such a regular on the HSU he was virtually an inmate himself. We went over everything we knew about the police evidence and kept returning to the same conclusion – we were shafted.

My only chance lay in Kevin seeing sense, taking the rap and getting me off. In many ways it was the noble course of action. I really had nothing to do with the vast majority of the two months of conspiracy and only got involved to do him a favour.

As police evidence continued flooding in, the screws allowed us a video recorder so we could watch copies of the taped exhibits.

'Something will come up,' Kevin kept repeating, refusing to accept what was staring him in the face. 'You'll see. There's no way they'll pin this on me.'

I became exasperated. 'I'll tell you what we'll do,' I said. 'You won't listen to me, but maybe you'll listen to a second opinion.'

I walked back to the pool table where Ramzy was playing a game with Roger.

'Ramzy,' I said. 'Come here for a minute.'

He followed me back down the spur to the TV.

'Sit down,' I told him. Then I turned to Kevin.

'Now bear in mind, Kev, he's not from our game and he'll look at this just like members of the jury will.'

'Have a watch,' I said to Ramzy, and I pressed the play button.

The video showed a high street on a roasting hot day in July. There were women walking around in miniskirts, summer dresses and vest tops, men in t-shirts and shorts, while to the rear of the shops a small, wooded area with a footpath leading into a park could be seen.

Suddenly, Kevin popped out from there. He was wearing latex gloves, a heavy jacket, a roll-hat and a pair of sunglasses. All he needed was a stripy jumper and a bag with 'SWAG' written on it. If it hadn't been so serious it would have been funny.

Just to add the finishing touch, the camera panned from where Kevin was standing, following his eyeline over the road to where a security van pulled up outside a branch of Barclays. Kevin then started striding towards it, full of purpose. I paused the video.

'Ramzy,' I asked. 'What do you think's going to happen?'

'It looks like he's going to rob that van,' Ramzy said.

'You don't know what you're talking about!' Kevin cried. 'You're thinking like a copper. That's what the filth would say!'

I thanked Ramzy and he left us to it.

'Do you know what I think, Kev?' I said.

'What?'

'I think you should go guilty and get me out of here. They're doing you for the whole two months. I was only there at the end. You're probably going to get life, but if you hold your hands up, you'll get a much smaller tariff. If you fight this, you are screwed, I promise you. You might never get out.'

He looked at me coldly.

'Don't you know who I am? Kevin Barnes *never* goes guilty.'

News of our situation trickled through to people on the outside. Even Uncle Micky spoke to Milner, trying to apply a bit of traction. Nothing worked. Everyone else could see the reality. The police had a lot on Kevin, but not much on me. Yet speaking to him was a waste of breath.

A week before the date for our hearing Dentif came in with the barrister from his office, a guy called Charles Conway. We discussed my options and decided that my best course of action was to go guilty and hope for a deal. If I did that, Conway suggested there was a 50 per cent chance I could escape a life sentence. The most likely outcome was somewhere in the region of 15 years.

In the days that followed, I stepped up my attempts to convince Kevin that he was on the path of madness, but it remained pointless. He was guarded and cynical and carried on as if he didn't give a shit. Our discussions became more heated and a few turned into all-out arguments. His attitude really bugged me. You can be like that when your own future is at stake, but not when it's someone else's.

'Kev! Get fucking real mate. This is damage limitation. We just have to think of ways we can get out of the situation as fast as possible. Look, if you do your bit and get me off, I'll get you out. I promise. I'll make sure you've got money. I'll look after you. You just have to do this one thing for me.'

'I'm Kevin Barnes,' he would repeat, stubbornly. 'I don't do that.'

With the hearing just days away, Dentif came back.

'What deal will they offer?' I asked.

He shook his head.

'Nothing John, it's the lot I'm afraid. They're going to get you for all of it one way or the other. But pleading guilty is still your best option. It's the only way you might avoid a life sentence.'

I nodded and accepted the reality. It was that, or live in jail until old age. Back on the wing I told Kevin of my decision.

'I'm going guilty.'

'I can't fucking believe it.'

'Listen Kev, you are fucked. And you're so fucked that you're going to drag me down with you. I've got no choice.'

Forty-eight hours before the trial we were given yellow and green jumpsuits to wear, put back into the van and driven through the prison grounds to the main reception block. Once inside, the screws led us to the side of the building and opened a thick, vault door in the wall. We passed through it on to a gently sloping corridor that took us underground.

Built from reinforced concrete, like a smaller version of the Blackwall tunnel, the Woolwich Crown Court tunnel is a giant echo-chamber. Every little sound reverberates down there, footsteps, voices, coughs, while all the while you hear the heavy, ever-present rumble of traffic on the road overhead.

Once we reached the midway point of the tunnel we came to another enormous door. A series of locks clicked from inside and it swung open smoothly and steadily, revealing another corridor that took us up into the court. We were there for a standard pre-trial hearing, but once they got us into the dock and the judge started talking through the preliminaries, Dentif stood up and said, 'Mr McAvoy wants to change his plea, your honour.'

'Very well.'

It was the hardest thing I had ever done. I looked over at the police sitting smugly in a line beneath me and despised their eager faces. Worse than that, I felt I was letting them win. The judge asked me to stand and the clerk read, 'Count one, conspiracy to commit armed robbery. John McAvoy?'

Before I had hope, even if only a sliver of it, now I was giving it up. I looked back at the police then up at the judge. It took me a long time to get the word out.

'Guilty,' I said, at last. I felt sick.

'Count two, possession of firearms with intent to commit an indictable offence. John McAvoy?'

'Guilty.'

'Count three, possession of live ammunition with intent to endanger life. John McAvoy?'

'Guilty.'

'Count four, possession of a stun gun with intent to commit an indictable offence. John McAvoy?'

'Guilty.'

I sat back down and the court blurred around me. Other things were discussed. I paid no attention. Before I could get my head together they started leading us back downstairs.

'How do you feel?' Kevin asked.

'I feel all right,' I lied.

'Don't worry mate,' he said. 'I'll be out soon and I'll send someone for you. I'll get you out and make sure you've got some money. I'll look after you.'

It was almost comical. Kevin was such a throwback, one of the old-school of villains. He hadn't adapted to the ways the law had developed. There was simply no way, with his prior record and the huge mountain of evidence piled against him that he was getting any result other than a very long sentence, but he remained stuck in this delusion that somehow everything would magically work out. He was so detached from reality I felt sorry for him.

'Okay mate,' I said and left it there.

They took us back through the tunnel. Returning to the HSU was tough. It felt different.

I was no longer on remand. I was a convicted criminal, awaiting sentence. It seemed darker in there, like someone had switched off a few lights. At 22 years old I knew it was very unlikely I would see the outside world until my 30s. While my friends and associates were making money and living it up, I would be locked away for the best years of my life.

Dentif returned a couple of days later. He assured me that my decision was the right one under the circumstances, but my mood was still low.

'Can you hurry them up?' I asked. 'I want to be sentenced so I can get out of this hole.'

He completed the paperwork, but the application was blocked by the prosecution on Kevin's case. They believed that if I received my sentence, I would then offer myself as a witness for the defence, take the blame for everything and get Kevin off. Once you've been sentenced, you can turn up in court and say what you want. There are no repercussions.

For me it was crushing news. Kevin's case was a drawn-out affair and I had to wait until it was over before any decision on my future could be decided, meaning I faced an uncertain period stuck in the HSU.

With things poised like that and no clear way out to aim for, I became miserable. Without a distraction I could easily have drifted into serious despair. And it was then that my exercise sessions began to take on a different character. At Belmarsh we were only allowed to use the gym three times a week, which was rudimentary at best, little more than a small room with a multi-gym and stereo in it, but I tried to make the most of it. I got a friend from outside to send me in some CDs, the kind of pumping dance music I had been listening to on pills in Spanish nightclubs, which I would have on full-blast while working out.

Needless to say, Hamza, who came along to train his legs, was not keen. 'Brother,' he would moan, between sets of squats, 'my ears, this hurts my ears, please turn it down.' I often got the impression that some of the younger Muslims enjoyed it, although they would never admit it. Dance music was a symbol of western decadence, after all.

As the gym facilities were so limited, I would use the exercise periods in the yard as fully as possible, beginning to find something in my outdoor circuits that had not been there before. It's not just that my fitness was increasing, although it was, or that the other lads found it harder and harder to keep up with me, although they did. It was that it had such powerful psychological effects.

Prison can be a savage thing to cope with, particularly if you are in long term. Banged up in my cell for hours on end, all sorts of things would pass through my mind. It's for those reasons so many prisoners suffer mental illness or end up attempting suicide. I believed I was strong-minded and resistant to such possibilities, but still needed something to take me out of there, to raise me beyond the walls. Some prisoners used drugs for that. Others would take up reading or art. For me, exercise became that thing.

I grew so attuned to it and felt so alive when I ran and jumped and used my body. I could almost forget where I was. For that hour, out in the yard surrounded by anti-helicopter wire and concrete I could zone out, or maybe zone in. I could lose myself in the moment, in my aching lungs and pumping heart and just be. Nothing else mattered.

Sometimes in the association area I would use the rowing machine or exercise bike, but they didn't particularly interest me. I rowed 500m for the first time in Belmarsh and found myself out of breath, but as the months dragged on and my fitness increased naturally, I would sometimes sit there for the full hour, just rowing or pedalling without even looking at how much distance I covered.

Soon I was adopting a rigid routine that involved two and a half hours of exercise a day. I would wake early, at around 5.30am and do a 90-minute cell circuit consisting of squats, burpees, sit-ups, step-ups and other bodyweight exercises. Then in the afternoon I would do my outdoor circuits in the exercise yard with the other boys. There was probably something compulsive in it. I was feeding a habit in the same way an addict does, but the effect on my state of mind was like voodoo.

Despite the upturn in my spirits and my new found interest, I still could not conceive of a life of normality, whatever that means. Having a job, travelling to work, paying bills, why would I? My frame of reference was what I grew up with and I had no plans at all outside of crime. I only thought to get out of Belmarsh as quickly as possible then move down through the security categories until they put me in an open prison, so I could scarper and return to the continent.

One afternoon, while Kevin's trial was going on, I sat in association chatting to Roger.

'I need to get of here, mate,' I said. 'I'm convicted now. I just want to go to a normal nick.'

'I know,' he agreed. 'There are some places where they let long-term prisoners cook their own food and have more time out of their cells. I'm the same. I want to go somewhere like that.'

That night I found it hard to sleep. The routine and tedium of life in the HSU nagged at me. I lay there twisting and turning, eating myself up with resentment at the system that had no place for me other than a cell. I'd show them, the bastards. One day, I'd show them.

At 6am my door pinged open. I was already awake. Five or six screws stood there.

'Morning John,' the one at the front said.

'What is this?'

'You're gone.'

'What?'

'Come on.'

I was dragged downstairs, strip-searched and cavity checked, then given a fresh green and yellow jumpsuit to wear.

'I'm being ghosted out, aren't I?' I asked.

They said nothing.

'Where am I going?'

They said nothing.

I was marched out, loaded into yet another lorry and strapped into another Hannibal Lecter box. The HSU screws handed me over to another bunch. Seven of them sat outside, eyeballing me.

'I'm getting used to this gents!' I told them, from inside my cage, feigning good spirits.

They said nothing.

Once the lorry started moving, these new screws began speaking among themselves. Boring chit-chat about pensions and what they were doing on their holidays. I looked from one to the other. They had the letters 'WD' on the lapels of their uniforms.

'WD?' I thought. 'It's Woodhill. I don't believe this. They're taking me back to Woodhill.'

I soon found out the reason for my sudden move. Probably in desperation, Kevin and his solicitor had adopted a defence tactic of blaming everything on me, saying I was the ringleader of the operation and he was following my directions. It was a poor strategy and didn't achieve much, but the authorities believed there could be problems between myself and Kevin if we continued to be housed in the same facility. I had been transferred to avoid the possibility of physical violence between us.

I don't believe we would have come to blows, but although I expected him to try something, I didn't see the point in his ploy. It was unlikely to change much for Kevin, particularly bearing in mind all the video footage of his activities, but if the judge and jury gave it any credence at all it could still affect the length of my sentence. As a trial gambit, it was foolish and selfish.

Milner phoned me during my brief stay back in Woodhill and offered me the chance to go QE.

'Currie is offering the Queen's Evidence option again,' he said. 'In return for a substantial reduction in your sentence, it would mean a guarantee of not getting life and the possibility of being out in a year or two.' He paused. 'I have to ask, John.'

I laughed and so did he.

'I tell you what you can do, Henry.'

'Go on.'

'I want you to do this word-for-word, okay?'

'Of course.'

'Ring Currie back and tell him to go fuck himself with a truncheon. I'll sit in here and do life if I have to.'

16

People Like You
Do Not Change

ONE of the benefits of being back at Woodhill was that security was far more lax. I had access to mobile phones every day and spoke to Aaron and others on a regular basis. He was back in the UK and went down regularly to Woolwich Crown Court, to listen to Kevin's case and give me updates. When the trial concluded, they took me back to Belmarsh.

'How do you think it went?' I asked Kevin, when I saw him.

'Disaster,' he said, shaking his head. 'Total fit-up.'

He and I were called in for sentencing a few days later, joined in the dock by a character I had never met before, a lanky black guy with a bedraggled, hangdog face. Gerald, it turned out, was the accomplice Kevin had been using before I came back from Spain, the one he had dropped for being a liability.

A walrus-faced judge called Carroll presided and Gerald was asked to stand first. He wore a squalid tracksuit. His hand shook uncontrollably.

'This is embarrassing,' I thought.

Gerald had previous convictions for kidnapping and like me was up for conspiracy to commit armed robbery. Carroll gave him a telling off and ten years, which I gauged against my own case. Ten years would not be so bad. I could probably cut it to five. I had already served two.

'John Michael McAvoy, stand up.'

I stood. All the familiar faces on the police bench stared my way.

'There are a lot of aggravating factors here,' Carroll said, his thick, white moustache undulating with the words. 'Firstly, your age of offending. I have to bear in mind that whatever sentence I pass down today, you're going to come out of prison a young man and on that basis I have to say that you will continue to pose a serious and persistent danger to society.

'I also take into consideration your severity of offending at such a young age. You've gone straight from being a non-offender, to committing some of the most serious offences on the statute book. That is not to be taken lightly.

'I must also sentence in light of your very deep-rooted connections to the criminal underworld. Connections of such a nature are not easy to break and will likely persist throughout your life, making your chances of re-offending very high.'

I began to get a queasy feeling in my guts.

'In light of all of this and the fact that the firearm in your possession had a bullet in the chamber ready to be discharged, I have no option but to pass down two life sentences, one for possession of firearms and the other for conspiracy to rob.'

Bravado forced me to smile. The police leapt from their chairs, fist-pumping and high-fiving each other. DCIs Foreman and Currie shook hands gleefully. I stood there and grinned, grinned for England. What else could I do?

'Now Mr McAvoy, if I were giving you a fixed term today,' Carroll went on, 'I would have given you ten years. But because I've passed a life sentence, I'm going to set a minimum tariff of five. May you use the time to re-evaluate your future.'

I sat down and processed the result. Life was a bit of a shocker. Although the tariff meant I could first be considered for parole at five years, whenever they let me out I would be on licence forever. Unless I got myself out of the country, they would watch me until my dying day. I would have to report to the probation services on a monthly basis and if I was even suspected of criminal involvement, I could be recalled to prison without trial.

Returning to the HSU was just as depressing as it had been the last time. The only positive was that the length of my tariff made it harder to justify keeping me there. Hamza shrugged and said I had to know what to expect. The authorities were preparing to charge him with setting up an Al Qaeda training base in Oregon, USA, which he adamantly denied.

'The truth is I've been having meetings with the MI5 since 1992,' he said. 'They know everything I've been doing and permitted it, but because of 9/11 they're using me as a scapegoat now. If they decide they want to get you, they will. I know they will send me to America eventually. It is the ordeal I must suffer in this life to prepare me for the next.'

Roger said he was applying pressure to get himself transferred, that it was inhumane to keep someone in the HSU for years on end. Other prisons had looser regimes with more time on association. That sounded good to me.

Over the next few weeks we had various official visits during which we argued our case. On one occasion, a female civil servant met with myself and Roger by the TV near the end of the spur. She was stocky, with short, gelled hair and wore a trouser suit and boots, which gave her a very masculine, almost transgender appearance. I had come to the conclusion that there was something a bit odd about most top government officials, as if they hid neuroses beneath masks of normality.

'How's your uncle?' she asked me. 'I remember him from 1990 in Leicester jail.'

It was a classic tactic. Start off with something known, to make you feel like they are authoritative, that they have done their homework and know all about you.

'Never mind that,' I said. 'I shouldn't be here. I should be on the main prison. I've got by far the smallest sentence in the place. I've already done two years and I only got a tariff of five. Move me off here, it's out of order.'

'Me too,' said Roger, who by then had also been to court, found guilty of murder and sentenced to 33 years. The judge had been horrified at his use of an AK-47, describing it as a 'weapon of war'. Roger refused to co-operate with police or divulge who employed him, which exacerbated the situation. Old Bill had uncovered coded references to an underworld figure known as 'Dad' but that was all they had. Their frustration led to Roger being given the maximum sentence possible.

'Let us back on to the normal wing so we can do some rehabilitation courses,' he said. 'It wouldn't even be an expensive transfer to move us out of the HSU and into the Belmarsh main prison.'

'Come off it!' she replied. 'We're not stupid! You can't fool us. We know people like you do not change.'

Roger and I exchanged a look.

'I can't believe you just said that!' Roger retorted. 'Isn't the whole purpose of the prison system to rehabilitate offenders and make them productive members of society? Are you suggesting that as a representative of Her Majesty's Government, you do not believe in your own system?'

She laughed but there was no humour in it. Her laughter was dry, like a bag of gravel being split with a spade.

'Of course some prisoners can be rehabilitated. But not guys like you. Not criminals who work at your level. Men who do what you do, do not change.'

She paused for a little while.

'You talk well and seem likeable but the first opportunity you get, you'll take it. If that means running for the wall, you'll do it. If it means bashing an officer, or maybe even worse, you'll do it.'

After the meeting I went back to my cell and thought about what she said. In some ways, she was right.

Still, over the weeks that followed I did what I could to advance my case. Roger was transferred out to Full Sutton in Yorkshire. Whenever Governor Arden ventured on to the wing I would approach him and demand to know why I had not been moved.

'L-l-listen John,' he'd say. 'The p-p-paperwork has to be s-sorted. It t-t-takes a while.'

For three more long months I continued my routine until suddenly, in the depths of the night, I was finally awoken by the click-click of spur doors opening, followed by the rhythm of feet on the floor. I lifted my head from my pillow and saw four screws at my cell door, fronted up by Boyband.

'You're gone,' he said.

I rose wearily and they took me out through the wing, down to reception and into a holding cell. I was strip-searched for the thousandth time, before Boyband gave me the now familiar yellow and green suit to put on.

'Why am I wearing this?' I asked. No one replied. They led me out through the metal detector and handed me over to another set of screws with northern accents. At that point it became obvious the main prison a few hundred yards away was not my destination.

The new set of screws loaded me into a waiting van and we set off. The journey seemed interminable. Four hours with all of them nattering like a bunch of old women. I closed my eyes and tried to ignore them.

We eventually arrived at Full Sutton near York where they placed me in yet another holding cell in yet another reception area. It was comforting to know Roger was already there, an eventuality they would have avoided if at all possible. The options for cat A and cat AA prisoners are few.

I hoped to meet up with him again but knew it would depend on our circumstances inside. Meanwhile the screws went through the stuff I had brought from Belmarsh. One shaven-headed, military-looking guy said, 'We're having your trainers.'

It was a nice pair of Nikes.

'Piss off!' I replied.

'You're not allowed those trainers in here.'

'I've just come from the maximum security wing at Belmarsh. How come I can have them there and not here?'

'No.' He was implacable. 'You can't have them. We're taking them.'

He left with the shoes and came back five minutes later with some plimsolls, the standard black, rubbery ones that everyone used to have at primary school.

'Come on! You're really taking the piss now.'

'That's the rules,' he said. 'Now let's go.'

I had the feeling he was trying to rile me and the receiving officer on the desk did little to change my first impressions.

'McAvoy?'

'Yeah.'

'I'm going to give you a piece of advice, son. Keep your head down. It's not in your interests having a surname like yours in this place.'

'What do you mean?'

'We had your Uncle Micky in here between 1997 and 1998. He had a lot of influence among other inmates and orchestrated a terrible riot. The prison was smashed to pieces.

'One wing was virtually burnt to the ground. All thanks to your uncle. We had to ship him out in the end. There's quite a few staff in here will remember all that.'

I nodded and smiled, wise to his game. He continued leafing through my file.

'Barnes!' he said. 'Was Kevin Barnes your co-defendant?'

I shrugged. 'Well if it says it in there, he must have been.'

'We had him here too, years ago. He was a proper piece of work. He killed the prison dog during a riot, snapped its bloody neck. He was involved in the Strangeways riots, violence, kidnapping. You've kept some right company, you have.'

There was nothing I could say.

'We'll put you on E wing,' he said, and closed the file.

The screws took me out of reception and through an enormous, broad corridor which led to the wing. Like the HSU, Full Sutton was very modern, highly polished and sterile. E wing was on two floors, with the association area in the middle. As soon as I walked in, every set of eyes fell on me, just like the movies.

I looked from one cold visage to another, hoping to see a familiar face or a flicker of recognition. More than that, I hoped to see Roger. 'John, John!' someone called from the balcony. I craned my neck and saw Mukhtar and Yassin, two of the suicide bombers from Belmarsh.

'At least I know someone,' I thought.

Mukhtar and Yassin showed me around and while they did, other inmates approached with a familiar question.

'Are you Micky McAvoy's nephew?'

Full Sutton was renowned as a tough nick, with hard men doing hard time, but I knew from then I would be okay.

As luck would have it, my allocated cell was directly opposite the one in which Uncle Micky used to stay. A bearded Scot called McAteer appeared in my doorway, a thick-set man with a pugnacious look, a gangland hitman bearing a reputation as a complete homicidal fruit loop. His forehead was riven with a jagged scar. He certainly looked the part.

'Are ye Micky's nephew then are ye?' he growled. I nodded. McAteer had famously killed a guy with a shotgun then taken a shit on his chest as a mark of disrespect, a semi-legendary bit of criminal folklore.

'I am, yeah.'

'I remember when Micky was in here. He was a top man. Do ye wannae come te mine for a cup o' tea?'

I shrugged and followed him to his cell, where he boiled the kettle. A bookmarked copy of a Jeffrey Archer novel lay on the shelf by his bed.

'Sorry pal,' he said. 'They only gae us UHT milk. Tastes like shite, but it's the best ah've got.'

'Do you know where Roger is?' I asked him.

'Roger who?'

'Roger Vincent.'

'Oh, him, aye, he's on A wing.'

'How can I get over there?'

'It's impossible pal. Forget it. If ye go te the screws and say ye wannae be transferred to another part ah the prison, they'll think ye've got ulterior motives.'

'No chance then?'

'If ye wannae see him, the best chance is tae go tae chapel on a Sunday. It's the only time lads from different wings can get together.'

Following McAteer's advice, the next morning I went down to chapel and saw Roger. I didn't get to speak to him, but caught his eye. He waved and mouthed something I couldn't hear.

About three days later, after I got myself settled in, both the senior officer and the principal officer of the wing arrived at my door with serious faces. I was sat on my bunk reading *The Times*, which I received daily.

'John.'

I looked up.

'Have you got a dispute with Roger Vincent?' the SO asked.

'No, why?'

'Because he's asked for you to go on his wing.'

'Yeah?'

'Are you sure you have no dispute with him?'

'Absolutely.'

'So if we asked for your opinion, would you want to be placed on the same wing as Roger Vincent?'

'One hundred per cent. Get me over there.'

'Okay, pack your stuff up, let's go.'

It turned out that Roger, in his short time in Full Sutton, had become an extremely influential inmate, commanding the respect of those around him. If prison officers had an issue with a prisoner they would approach Roger to mediate for them. For that reason, the staff also did him favours. That was the quid pro quo.

It was great to see Roger again. Although he knew he was facing 30 years, almost half a lifetime behind bars, he maintained his positive manner, wit and intelligence. You had to admire him for that. In all my years of life, in or out of prison, I have never met anyone as genuinely affable, honest and trustworthy as Roger Vincent. I know that for people from outside that world, describing a convicted contract killer in those terms might seem contradictory, but they don't know Roger. Roger the hitman and Roger the person were two sides to the same man, I suppose, but the Roger I knew could not have been more pleasant to be around.

Life settled into the familiar routine pretty quickly. I fell back on my habits of reading and exercising and found that status had its perks. With access to money from the outside, I had a kid that I paid a fiver a week to polish my cell floor. Roger and I had another couple of lads that cooked and washed up for us in the inmates' kitchen, an arrangement that worked well for everyone. We used our cash to buy in food, which our boys could eat for free if they prepared it. We might have been prisoners, but we wanted to live as well as possible.

Yet with a larger inmate population than the HSU, comprising only of high-risk convicts, Full Sutton housed some real maniacs and there was a feeling that things could erupt at any time. Violence was everywhere, in faces and conversations. The men wore it on their skins.

The slightly freer regime made it a better place to live, but I had to learn to exist within a very delicate, volatile atmosphere. In the criminal lifestyle you have a different relationship with violence than regular people anyway, but living in such claustrophobic conditions with such dangerous guys brought high levels of stress. Alertness was key at all times. Threats could come from any angle.

The kitchen area in particular was a real boon. Being able to buy in your own food from outside and cook it yourself saved you from the godawful slop from the prison kitchen, but presented some serious dangers. Inmates could book knives to use for chopping ingredients. They would have to sign them in and out of the screws' office, but that gave them limited access to dangerous weapons. I had only been on Roger's wing for a week when I witnessed my first major incident.

It was a Saturday afternoon and I had been down to the gym for a workout, before heading up to the kitchen area where I busied myself making an omelette. Omelettes were the one thing I was particular about and insisted on cooking myself, with a certain ratio of whites to yolks that I read was good for fat loss. An Asian kid arrived, started cooking next to me and we acknowledged each other silently before carrying on with what we were doing.

Moments later, two black lads walked in, young guys, in their early 20s, convicted murderers on long sentences and I knew, straight away, by their stealth, their gait and attitude, that something was going to happen. The Asian had focused on his food-prep, chopping onions and garlic and was oblivious.

They advanced on him swiftly and silently from behind. It was like watching a documentary in which leopards stalk a gazelle drinking from a lake.

Despite the sense of impending carnage, there was no way I could warn him and it did not occur to me to do so. One of the first rules of prison is not to involve yourself in other people's business. Who knew what had happened between these three to provoke the situation? In those circumstances all you can do is stand by and let nature take its course.

Before he had any chance to react, they were on him, hitting and hitting him for at least 15 seconds. From my position it looked like they were punching him, savagely and ferociously below the waist, but as they withdrew I saw blood-soaked blades in their hands. They had stabbed him more than 20 times in the buttocks and on the upper legs.

Screaming, the Asian kid sank to the floor, his grey tracksuit bottoms turning a repulsive burgundy, his face going white through loss of blood. The attackers ran out as the screws heard the commotion and charged in, pressed the panic button and carried the victim off. Thick, arterial blood from his wounds leaked on to the tiles, leaving a macabre trail. I was convinced the kid would die.

'Bang up!' the screws shouted.

My overriding emotion was not shock or fear, but frustration. The incident meant the wing was placed on instant lockdown and I was unable to finish preparing my omelette. I was hungry.

The principal officer came to question me, famished and irritable in my cell shortly afterwards.

'Come on McAvoy, what happened in that kitchen?'

I shrugged. 'I didn't see anything.'

'My officers said you were standing next to him. You must have seen something.'

'No.'

'Why aren't you talking? Was it you?'

'Does it look like it was me? I haven't even changed my clothes. There was claret everywhere.'

'Well if he dies you'll have it on your conscience.'

'Fuck off, I didn't even see it.'

For the rest of the afternoon cell doors opened and closed while they conducted their enquiries. Eventually they checked the CCTV cameras and nabbed the guys responsible in early evening. The two black kids could not have cared less. The pair of them were serving more than 30 years each anyway and had lost all sense of consequence.

I found out later the incident had been triggered by a game of pool. The Asian had accused one of the black boys of committing a foul, hitting the object ball with his cue, which he denied. There had been a minor exchange of views, the Asian accused one of being a 'cheat' and the individual felt disrespected.

'Apologise,' he had demanded.

Rather than say sorry, the victim had repeated his trivial accusation and walked off. That was all it took.

The first social rule in prison, particularly a high category one, is to respect the hierarchy. Violent criminals, particularly those with lots of money, armed robbers and gangsters, are at the top. Sex offenders are at the bottom. Drug addicts are just above them. Everyone else fits into the pecking order as best they can from there.

Jostling for position occurs all the time. There might be a queue to use the hotplate, for example. In normal society it would just be a queue, but on the inside it is a demonstration of social standing. Maybe a top prisoner can jump it, while one with less status will be kept waiting. Any perceived slight, any attempt to buck this system, can be met with extreme violence. If the wrong guy tries to step in front of someone else he will have to fight for his life and face repeated future reprisals if he wins.

Blood is a prison currency and some of it is worth more than others. Favours will be asked and barters paid for in food or cigarettes. It's not uncommon to see someone half-killed or maimed over a pouch of tobacco or a can of tuna.

'Let's go in the showers and have a straightener,' someone might say, in a petty dispute. But if he's talking to one of the main men he would get short shrift.

'I'm not about that. I'm not fighting you man against man, why would I? But if you want to have it, we can have it. If me and you have a problem it could come on you anytime, anyway. In fact, forget we're in prison. We're not in reality here. I'll find out where you live and we can take it to the real world. I'll get my boys to come up. They'll find your people. I'm not gonna just walk into the showers like an idiot.'

Shortly after the kitchen incident, a lad was attacked in the toilets by a heroin dealer with mental health problems. That one was caused by the victim paying for his drugs debt with chicken drumsticks, but being two short. His face was slashed and he received seven separate wounds around his ribs and abdomen. He had to have 180 stitches. On the outside those two chicken drumsticks probably cost about £1.50, but in Full Sutton their value was mutilation.

This sort of thing, heads slammed in cell doors, beatings to the point of unconsciousness or broken bones, stabbings with faeces on the blade to cause septicaemia, all of it becomes normal. In that environment it happens every day. Even for those like Roger and I, whose status placed us above reprisals, the anxiety of living among it can get to you. You are always looking, just in case someone has your number. Nobody can live in that world and be unaffected by it.

Two doors down from me lived a psycho called Mickey Boyle, a diagnosed paranoid schizophrenic with a hopeless heroin problem. I kept him sweet by giving him the TV supplement from my newspaper every Saturday.

'Thanks so much mate,' he would say. 'That's very kind. If you need anyone killed or anything, just let me know.'

Boyle had been transferred to Full Sutton after a serious assault in his previous jail. Apparently a guy in a nearby cell had a heroin packet secreted in his anus and made the schoolboy error of telling Boyle about it. Mickey predictably insisted he remove it from his innards and hand it over free of charge. He refused and that was where the trouble started.

Affronted by this audacity, Boyle had taken him hostage, barricaded the guy's cell door and started slashing his face with a *shank* (a home-made prison knife). After the first few incisions and faced with the prospect of losing facial features or losing his stash, the victim made the wise decision to hand over the heroin.

When his victim had shit-out the drugs, with screws waiting outside to apprehend him, Mickey then refused to leave the cell unless the prison governor personally brought him silver foil, a lighter and a spoon to cook up with. The governor did as requested.

Mickey took his time, spent ten minutes sorting his fix, then opened the door with a beatific grin and let the hostage go. As the screws barged in, batoned him, tangled him up and threw him in the block, he was rushing his knackers off and barely even noticed.

For HMP management, Mickey Boyle was the very worst kind of prisoner. He had undergone various psychological exams, been declared mentally ill, spent time in Broadmoor and was waiting for a bed to become available in Rampton, a high-security psychiatric unit in Nottinghamshire. In mainstream prison terms, this gave him great power. Officially he was a medical rather than a criminal case, meaning he could do virtually anything and there was little the screws could do back.

Despite its chaotic unpredictability, I still preferred life at Full Sutton. Most important was that we got to use the gym frequently, while the facility itself was much better equipped and had staff that knew what they were doing. Like a fitness suite on the outside, the gym was divided into two rooms, one with weights and strength training equipment, the other with cardiovascular machines.

Most inmates wanted to build muscle and pump iron, so the weights room was always packed. I quickly grew bored of having to

A lurid *Sun* article about Billy's activities

THE Sun

Friday, September 25, 1981   12p   TODAY'S TV: PAGE 10

GUNMAN BILLY LIAR IS COPPED BY THE CAMERA

GOTCHA!

30,000 more steel jobs to be axed

ANOTHER Sun EXCLUSIVE

By PETER McHUGH

BRITISH STEEL boss Ian MacGregor is to axe 30,000 jobs and freeze pay in a final bid to save the tottering State-owned corporation.

He has told the Government that British Steel's 130,000 workforce must be pruned to around 90,000 within months—and the giant complex on Teesside will have to shut completely.

But last night steel union leader Bill Sirs threatened a national strike if the plan goes ahead.

And Railmen's leader Sid Weighell claimed any walkout would be backed by his members as well as Britain's miners.

Debts

Mr MacGregor has told the unions that the corporation's debts are now so horrific above £1 million a week—that NO payrises can be offered this year.

The steel chief outlined his crisis plan to new industry Secretary Patrick Jenkin and has been promised full Government support.

Personal letters spelling out the crisis have been sent to all employees.

Mr Sirs and Mr

Continued on Page Four

16 years for crook freed by 5 juries

THIS is the moment when justice finally caught up with one of the underworld's most slippery villains.

William "Billy Liar" Tobin lies on the ground with his gun beside him—captured by police during an attempted £800,000 armed robbery.

It was the end of the road for

THE GOOD LIFE
See Page 7

the cheeky Mr Big from South London who in FIVE years had been charged FIVE times with major crimes—and FIVE times had got juries to acquit him.

Detectives were tipped off by one of Tobin's gang and filmed

the whole raid—on a security truck in Dulwich, South London—with a video camera.

As prosecutor Kenneth Richardson told an Old Bailey jury: "If you can't convict on that evidence, the police might as well give up."

Yesterday Judge John Leonard handed out a 16-year sentence for attempted robbery and possession of firearms.

£30,000 BINGO! Is this your lucky day?

See Page 12

My stepdad Billy Tobin's arrest on the front page of *The Sun*

THE Sun

Tuesday, September 29, 1981.   12p   TODAY'S TV: PAGE 14

THE JURY FIXERS

Supergross yesterday

Black Monday! Shares in steepest dive for 52 years

By ROGER CARROLL

PANIC selling sent share prices plummeting world-wide yesterday in the steepest dive since the Great Crash of 1929.

In the first hour of Stock Exchange trading on Black Monday, nearly £4,000million was wiped off the value of British companies.

But last night there were hopes that Wall Street could calm the slide.

Share prices in New York made a sharp recovery, with the Dow Jones index closing at £42.56 — more than 10 points up.

Panic

THE LONDON losses yesterday were on top of the disastrous £14,500-million fall of the previous fortnight.

And the message from investors in Hong Kong, Tokyo and Sydney was the same Sell! Sell! Sell!

In London prices began to tumble even before trading officially opened.—

Continued on Page Two

SHANKS, KING OF THE KOP IS DEAD

—Back Page

Squealer tells of sex blackmail

By MICHAEL FIELDER

RUTHLESS underworld bosses are nobbling Britain's juries.

They are using sex, cash and threats to blackmail jurors into giving wrong verdicts.

And they have even bribed court staff to hand them secret information to help defeat justice.

DOSSIER

The Sun has put together a frightening dossier.

The information comes from a man in the know — the Supergrass who helped police put away notorious gangster Billy Tobin at the Old Bailey last week.

The Squealer, who has a £50,000 underworld contract on his head, says: "This is the only decent thing I have done in my life."

He reveals "Jury nobbling has become big business in the past years."

And he tells of:

● HOW daily birth are used to "chat up" jury men and have sex with them to swing verdicts — the names one woman who was used regularly at £300 a time.

● HOW gamblers on juries are picked out as likely bribery targets.

● HOW respectable-looking "front men" are hired as fixers.

Mr X also tells how Billy Tobin had boasted: "There's not a court in the country which can convict me."

JAILED

Tobin, 29, was convicted of attempted robbery and jailed for 16 years last week after being captured in a police ambush during an £800,000 hold-up.

He had been acquitted by juries FIVE times in FIVE years.

During Tobin's trial last week two women

Continued on Page Two

'The only honest thing I have ever done'

THE SQUEALER

THE FULL AMAZING STORY Centre Pages

Back on the front page of *The Sun*

Some pictures of Billy as I remember him from childhood, at a family gathering with my sister Donna

As a toddler with
Arsenal and England
defender, Kenny
Sansom

Me in the Highbury
dressing room with
a few of the Arsenal
players

Happy times, in
Marbella with Aaron
(on the right)

Happy times in Marbella with Aaron

My cousin Bill visiting me during my time at HMP Full Sutton

A notice put up in the Lowdham Grange prison gym to inform other inmates of one of my world records

In Lowdham Grange with some other inmates, after breaking my first world record

In Sudbury prison sports hall, with officer in charge of the gym, Mark Sherriff

Being presented with a plaque by the governor at HMP Sudbury

With Laura Wheeler who gave me so much help and guidance

My first time in a real boat, at Burton Leander in 2011

Best man at Johnny's wedding while still an inmate at HMP Sudbury

With Johnny after my release from jail in 2012. He's been a great friend to me

With assistant coach Mike Hill at
London Rowing Club 2012

With some of the guys I first rowed with at LRC.

At the London Rowing Club, which has remained an important part of my life, even since I stopped
rowing

At LRC with coach Brian Ulliott (on the right)

Oonagh, my flatmate who showed so much trust and faith in me

In a single scull on the Thames, 2012

With my friends Jack and Ben from LRC at the
Henley Royal Regatta

Rowing in a crew on the
Thames with some top
class rowers

Cycling at Ironman UK 2013 after only four weeks' training. Those Lancashire moors get bloody windy!

With Darren Davis, just after finishing my first Ironman in Bolton, 2013

In my first Ironman event, 2013. I still had my rower's build!

Talking to Terry Williamson after my disastrous Ironman UK 2014

In the medical tent with Darren after Ironman UK 2014. My experience that year taught me to respect the event. I am not superhuman!

Crossing the line in tenth place at Ironman UK 2015. After my disaster the previous year I proved a lot to myself by staying disciplined and achieving a positive result

At the summit of the Col de la Colombiere, May 2016

With Hywel Davies at Col de la Forclaz on his Alpine training camp

On my new Wyndy Milla custom made bike at Ironman Staffordshire 70.3 in 2016. Finishing sixth was a real boost

Another shot of the mean machine, this time on the urban stretch of the Ironman Frankfurt bike course

Coming into the 'special needs' nutrition station on lap two of the Frankfurt marathon. Darren is holding my energy gels

My coach, Keith Sanders, supporting me at Ironman Frankfurt, with female world champion Miranda Carfrae

Crossing the line at Ironman Frankfurt 2016 was a fantastic feeling. I knew I had arrived as an international athlete

Signing with Nike in 2017 was an amazing moment and cemented my status as a professional athlete. It made me even more determined to use my story for good. Just five years earlier I had still been an inmate.

queue up for the dumbbells, benches and bars so would take myself off to the cardio room instead, where I pounded the treadmills, exercise bikes, rowers and elliptical machines. Whatever I did, I would sustain for the full hour, having increased my fitness in Belmarsh, but it was totally unstructured. Exercise was still simple escapism for me, rather than being anything you could call *sport*.

That first began to change when I learnt of the Full Sutton Christmas competition. Run by the gym staff every year and a big deal among inmates, it consisted of a *Superstars* event for fitness with a separate strength/powerlifting contest. Victory in either was seen as a major badge of honour on the wings. Some men had been in there 20 years, training as hard as they could and the comp was the pinnacle of their year.

The fitness challenge consisted of a variety of cardiovascular activities, some with minor resistance, while the strength one, which was adjusted for bodyweight, involved squats, bench presses and deadlifts. The gym officers at Full Sutton were serious guys and knew what they were doing. Both tests adhered to national standards.

I entered both purely to maximise time out of my cell and surprised myself by coming third in the strength comp, even though I had not trained for it, beating some huge, hairy gorillas who pumped iron on a daily basis. Compared to them I was relatively small, but even at 5ft 9in and 73kg, I was able to bench press 140kg, squat 190 and deadlift 200. The screws were very impressed by my natural power, which did wonders for my ego, but it was the following day, during the *Superstars* event when things really got interesting.

Greg and Norm, a couple of scallies from Manchester, had the reputation of being the fittest boys in the prison. Norm had won the comp for the previous three years and was hot favourite, while Greg was most people's tip to come second. The challenge consisted of a 500m row, a 1km treadmill run, 25 reps of 65kg bench press, 50 reps of lat pull-down on a medium weight, 50 reps of shoulder press with a 30kg bar, 50 bunny hops over a bench, 50 step-ups holding dumbbells, then finally another 500m treadmill run with a steep incline. The idea was to complete all the exercises in as quick a time as possible.

Norm went first and looked impressive. He was lithe and lean, with barely any visible body fat, like a greyhound. Greg followed and failed to beat Norm's time, as did four or five others. The general feeling in the gym was that Norm was a dead cert again, but as the time for my turn neared, something kick-started inside me.

From my chest rose a burning need to prove myself, a determination that appeared out of nothing. I had no idea whether I was capable of beating Norm, but was gripped by a passionate knowledge that I had to. I would win that competition no matter what.

At the moment when the screws read my name and told me to prepare myself, I had a similar sensation to how I used to feel waiting for a robbery. There were no nerves, just focus. Everything other than the circuit and what I had to do faded into the periphery. It was all or nothing, life or death.

It was on.

I absolutely tore the arse out of those exercises. Everything around me smudged. Time compressed and became meaningless. Before I knew it I was finishing on the final treadmill and turning to the screws. The whole line of them gawped at me in disbelief, open-mouthed like a row of baby chicks.

The officer in charge of the gym, a national fitness competitor called Mark Elliot, double-checked his stopwatch then broke the silence.

'Fucking hell John,' he said at last. 'That is really quick.'

'So have I won?'

'That circuit you have just done is a nationally recognised circuit used in super-fit competitions. The time you clocked would put you in the top three or four in the country.'

I was elated.

'To have done what you have just done, while in prison, on a regular diet, with no specialist training is absolutely outstanding.'

'Yeah, that's great. So how much did I win by?'

It turned out I had obliterated Norm's time by 43 seconds. Officially I was the fittest prisoner in Full Sutton jail by some distance, which gave me massive kudos among the boys. The staff presented me with a box of chocolates as a prize. At that point, that was enough.

17

Goddamn Democracy!

MY new-found passion for fitness gave me a new outlet. For the first time, in winning the competition, I was able to think positively about myself in ways unrelated to crime. As a diversion it was only temporary, though.

With Roger I could speak about most things and our conversations often spread to topics far beyond the mundanities of prison life. We talked politics or war, economics, social issues even, but in many ways, he was an exception. Other than Roger most dialogue around the prison was either crime-related, drug-related or connected to some perceived slight endured by one of the prisoners.

'I don't like the way so-and-so looked at me. I reckon he's planning something with that kid from Hull. I'm going to have to do something about it.'

When that constitutes 99 per cent of what you hear around you, it worms inside your head and stays there. The ever-present threat of violence, who did what to whom, obtaining spliffs or smack, these are the dominant themes of prison conversation. When you're inside, to a large degree they are your world. My overriding focus was still on organising my activities for when I got out. The way I saw it, I had a minimum of 18 months left to serve. The first chance I got, I would escape then be straight back into the game and making money.

A few months after my arrival, early in the new year, we were informed that every Friday the prison would have to shut earlier as government cuts affected staffing. This entailed a change to our routine. We would remain on lock-up throughout the morning, get three hours out of cell from 12 until three, including lunch, then be banged up again for the rest of the day.

At first inmates were unconcerned, until it became clear that it also meant that Monday to Thursday their work shifts would be 15 minutes longer to compensate for the lost time on Friday. To me, it was no big deal, but for men who had been there for decades and were thoroughly institutionalised, this kind of disruption to their routine was intolerable.

Shortly after the news was announced, I was sitting in the TV room with Roger on association, when a couple of the old-timers came to confer with him.

'We're not happy about this Roger,' they said.

'I thought you wouldn't be.'

'We want to have a sit-out.'

He sighed. A sit-out is a well-known form of prison protest, in which inmates refuse to return to their cells after association. It is regarded as a very serious contravention of prison rules and can lead to major disturbance.

'Is it really worth the aggro?' Roger asked. He tried to dissuade them, but they were adamant. Soon the wing was abuzz. Mutiny was in the air.

Everyone sought affirmation from everyone else. Boys egged each other on. A sit-out will not work if only some prisoners do it. To be effective, the whole wing had to unite against the screws.

That put me in a very awkward situation. If, like Roger, you were serving a long sentence anyway, or like Mickey Boyle you had mitigating circumstances which meant potential consequences were limited, you could participate with little fear. I was only looking at another two years by then. The last thing I needed was added time. It became clear the consensus was to go ahead so, reluctantly, I agreed. It was either that or become a pariah on the wing. The day was set for Saturday.

On Saturday afternoon everyone assembled in the association area. Some sat on seats while some absent-mindedly played pool or stared at the TV. The tannoy system came to life – *bing bong!*

'Ten minutes remaining of association.'

There were a few exchanged glances before everyone resumed what they had been doing.

Bing bong! 'Five minutes.'

The atmosphere became more tense. Usually prisoners began moving at that point. By the final set of chimes, when prisoners were meant to be in their cells, no one had left.

Within a minute the SO and the PO came to the association area and asked what was going on. We all sat in silence. No one wanted to assume responsibility and be earmarked as the ringleader.

'Okay,' the SO tried again. 'I'm giving you a lawful order. Are you going to bang up?'

No one replied.

'This is your final warning,' he said. 'Are you going to obey a lawful order and return to your cells or are you refusing?'

Again, no one spoke. They left, locking the door behind them.

At first the mood was jubilant. Throughout UK prison history these sorts of events had demonstrated a tendency to spiral out of control, but at that point no one was hurt and we felt we had got one over on the screws. Everyone relaxed, cracked a few jokes and waited to see what would happen next.

Within a quarter of an hour the door locks clicked again and all the prison officers filed in, every last one of them. Inmates immediately tensed up. What was this, a face-off? The screws lined up along one wall and the SO stepped forward and spoke again.

'Okay lads,' he said. 'As I'm sure you know if this situation continues the governor will have to take action. We're still hoping it doesn't come to that. Can one of you please tell me what this is all about?'

This time, an American drug smuggler called Jimmy stepped forward. Jimmy was not one of the leading inmates in the jail but he was well enough liked, a long-haired Californian pot-smoking hippy, who had been nicked for sailing a boat from the States right up the Thames with a ton and a half of cocaine on it. We all loved that. Jimmy was not one of us, but he had a set of balls. He walked into the no-man's land between us and them and began to speak.

'Look man, it's very simple. We are not banging up because we're not going to do this 15 minutes extra work thing. This isn't a labour camp man. This isn't Soviet Russia. I mean what the hell. This is the UK, am I right? We have rights here don't we?'

'It's the only way we could work it,' the SO said. 'Government cuts have meant...'

'...government cuts, government shmuts! Come on man. It's 15 minutes. It doesn't mean much to you but it does to us. We're living in this place, this is home to us. There was no consultation here, no due process, no recognition of our status as human beings.'

Jimmy warmed up to the situation and started to really enjoy himself. As he spoke, cheers and shouts came from the other inmates. He was inspiring them, riling them up and loving it. The atmosphere grew more rowdy and the screws grew more uncomfortable.

'Goddamnit motherfucker!' Jimmy shouted, the veins on his neck standing out. 'This is a goddamn democracy! We're gonna fight for our rights man!'

A group of young black inmates shouted 'brap, brap' and pointed their fingers in the air pretending they had guns. Even some of the old lags were getting carried away. I turned to Roger.

'Fucking hell mate,' I said. 'This is gonna go tits up.'

Roger nodded, 'It's not looking good.'

Sensing there might be trouble if they remained, the screws began to sidle out. Once again, we were left alone, the lunatics running the asylum. From there most of us knew which way it would go. In those circumstances the governor will call in a special tactical unit assembled by the wider prison authorities. The squad would simply bide their time, wait for the right moment, probably throw in a few pepper spray canisters to soften us up, then charge in, armed to the teeth and absolutely hammer us.

Hours ticked by and some of the youngsters pushed the fridge-freezers and the pool table against the door to act as a barricade. They opened up the ice boxes and started pulling out home-made prison knives they had stashed in there.

'Fuck this shit!' one was saying. 'I ain't got nothing to lose, let's do these battymen!'

If officers had arrived at that point, a small-scale war would have ensued. There was no doubt about it, but by then we had been in there for six or seven hours and a couple of the older, non-violent inmates, fearful of what was coming, came and spoke to Roger. Roger sympathised and took it upon himself to assuage disaster, going over to the kids brandishing weapons.

'Look boys,' he said. 'We're all in this together and if it's on, it's on, but you have to appreciate that if you take it to that level, you're bringing in others who never really wanted that. There are guys here who don't want the shit kicked out of them or to be slung in the block and if you start going at screws with shanks, that's what it'll mean.'

Roger took the one he assumed to be the top boy to one side, a kid from Birmingham with baleful eyes and big, bony hands.

'You have to understand,' Roger said. 'If one of those bastards gets cut, or worse, if you rub out a screw, we will all get fucked for it. Some of your lads don't care, they're never getting out anyway, but there are guys due to be released soon. They didn't sign up for this. They were happy to stand up for our rights, but not to see someone get murdered.'

Roger's powers of communication rarely let him down and after a good 20 minutes of speaking sense, he somehow managed to calm the hot-heads. Eventually he got them to move the freezers back and put away their knives. Then he banged on one of the doors. When a voice came from outside, he called, 'We're going to bang up now.'

About an hour later, the SO returned. With the atmosphere still tense and delicate, he called us one by one to return to our cells.

'Open your mouth,' the SO said when my turn came. 'Now put your hands by your sides.'

Two officers gave me a thorough body search and showed me out of the door on to the corridor to the cell block which was lined with officers on either side. I walked between them, hands above my head, fully expecting fists or feet to come flying my way at any time. It didn't happen.

It was a relief to get to my cell unharmed but we still faced a torrid night. All through the hours of darkness you could hear the bang, bang of cell doors opening and closing as they came for the ones they believed to be the organisers. Jimmy, the American hippy, was ghosted out, as were eight or nine others. He only had a year of his sentence left at that point too. That's what you get for trying to step up. In total 200 prisoners had refused bang-up that night and while it lasted it had been the biggest protest in Full Sutton's history. The snatch squads had assembled and were waiting outside for the order to hit us. At the point when everything calmed down, we were literally minutes away from gas canisters, anti-riot shields and batons. Anything could have happened. Roger's intervention saved us all from a battle we could not have won.

The following day the wing was placed on lockdown and each of us was charged. The screws marched us down to see the SO, one by one. He sat in his office scowling, flanked by officers, a proper kangaroo court.

'McAvoy, you're charged with refusing a lawful order, how do you plead?'

'Not guilty.'

'Not guilty! What do you mean not guilty?'

'I mean not guilty.'

'Explain yourself.'

'I was under duress,' I said. 'I was under serious threat to my life. I had to join the protest or the others would have killed me.'

He gave a little laugh.

'Would they now? Let me tell you something McAvoy, everybody who walks through my door today is going to tell me they were under duress, every last bastard one of them. But you can rest assured that there is not one inmate on this wing who will be found not guilty.'

'It's nice to know I'm involved in such a fair-minded legal process,' I replied.

He fixed me in the eye.

'Guilty!'

In the aftermath they began applying traction to some of the inmates they thought they could pacify and offered me a job as the wing cleaner, in exchange for extra exercise sessions. The lure of added gym time pulled at me and I accepted. Fitness was the only thing keeping me sane.

Not long after that they downgraded me from category A to category B. Things were moving in the right direction.

Attending the gym daily saw my stamina continue to improve and during my two and a half years at Full Sutton I won the Christmas fitness competition all three times I entered it. They even made me compete with a handicap, to make it fairer. I still won.

The time passed slowly, but steadily.

I knew that playing the game would help my case for early release, so I attended rehabilitation classes and courses. Advanced Thinking Skills, Victim Awareness and Anger Management, most of the sessions were an absolute joke. We would go down to the chapel and sit with the vicar in a little circle of hardened criminals. There were guys there for killing policewomen, rape and murder, drug trafficking, armed robbery, all the worst crimes on the book. Some of them were multi-millionaires and every single one of them was gaming the system.

'So,' the vicar would say. 'You've had some time to reflect. What do you think about your crime now, John?'

'Oh I'm really terribly sorry. I should never have done it.'

'Do you feel any shame?'

'Oh, yes. I'm very ashamed about what I've done, Reverend. If I could turn back the clock, I would.'

It became a competition among the prisoners to try to out-do each other with fake sincerity, sharing smirks and winks, but the old boy never got the joke. To us it was obvious, we were just spinning lines to get boxes ticked on the paperwork, but he fell for it. Sometimes they made us do role-plays.

'Now John,' the vicar would say, 'you pretend to be a shopkeeper. And Danny has been stealing from your shop. What would you like to say to him?'

The whole thing was absurd, stemming from the authorities' need to be seen to make an effort to rehabilitate. I can appreciate it's not an easy task, but in my view there's an inherent contradiction which those in the system never saw. If rehabilitation means to prepare someone to re-enter society, you cannot achieve that while locking a man in a small room for 22 hours a day and denying him basic freedoms. It's impossible.

The biggest sticking point for many guys is that although the courses stand you in good stead at parole hearings, by agreeing to do them, you tacitly admit your guilt. You cannot apologise for your crimes and empathise with your victims while maintaining innocence. That can mean a catch-22 situation for anyone hoping to lodge an appeal. As far as prison authorities are concerned, you have been convicted by a judge. It doesn't matter what you say. If you will not admit guilt, you are 'in denial'.

After completing the courses, I attended a sentence planning hearing where they confirmed I had taken advantage of everything that the prison could offer and would soon move on. My tariff was virtually spent and I could begin to move down through the security categories.

Before that could be ratified I had one last Full Sutton hoop to jump through – the 'kinetic self-change programme', a really stressful series of sessions often forced upon inmates imprisoned for crimes of violence. A psychologist was brought in for one-on-one consultation to see if I met the criteria to be classified as a psychopath.

While I had always treated prison courses light-heartedly, that one was nerve-wracking. Being diagnosed as a psycho would have a detrimental effect not only on my chances of release from prison, but for the rest of my life. There was a danger of having years added to my sentence, or being assigned to the mental health system and ending up somewhere like Broadmoor. With the door possibly opening up before me toward eventual release, the psychologist would have the power to either push me through it or slam it in my face.

I was surprised in our first meeting to see the guy was no more than about 23 years old. I guessed he was just out of university and he feigned an awkward friendliness which came across as nervous. We spoke about my life up to that point in general terms, before he began asking specific questions.

He wanted to know if I used to wet the bed, how I felt about fire, if I had ever enjoyed hurting animals, all that sort of thing. I answered honestly, but most of the questions made it obvious what he was looking for. If you are put in that situation and you say, 'Yes, when I was a kid I used to disembowel hedgehogs for a laugh,' you know what result you are likely to get.

At the end of it all, his report stated I had demonstrated an instrumental use of violence as an armed robber, which in some cases was an indicator for a positive diagnosis. Fortunately, the responses I gave were enough to convince him otherwise. The sigh of relief I breathed when the confirmation came through was genuine. He had given me the green light to move on.

What he did say was that he thought I lacked 'consequential thinking skills' and was lucky that during my criminal career I never actually had to physically hurt anyone. I suppose that was true. I had threatened people with harm and brandished weapons capable of deadly force, but never had to use them.

He stressed that I had been in situations with firearms where one wrong move could have led to chaos and it was difficult to argue with that. Maybe if I had shot someone, at some stage, it would have changed me as a person. That can only be speculation.

He also talked a lot about the mental harm I had caused my victims. How a security guard doing his job, who suddenly finds himself threatened with a gun and fearing for his life would be traumatised by the fear and shock. I had to admit it was something I had not spent too much time considering and as I pondered it, I did feel genuine remorse.

In our world we dehumanised the men doing those jobs. We only saw companies, who we thought of as targets. We would call a Securicor van a 'blue', a Post Office one a 'red', a Securitas a 'white'. When we talked about smacking a blue for £150,000, the concept that the men operating that van were human beings and might have families did not really play a part. We glossed over it. When I acknowledged that as the reality it troubled me and still does, even now.

With all that out of the way I was placed on the transfer list. The SO asked if I wanted to go to Lowdham Grange, a cat B prison near Nottingham. It was privately run and had a reputation as being one of the best equipped cat Bs in the country, so I accepted the offer.

The move excited me. After five years in maximum security I finally felt I was moving forward and packed my stuff eagerly. The only negative was saying goodbye to Roger. We had spent a great deal of time together and become close.

Regardless of what he had been convicted of, to my eyes he will always be one of the most honourable men I have ever met. The sadness shone out of his face as I shook his hand. Both of us knew it was unlikely we would meet again.

18

14 November 2009

I WAS accompanied on the drive to Lowdham by Andy, a kid from Manchester being transferred with me. When we arrived at the latest stop on my tour of penal institutions, the manner of the officers who met us was so different to what we were used to. I almost felt I was home.

'Do you want tea?' one said as they showed us into the building.

'Tea?' I couldn't believe what I was hearing.

'Yeah,' he nodded. 'Would you like a tea and something to eat?'

'Err…okay.'

'Milk and sugar?'

After refreshments, they began going through our belongings. There were items in there I had never been allowed to wear, trainers and t-shirts that Mum and aunties sent in for birthdays, things from my old life that were forbidden in high-security environments. At Lowdham, all of it was allowed. I could hardly believe it. In comparison to where I had come from it felt like a holiday camp.

With our clothes piled up into trollies they sent us over to F wing where we would be staying. A screw opened a door at the back of reception and that was it, we were outside, beneath the sky! There was no strip-searching, no helicopter wire and we were accompanied only by a lone female officer. Freedom seemed closer than ever.

Each cell at Lowdham had its own phone and you were able to make and receive calls from the outside world, an unbelievable luxury. Beyond that, pretty much every guy in the place had a mobile, although they were officially prohibited. To begin with the change in culture was disconcerting. We were out of our cells more. We had more time to ourselves. It took me a couple of weeks to adjust.

It all meant that I was able to begin to make small arrangements for my eventual release. I could speak to Aaron, Johnny and others, not that I would openly talk business, but there were ways and means.

I had a gym induction and took a job as wing cleaner, as I had at Full Sutton. With about 14 months to serve until my parole hearing, although I hoped for the best result, I thought it unlikely I would be granted release at that stage. What I expected was a reduction in status to cat D and a transfer to an open prison, at which point my arrangements on the outside would kick in and I would bunk out, get myself a fake passport, head to the continent and disappear. That made a lot more sense than trying to organise an armed escape from Lowdham, although it would have been perfectly possible, as it would draw a lot less attention from the police and media.

For the first six months I purposely kept myself below the radar, spending a fair amount of time in the gym, as had become my habit. One day I got talking to an inmate called Mickey Steel, who was always rowing on the machines. He explained that he was pulling a million metres for charity, so the officers allowed him extra time out of his cell. He was in the gym half the day, every day.

The idea attracted me straight away. I spoke to one of the gym staff and asked if I would be able to participate as well. They were thrilled that I wanted to join in, as charity work looks great in your file, demonstrating a level of empathy for others. I chose the Rainbows' Children's Trust, a hospice for children with terminal illnesses, as my cause. Lots of the boys from the prison sponsored me meaning I raised £400 and was able to begin.

As a result of signing up I became entitled to gym sessions seven days a week, an opportunity I used to its fullest. I went at it hard, with the intention of doing the million metres as quickly as possible. To begin with I set a target of 32km (20 miles) of rowing a day.

Within a month I completed my first million metres, but was enjoying the extra time out of my cell so much that I asked if I could do another million.

When I blasted through that as well, I asked to do it again. My energy and dedication attracted attention. I had rowed three million metres in three months, which is no mean feat for anyone.

Darren Davis, the officer in charge of the gym, seemed particularly intrigued and began speaking to me often. He explained that 5,000km is the equivalent of rowing the Atlantic. I asked for permission to go for that too.

The end result was that for five solid months I hit the gym every day, rowing and rowing and rowing. I understood nothing about technique or water skills, but my fitness climbed to even greater heights and without realising it, I built up muscle memory as my physique moulded to the demands of the discipline. My body and mind underwent a process of adaptation.

One day, at about the 3.8 million mark, I was tearing through my metres while Darren sat behind me, watching intently. I finished a 10km session and he came over to examine the digital display on the machine.

'John,' he said, a trace of excitement making his voice quiver slightly. 'That's extremely quick, do you realise that?'

I looked at the time, which did not mean a great deal to me. 'Yeah, I suppose it is.'

When I returned to the gym the next morning, Darren approached holding a piece of paper.

'Look at this,' he said.

He had printed out a list of British and world records for indoor rowing. Together we read through. The times were similar to mine. In some cases, they were even lower.

'I can beat most of these now,' I said.

'Can you really?'

'Yeah. That 10k time for example. I'm within seconds of that.'

We spoke no more about it that day and I pulled my metres as usual, but Darren had planted a seed of something in my mind. British records? World records? This was not just exercising in the yard or winning prison competitions. I could perhaps be the best in my country at something, maybe the best anywhere. The thought captivated me and during quiet moments in my cell, I kept returning to it.

For the next few weeks things continued the same way. Darren had opened my eyes to how fit I really was, but for John McAvoy the criminal, it was a diversion, not a signpost.

I received a letter from Aaron written in a code we used. It talked about visiting girls in different places, but the real gist was that we were ready to rock 'n roll. As soon as I got my transfer to an open nick, he would be there. We had a passage to Germany lined up and a few bits to get me started, so I could hit the ground running. At that time I was just over five years into my sentence.

When people talk of a day that changed their life for the better, they usually mean some great success, achievement or slice of luck – winning the lottery, getting married, the birth of a child. For me that day was 14 November 2009, a Saturday. And it was nothing like that.

It began normally enough. I rowed 20,000m in the gym, had some food then watched the first half of an Ireland v France World Cup qualification match in association. Despite having been born and raised in London, I always supported Eire, a McAvoy thing. As the ref blew the whistle I went up to my cell, to phone my cousin Bill.

'Are you watching the football?' I asked him. 'I can't believe how well they're doing. They might even win it!'

Curiously, he did not share my excitement.

'Mate,' he said softly. 'I've got something to tell you.'

'Thierry Henry's hardly been in the game, I can't...'

'John.' He sounded so serious. 'I've got something to tell you mate.'

'All right.'

'Are you on your own?'

'Of course I'm on my own, I'm in a fucking prison cell!'

'Aaron's gone.'

The words touched me too deeply, too suddenly, like a knifepoint in my ribs. I pushed them away.

'What do you mean he's gone?'

He said it again, more slowly.

'Mate...listen...he's gone.'

'Gone where?'

'John, I want you to listen to me mate. Aaron's dead. He was on a job. It all went wrong. He's gone.'

'Nah, he can't be. I got a letter off him a couple of days ago. You've made a mistake.' My voice started to crack. 'What's happened, Bill?'

'I don't know all the details. It was in Holland. There was a car crash. I'm sorry mate. I'm sorry.'

I put the phone down and sank on to my bunk. Disbelief gave way to anguish. Tears trickled down my face.

As usual the floodlights were on outside and the bars on my window cast a stark, striped shadow across my cell. I sat there and wept. Aaron Wild, my best friend, the charmer and ladies' man, ex-private schoolboy and nearly a city banker, who belatedly joined me on my path, was now only a memory.

At just 27, he had lived fast and died young.

Part Three
Running Away

'The strange dance between traumatic arousal and reward also exists in one of our most valued cultural pursuits, high level athletic competition...The release of epinephrine in the face of an extreme survival threat may be associated not only with feelings of anxiety and fear, but also with excitement and exhilaration.

'Those sports that involve maximal sustained physical exertion and effort and that are associated with the most extreme anaerobic pain are also closely linked to the cycle of traumatic arousal... In these instances, the stimulus appears to be pain. The necessary practice of intense training to achieve sufficient fitness levels to achieve a reasonable level of competition in these sports is by definition painful, at times agonisingly so.

'In conversations with trainers and physicians who treat elite endurance athletes, I find a kernel of evidence that this pursuit of fear or pain-based arousal and reward is often related to a history of trauma.'

Robert Scaer, *The body bears the burden* (Routledge)
p.126–7

19

Metamorphosis

I BARELY slept. Images of Aaron and I together tortured me throughout the night, parties we had been to, jobs we had done, our time in Spain. I felt lost. An urge rose in me to lash out, to smash everything. I resisted, gripping the sides of my bunk with such madness my forearms felt they would burst, burying my face in my pillow. I did not want to be one of those prisoners that loses control and behaves like an animal, but for the first time in my life I had no idea what to do.

Those dark, lonely hours became an endless void into which I sank and sank and sank. They took an eternity to pass. As night crawled towards morning I would look at the bars on my window and the giant shadows they cast across the floor and wonder. What was I doing? What were we all doing? In reality, away from the bluster and cockiness, who did this work for, this way of life?

There was adrenaline and danger and moments of great triumph, but at the end of it all, what? Aaron was dead. Micky had spent a large part of his life in jail. Billy and Kevin were locked up. Roger would be inside until he was an old man. I had already spent most of my youth behind bars.

I began to see it, really see it. It was not just a platitude repeated by police and authority figures, a lie propagated by the system. It was true.

There was no happy ending.

We were not all going to end up cruising around the world on yachts, with luxury villas in Barbados and supermodel girlfriends. In this life I had chosen there were only two outcomes. Sure, you might have a few good years, but ultimately you would either lose your freedom, or your life. It did not end any other way.

That night stripped layers from me and when the sun rose, what remained was formless, raw and vulnerable. As I emerged, bleary eyed and sweaty from my cell, the world was not the same as it had been. While I queued to collect my breakfast, neither was I.

I phoned Mum and she confirmed it all with a shaking voice. Aaron had been around to see her only a few weeks prior and helped her out with money. I asked her for details, if she knew exactly how it happened. But at that stage neither she nor anyone else had any idea.

I called my cousin Bill again. He had spoken to Johnny and a couple of others and pieced together some information. It seemed Aaron had been on a robbery out in Holland, as during his time on the continent he involved himself in work outside of drugs. The job had been initially successful but a problem had arisen on the getaway. Everyone suspected the police had rammed him off the road.

Throughout the day I seesawed between anger and grief. Andy and a couple of other guys on the wing tried to console me, but there was nothing anyone could say to make me feel better.

That evening, the story was reported on *News at Ten*. They talked of a gang of British robbers that were killed attempting a getaway and still photographs were shown of them in action, close-ups taken from CCTV cameras.

They wore balaclavas, but even so I could tell which one he was. Through the opening in the material I could see his eyes. He had a can in his hand, spraying the camera lenses to obscure the footage.

Seeing him like that, in the very last moments of his life, brought home the finality. Aaron was doing exactly what you would expect him to do in that situation. I could put myself in his position. I would have been doing the same thing.

When the lights went out that night, my second night, the image recurred in my mind constantly. Aaron in the balaclava, Aaron on a job, Aaron alive – his eyes kept me awake.

I had looked in those eyes and promised loyalty. I had seen them happy, excited, frazzled on drugs and narrowed in concentration. I had seen them light up when a pretty girl walked by, but now no one would ever see them again.

I found myself replaying the scene from Plaza beach like a movie in my head.

If anything ever goes wrong, if you go down, I'll come for you, alright? That's the way it has to be.

Of course mate. Me too. I'm always there if you need me.

At the time it had meant so much. Now it seemed like hollow, drugged-up nonsense.

The following morning, shattered from two nights of poor sleep, I came down for breakfast, got my tray and sat at a table with a bunch of the lads, as usual. I had no desire to talk, so just listened to what went on around me. It was typical prison chatter, stabbing so-and-so because he did this, where to get drugs, mates doing robberies on the outside. As I sat there picking at my food, I felt suddenly and acutely aware of the huge weight of their negative energy.

A voice inside my mind said, 'This is all shit. Listen to these boys, to their concerns and interests. Aaron threw his whole life away for this. For fuck all. For piles of pieces of paper covered in pictures of the queen. This is where it ends.'

For the next few weeks solitude became my habit and I cut a detached figure on the wing. Battles raged within me. How many times had I been involved in chases, had police pointing guns at me? How close had I come to the same fate as Aaron?

I looked at my environment, really looked at it, at the people I lived with. It was nothing more than a human storage unit and I was rotting in it. I was a young man. Guys my age were meeting girls, forming friendships, building lives. I was around scum, people who thought of nothing but themselves, their own needs, their urges. I looked at myself, at all I had done, at the Rolex on my wrist and no longer liked what I saw.

There had been some nice cars and some top nights out, but should life only be measured in things like that? I had so many questions but few answers. At times I was almost depressed.

I continued training, but from then it became something I did alone. When I went to the gym or out on the yard to do circuits, I would gently shun other inmates who came to join me. It was about me, my process and forging something new.

They brought Aaron's body back for the funeral but I was unable to attend. His sister asked me to write a eulogy and I expressed myself as well as I was able.

My education had been Billy's lessons, Billy's knowledge, not Shakespeare and poetry. I wrote simply that Aaron was a good person, a funny, charming, talented young man who got swept up into our life. He had found out where that life really ends and by finding out, he had showed me. By dying, Aaron taught me the one lesson that Billy never could.

In place of going to the service I asked to visit the Catholic chaplaincy at the prison, so I could speak to the priest. He read a prayer and told me to share my feelings if I wanted to. It was nice of him and gave me some closure, but I knew my answers were outside the Bible.

As a kid I had regarded myself a Catholic, as a matter of upbringing. Even when I was out robbing, I used to pray to God to protect me, which sounds crazy, but I never really had faith. My change had to come from within.

As I neared the end of my five million metres, with Darren's encouragement, I began to notice that my stints on the rowing machine took on an almost mystical aspect. Throughout my time in prison I exercised as a form of escape, but now it was myself I was escaping from, as much as the walls around me. When I rowed, my mind would clear of all the searching and questions and ruthless self-examination.

I would push myself harder than ever before, find the pain barrier and row through it. When I did that I felt free of everything, becoming a better, cleaner version of me, like putting coffee through a filter.

There was a guy on the wing called Hussein, a well-educated, middle-class kid from Bournemouth, convicted of organising a massive drugs ring. They had given him a long sentence but his background meant he kept his distance from others. Our mutual isolation brought us together. I went down to association one day and found him there on his own.

'You know what,' I told him. 'I'm done.'

'What do you mean?'

'I am never committing another crime. I'm finished with this.'

We sat in silence for a while.

'It's very hard, you know John,' he said at last. 'You say that, but you'll come out and have all the old faces around you. If you haven't got a trade to fall back on, it's tricky. You have to make a living somehow.'

He had a point. I left school with no qualifications and had never had a proper job. There was no obvious way for me to make it work. I just knew that I had to.

Down in the gym I began talking more and more to Darren, who showed himself to be a genuinely interesting, deep-thinking man. In my state of need I welcomed his input into my life and came to see him as more than just a screw. It was the first relationship I developed with an officer in all my time in jails.

Outside of work he led an active life, taking on a number of extreme challenges. He had been on expeditions to the South Pole and Everest. He was one of the first men to have climbed the Watkins mountains in Greenland and had cycled from Land's End to John O'Groats. The breadth of his experiences fascinated me.

Darren read a lot of books on endurance sport and human endeavour. He began telling me stories about Lance Armstrong, James Cracknell, Graham Obree and others. I found them fascinating and he would bring some in for me to read, which I took back to my cell and consumed hungrily. One, called *Formula* by Geoff Thompson, affected me deeply.

The book talked of the changes that were needed in life to find a measure of happiness, of the things that should be avoided, that sap your energy, like fast food and soap operas. How selfishness and thoughtlessness create a spiral. Within it I recognised so many things that were relevant to me. Need for renewal made me absorbent and I soaked up everything.

My respect for Darren grew as I recognised how he was one of the few officers to treat work as a vocation, rather than a job. He was not earning a few quid to pay the bills. He really wanted to help people. He ran personal training courses for inmates, so they could gain PT qualifications and hopefully find work when released. Assisting young men to break out of the destructive cycle of crime, prison and re-offending mattered to him and you could see that in the way he spoke and moved.

National figures placed recidivism at 59 per cent, meaning that more than half of UK inmates would go on to be re-convicted for something else. Once you had been inside a couple of times, as I had, particularly at my level of crime, the perceived wisdom was that you would never break out of it. You would spend most of your life behind bars.

Few would have given me a chance, but Darren's positivity drew him to see something in me. His sincerity and willingness to help started getting through. The fact he was in a uniform was irrelevant. He expanded my horizons.

We spoke in depth about my rowing and how well my stamina had developed. Darren was convinced I had talent, that I was capable of achieving something notable. By the time I finished my cross-Atlantic indoor row, we had discussed the possibility of challenging some of the times we looked at before. Both of us found the idea exciting. Breaking records from the prison gym would be a wonderful statement both about me and Lowdham Grange.

Darren phoned Concept 2, the world's leading manufacturer of rowing machines, who maintained the database of indoor rowing records. They confirmed it would be possible, as long as there were at least two witnesses, a photograph was taken of the machine's digital display and my results were validated by an independent party.

The news thrilled both of us and within a couple of days we decided I would attempt the British record for rowing a marathon (42km), held by a naval officer called Vincent Brumming. I did no special training as I spent so much time on the rower anyway. We simply sat down, switched the machine on, Darren and another officer stood by with stopwatches and off we went.

In no time I got into a zone, finding my rhythm quickly and flying through it for a couple of hours, all the way to 35km. At that point my energy levels depleted and I started cramping. Officers sent an inmate to grab a few sachets of sugar from the canteen, not necessarily a solution I would recommend, but on this occasion, with no alternative, throwing refined sugar down my neck did the job. My pace picked up again and I finished strongly. As I replaced the handle into the bracket and relaxed, the officers and gym orderlies erupted into applause. Darren smiled proudly. I had smashed the record by eight minutes.

I felt incredible, the same way, if not better, as I used to feel coming off a job with £200,000. I had done what I set out to do and not only achieved it, but exceeded it. At that point in time, there was no one in Britain who could indoor-row a marathon faster than me. Not bad for a chubby kid who hated PE.

Around the prison, people were shocked by my accomplishment. Wholesome success stories were not the sort of thing that happened in that world. Some were unsure how to react, but the recognition I did receive gave me contentment. When I sat alone in my cell that night, with my aching muscles and blistered hands, I acknowledged a private truth to myself.

I was really, really good at something.

Concept 2 sent me a certificate which I placed on the wall and soon Darren and I planned my next move. We chose the half-marathon, which would mean rowing at a higher intensity and using more power as opposed to raw stamina. Like the first time we made no special preparations, but I obliterated the previous record, smashing it by four minutes.

After becoming a double British record holder, I started to read more endurance sport specific books, eager to find out about training methods and nutrition. Obviously in prison I was hampered to a large degree and unable to explore these things as fully as I would have liked, but carbohydrates, protein, muscle recovery and physiology began to occupy my consciousness in the same way that robbery plans and escape routes once had. It fired my enthusiasm and excitement.

I learned about electrolytes and body fluids, so would get bottles of water then add a small amount of Ribena, some sugar and salt to simulate energy drinks. I even experimented with protein-rich versions by adding a little tuna. I became conscious of the food that I ate, which in prison was rarely healthy, but tried to increase my intake of lean protein as much as possible. People like Lance Armstrong, James Cracknell and Ben Fogle became my heroes. Armstrong may have been discredited because of drugs, but his mental strength inspired me. These were people who had literally pushed the boundaries of human endurance. It blew my mind how physically and mentally strong they were, how much they were prepared to commit to achieve their goals. I lapped up everything I could about them, sometimes reading 500-page books in a weekend.

The walls of my cell were soon covered in quotes. 'Pain is temporary, quitting lasts forever.' 'If you worry about falling off the bike, you never get on.' As I did all of this, I reached even greater levels of intensity in my rowing. Two other British records followed quickly, the 10,000m and the most amount of distance covered in 30 minutes. Darren made repeated comments about my extraordinary cardiovascular capacity and unshakeable mindset. He was enjoying the ride as much as I was and at national level, I was sweeping all before me. The momentum helped me leave Aaron's death behind.

Over the months, as my inner conflict fermented into intense passion for sport, I watched a programme in my cell about

Ironman triathlon. The whole history of the event fascinated me, having come about through an argument over whether long-distance runners, cyclists or swimmers were fittest. The resulting tri-discipline competition was considered the toughest one-day endurance challenge in existence. When they ran the first one, in Hawaii in 1978, it was a struggle simply to finish, but over the years it had developed very much into a race.

A marathon on its own has a certain mystique, perhaps because the first ever marathon runner, Pheidippides, died after completing it, but for Ironmen the marathon was just the final act of an epic three-part play. The sheer distances involved presented such an extraordinary challenge. It was said that during the race, athletes were at war with themselves, not competing with each other so much as the course, the weather conditions and the inner compulsion to quit when things got tough.

The programme showed clips of the world championship race in Kona, Hawaii, giving a sense of the enormous ordeal competitors endured. Some collapsed, some ran on through cramps and delirium. The winner yelled in triumph then broke down in tears.

'A sport that forever changes those who attempt it,' the commentator said. Shivers ran up my spine.

'One day,' I said to no one, in my cell, 'one day I will do that race.' It was a hope, rather than an expectation, but proclaiming it made it seem real.

I mentioned the idea to Darren, my confidante. He approved. Grinning, he then produced another sheaf of paper. He had taken the time to print off the biographies of all the people whose times I had beaten in collecting my four British records. One name in particular stuck in my head – Hywel Davies, a Welshman, a highly respected endurance athlete. These were men who had run marathons in two hours and 30 minutes, completed Ironman races in under nine hours and achieved many other feats of athletic excellence. I read them avidly.

'Think about this,' Darren said. 'You've beaten them. Look at these men and what they've achieved. You're better than they are.'

I nodded as a strange feeling grew inside me. The same sort of feeling I had all those years before when I watched *Fool's Gold* and found my grandad's newspaper clippings.

So this is who I am?

'It's a big deal John. You've got no real sporting nutrition, you're in a massively stressful environment and you're beating men like this. What does that say about you? Imagine what you can do when you get out.'

Suddenly, I had positive goals and an understanding of the discipline required to achieve them. It awoke something in me I had not known was there and we discussed where we could go with it. I felt strangely drawn to really big distances, wanting to stretch and test myself as far as possible, to establish my limits. I told Darren I wanted to tackle the world record for the longest distance rowed in 24 hours. The man who held it was a guy called Nigel Roedde, a 23-year-old from Northern Ontario in Canada and a real-life trans-Atlantic ocean rower. He had actually set the time while training for an attempt to cross the ocean between Morocco and Barbados.

Darren was initially sceptical, not because he didn't think I could do it, but because he couldn't see how I could attempt such a thing within the confines of the prison regime. I was still a category B inmate and for me to be allowed out of my cell for a full 24-hour period would require a major bending of prison protocol.

Darren spoke to the governor, pitching it to him on the basis that it was excellent publicity and would provide a boost for prisoner morale. From the viewpoint of prison inspectors, it would demonstrate that Lowdham Grange was a forward-thinking establishment that could demonstrate real rehabilitative powers. Such opportunities are rare.

Bearing in mind my prior successes, the governor cleared permission, provided Darren stayed up through the night with me, as no other gym staff would do it. That meant Darren sacrificing his day off on an unpaid basis, which he offered to do without hesitation.

'I'll tell you what I'll do,' Darren said. 'I'm going to put the exercise bike behind you and I'll cycle while you row. We'll keep each other going.'

A date was set – Saturday 19 February 2011 – and it was on. Everyone in the prison knew about it and my exploits became the subject of banter and discussion. Could I do it? Could a regular prisoner break such a demanding world record? It gave the boys something to talk about other than home-made knives and where to score their heroin.

On the morning I arrived in the gym ready, focused and a little unsure of what to expect. I had never even been up for 24 hours straight, apart from when I was off my head on drugs, let alone exercised for that long. The longest row I had completed was the marathon, which took me two hours 39 minutes.

I knew there would be a pain barrier, maybe several of them, but other than that I was in the dark. I had no clue how my body would react, or my mind.

We decided to start at 4pm so my sleep cycle would not be too messed up. The idea was when I finished I would be able to have a bit of food, then go to bed and get a normal night's sleep. Darren seemed to know what he was talking about so I trusted him.

We planned that I would row 50km in one hit, have a short rest, then row another 50km. At that point, if everything was working, I would already be ahead of the world record. We knew the splits I had to hold to beat the time and Darren had written it all out on to the whiteboard in the gym.

I bought supplies from the canteen to keep me going – Mars bars, flapjacks, a few bags of sweets – and laid them out next to me, along with several bottles of my home-made sports drinks. It was not a perfect set-up, by any means, but I would need to put fast energy into my body during the attempt and they were the best options available.

I climbed on, sat down and waited with a sense of total focus. At 3.55pm Darren stepped forward. 'Okay John, you've got the ability to do this,' he said, 'and I believe you're going to do it. It's all about being steady. Remember to eat and drink at regular intervals. I'll keep you on top of it all, so don't worry about the numbers.'

The minute hand ticked around to four, Darren gave me the signal and I began assuredly, with power and drive. Quickly I entered my inner space, where nothing mattered other than movement.

After the first seven hours and 100,000m, I felt brilliant. Alive, sweaty, but full of energy and resolve. Yet I knew it was still only 11pm and the toughest part of the row lay ahead. Darren warned before I started that the period from midnight to six was when the real test of my psychological strength would occur. It doesn't matter how physically fit you are, but at that sort of time, your brain starts telling your body that it's time to go to sleep. As a result, everything slows down. If you can force your way through that trough, by morning you start peaking again.

Every hour I would take in some sugar and fluids, but that could not stave off the inevitable. By 12.30am I began to feel seriously weary and by 1.30am, I was toiling. An hour after that, I found myself in a very dark place, barely able to keep my eyes open. My head lolled.

I never liked to ask others for help but felt the need to utilise Darren's experience.

'I feel like shit,' I told him. 'I don't think I can do this.'

'Listen John,' he said. 'I promise you, if you keep going, you will feel fine in three or four hours. Your body can do this, no problem, but if you let your mind shut down, you're done for. Just grind it out, keep telling yourself you can do it. You'll get there, I know you will.'

I ploughed on grimly. Darren spoke now and then, just to make sure I was awake. Mostly I didn't reply. All sorts of things passed through my mind, memories of Aaron, being with Elodi in Spain, growing up with Billy. People talk about life flashing before your eyes and I guess it was something like that. I was lost, cocooned in a little internal world while I pulled and pulled that handle.

At around 3.30am my bubble was popped when the door opened and a DST (designated search team) strode in, a small group of officers who patrol the prison at night. They scour the building with dogs, opening up toilets, checking light fittings and searching behind radiators. It's their job to unearth any illicit items stashed around the premises by inmates, in particular drugs or weapons.

'What the hell's going on here?' one of them asked.

'We're attempting a world record,' replied Darren. Briefly, the officer didn't know what to say.

'You what? That's a prisoner there. He shouldn't be out of his cell, it's three in the morning.'

'I know, it's been cleared by the governor.'

'No one told us. Are you sure you're all right to be with him on your own?'

'Thanks lads,' Darren said. 'I think I've got this.'

His sarcasm made me smile and they left us to it.

Soon I found myself sinking again and at about 4.30am, everything went briefly black. I paused, taking a shaky sip of my energy drink. Shadows danced behind my clouded vision. My back and legs screamed for me to stop. I could have fallen asleep in a second.

It may have been a dream, a sudden lapse into unconsciousness, but before me I saw the home office lady who came to visit Belmarsh.

People like you do not change.

As she faded away I picked up the handle again. I tried to look in front of me, to raise my head. Darren was talking in the background but his words failed to register. Through the darkness DCI Currie from the Flying Squad appeared, smiling at me in all his smugness and self-satisfaction.

Listen me old mate and listen well. You are fucked. Well and truly. You do know that don't you?

And then the judge.

I have no option but to pass down two life sentences.

Suddenly I was rowing, stronger than before. Pulling with the back and pushing with the arms. 'Fuck you, Currie,' I thought, gritting my teeth. 'Fuck all you cunts.'

The desire to prove them wrong, a fierce, desperate, all-consuming desire re-energised me. They didn't know me. They had no idea what I was capable of. I could feel myself waking up.

As I rowed on into morning and the darkness left, my thought patterns returned to normal. I didn't hate Currie, not really. I didn't hate any of them. In some ways I owed them one.

Currie may have thought he destroyed my life, a fact he seemed to derive enjoyment from, but that destruction had started my recreation. A new John was emerging and I was reaching my potential in ways I never thought possible.

By ending me, Currie resurrected me.

At 6am the gym officers arrived to start their shift, shock on their faces that I was still going. Their surprise, excitement and encouragement spurred me on further. Just as Darren had said, my brain aligned with my normal sleep patterns and I felt great again. As the staff chatted among themselves around me, I knew I was going to do it.

By mid-morning, fellow prisoners started showing up. Andy from Manchester appeared and a few others. They became my cheering section as I neared my goal.

It was around 2pm, 22 hours after starting, that I was informed I had broken the world record. I no longer felt tired. All that was long behind me and after 243,000m, I let out a yelp of delight.

'Forget you've broken it,' Darren said. 'You've got two more hours to put as much distance between yourself and the rest of the world as possible. Make your record unbreakable. Everything you've got left, give it now.'

From then on I rowed on pure euphoria, adding an extra 21,000m. When I finally climbed off that machine on weak legs, shook Darren's hand and thanked him, I was giddy, light-headed, almost as if I could float away. All the boys wanted their photo taken with me. In some ways it didn't seem real.

I had become a world record holder.

20

A Gift

I COLLAPSED on to the floor mat next to the machine. As my adrenaline subsided I began to get a sense of how utterly fatigued my whole system was. It was a tiredness beyond tiredness, as if my very bones craved sleep. People in the gym filtered away and again I was left alone with Darren.

'Can I ask you something?' I said.

'Sure,' he replied.

'How did I really look, in the middle of the night?'

He laughed. 'Honestly? You looked like death. I was worried you were going to pack it in. Thank God there were no mirrors in front of you. If you'd seen the state of yourself you'd have given up in a second!'

I chuckled. He leaned in and spoke more quietly.

'You've got a gift, John,' he whispered. 'A talent. Most of us spend our whole lives trying to find something we're supposed to do. You've found it. You are exceptional. You could be one of the very best. You have to make the most of this.'

I nodded.

'But listen,' he continued, 'and I mean this. If you get out in a year or two and end up re-offending, it will be the biggest travesty I have ever seen in all my years as a prison officer.

'People get locked into crime because they have no choice. You do.'

As we walked back to the cells, I resolved that when I regained my freedom I would distance myself from all my old associates. Leaving the game would be hard and would mean severing ties with people I cared about, even people I was related to, but if it was going to work, that was the way it had to be. I couldn't just go back down to my old area and hang out in BlueEye and El Pirata socialising with the same faces. If I did, I would be back involved in no time.

Ever since Aaron's death I had known I wanted something else, I just hadn't known what. Now I knew, with absolute certainty. Sport was my way out.

Darren took me back on to the wing and when we arrived the boys all started clapping and cheering. It stopped me in my tracks and a lump rose in my throat, which I swallowed, hard. It was so unusual to feel an atmosphere like that in there. That touched me. My exploits had roused a positive, cheerful mood in a place where that never happened. Seeing the lads together, smiling, even if it was only fleeting, showed what my sporting ability could do. As well as benefitting me, I could inspire others and make them happy.

The guys in the canteen had kept loads of food back and I was served with more potatoes and chicken legs than I knew what to do with. I took it all up to my cell and sat on my bunk, where I ate through some of the pile hungrily. As my system adjusted to the process of digestion I became completely exhausted. Within minutes I was asleep.

Early the next morning the governor knocked on my door.

'Well done mate!' he said, beaming and offering his hand. 'We're all so proud of you. What you've done is unbelievable.'

I thanked him and for most of that day existed in a state of weary elation. The congratulations and backslaps continued, while I basked in my glimmer of glory. But that night, after bang-up, my left arm and face went numb. My heartbeat faltered while at the same time, my mind became sharply alert.

The thought occurred that I could be having a stroke. I was moments away from pressing the alarm button when the feeling began to pass, but it had frightened me.

The prison doctor explained that I had exhausted my adrenal gland, which secretes insulin. As a result, adrenaline was being released into my body when I was resting, which was causing irregular heart activity. I had to be monitored for a few days and eventually it abated.

That was my first clear insight into the physical toll that top level endurance sport can exact. The demands are different to those on a footballer or tennis player. Not only while you compete, but during the days that follow, you feel the effects of high performance. Muscular, cardiovascular and even nervous systems all undergo extreme strain. Recuperation and proper nutrition are key, but the latter was near enough impossible to organise in prison.

Within a week I was back in the gym and again enjoying my regular chats with Darren. I found his commitment to physical and personal improvement uplifting and looked forward to speaking with him more than anyone else. It was more than a case of shared common interests. He had helped me achieve the most significant accomplishment of my life.

Admiring attention continued for the next couple of weeks. A rower at university in Southampton tried to break my record but failed and a photographer was sent by prison authorities to take pictures of me in the gym. I enjoyed my status as some sort of star inmate. Yet despite another visit from the governor and many plaudits from other staff, it was not all fun and excitement. At times I even found old resentments returning. *The system* was a hard thing to like.

My success was wonderful, but moments of pure, fist-clenching frustration still occurred, usually after lock-up, back in my cell. Gazing down at the shadows of the bars on the floor, part of me remained bitter, even angry. I knew I had changed and internally, I was no longer a criminal. It was as simple as that. All criminal thoughts and ambitions had left me and if society could know that, I should be free. Yet still I was kept there, caged and denied. It didn't seem fair.

To compound all of that, I knew by then I had a genuine ability, something to give to the world, but the prison environment was preventing me from using it to its fullest. I was 28 years old, in the prime of my athletic life, but incarceration would stifle my development.

As always, to cope I zoned in on training, reading and researching. Each session was like a mini rebirth – sweat out the old, drink in the new. Impurities gone, frustrations evaporated, flushed out by clean water and fresh perspective.

My parole hearings were scheduled to begin at the end of March, by which time I had already served more than the five-year minimum tariff Judge Carroll had laid out. I waited to hear what lay in store and appointed a new solicitor, from a firm in Nottingham, a pleasant, white-haired lady called Irene Tolley.

She confirmed what I suspected. It was unlikely I would be released, even though my tariff was served. The most probable outcome, which we could request, would be transfer to an open prison. That was better than nothing. At least it represented progression and I was eager to make it a reality.

Just three days before my hearing was due to commence, HMP bureaucracy intervened to disrupt my plans. I received a request to go to the office and arrived to find the wing officer sitting with the probation clerk. Both had grim faces.

'Sit down, John. We've got some bad news for you,' the PO said. 'Your parole hearing's been deferred.'

'What? Why?'

It emerged that years before, when I had been sentenced and returned to Belmarsh, the officer responsible for my paperwork had misunderstood the situation, leading to an error on my file.

Judge Carroll handed down a discretionary life sentence (as opposed to a mandatory which is given for murder), but the officer had recorded this wrongly, as an IPP – an indeterminate sentence for public protection. This mix-up meant that the magistrate booked to chair my parole hearing did not have the necessary authority to do so. Any life sentence review required a crown court judge. None of this was my fault but it meant that progress would be delayed.

'In reality,' the PO went on, 'you should never have been moved to this prison in the first place. We don't accept discretionary life-sentenced prisoners here.'

His words stirred up my reflections on fate. Although it was a massive annoyance, if the officer at Belmarsh had done his job properly, I would not have transferred to Lowdham, I would never have met Darren Davis and perhaps I would never have started indoor rowing.

This screw-up meant that I served several extra months at Lowdham Grange before my hearing was able to be convened. Every day I would go to the office and ask for news. Every day I was met with shrugged shoulders and blank faces.

It was disheartening, especially after all the effort I had made in the gym. I felt let down and I think the old me would have become openly hostile and confrontational, but my positive relationship with Darren prevented that from happening. I had a prison officer I could speak to, who I liked, who understood my exasperation and knew how to help me channel it.

To alleviate the stress, I naturally used training, my new go-to solution for all problems. I broke two more British records in no time. They weren't really challenging enough, so I spoke with Darren about going for something bigger.

'What do you fancy?' Darren asked, showing me the list of world times.

'One hundred thousand metres?'

He nodded. 'It'll be a very different challenge, in some ways more intense than the last one. You'll need your foot on the gas for a sustained period.'

'I know.'

The pre-existing record stood at six hours 48 minutes, meaning that to attempt it, the only special arrangement needed was a pass to be out of my cell over lunch. For this one I would be able to attempt some specialised training and with Darren's help began to read up about training zones. They would not allow me a heart-rate monitor in prison, which was a small hindrance, but at least with the knowledge I was able to approximate proper methods.

We concentrated on training my body to hold a fast split time of one minute 52 seconds per 500m, which I did until it felt easy. If I could sustain that for the whole distance, we knew I would have it in the bag. I performed lots of 20–30km rows working at that split, seeing how it felt. The idea was I would be keeping my heart rate at about 150 beats per minute for six and a half hours which would have to be gauged on feel.

To manage my nutrition, I exchanged my tobacco allowance for meat from the serving hatch and had five or six kids giving me chicken legs, along with cans of tuna, mackerel and plenty of porridge. It was not a perfect diet by any means and certainly not by the standards of high-performance meal plans in the wider world, but it was protein rich and as low-fat as I could manage, with plenty of omega oils from the fish.

Darren said he would bring some energy gels in for me to maximise my performance on the day, which strictly speaking, he was not supposed to do, but the positive publicity generated by my success would encourage the authorities to turn a blind eye. I felt very confident. We may not have had a professional set-up but I was sure I was capable of professional standards.

I woke early on the morning of Sunday 1 May 2011 and ate a large porridge breakfast. At 8.50am I walked into the gym, laid out my provisions and stretched. There was no messing about. Darren set up a camcorder and wished me luck. Bang on 9am, we began.

Up until 50km I rowed freely and smoothly, held the splits with ease and did not even feel like I was exerting myself. That all changed when I hit 75km and when it changed, the change was drastic.

The failings of my nutritional regime meant that I lacked replacement electrolytes, while profuse sweating was losing me lots of salt and potassium. My obliques and hamstrings started cramping up, then to make matters worse, shortly afterwards my *latissimus dorsi* muscle across my upper back went into spasm. It shook uncontrollably as I rowed, contracting and flexing like someone pinging a rubber band. The pain was excruciating, making me grind my teeth. My speed sagged.

'Just ease up and stretch out,' Darren said, with worry on his face. 'You're well within record pace, just relax your body then continue when you're comfortable.'

'No,' I told him. 'I ain't stopping. I'll keep going.'

The last 10km was sheer, prolonged agony, spreading from my body to my mind, shrinking my field of vision to a tiny spot on the wall, which I fixed my eyes upon. Silently, I counted strokes, while Darren kept shouting out my progress. It felt like my teeth would be worn down to nubs, but if I relaxed my jaw I would have screamed. All I thought of was reaching the end and being able to stop.

When the electronic display flashed '100,000' I released the handle, allowing it to clatter back to its holder, and let out a growl of pain. I rolled off the seat and on to the floor, letting my back flatten itself. Still, it convulsed. Beneath the physical torment came a wave of joy. Darren confirmed I had beaten the world record by 18 minutes.

The feeling was the same as before, elation mixed with satisfaction. Alongside that lay a sense of destiny. With two world records to my name, this new direction had to be leading somewhere? My destination remained unclear, particularly while parole was delayed, but I felt sure it was not in a prison.

Arriving back on the wing I was treated to another hero's welcome. Men whose normal posture was to demand respect, aggressively if necessary, gave it to me freely. I made a conscious effort to control myself, to accept their acclaim without swagger. These things were becoming habits.

Just as the excitement from that one started to fade, my parole hearing was convened in June 2011. A female criminal psychologist led the discussion.

'You're a very interesting case,' she said, looking right through me over her glasses, as if I was transparent. 'You've come in here with no drink or drug problems and no mental health issues. You can read, you're articulate, you're well dressed. You weren't abused as a child. What's it all about?'

'It used to be about money,' I told her. 'Isn't that what motivates most people?'

'Perhaps, but what I'm seeing with you is that you treat criminal activity like a corporate venture. You see crime purely as a risk to reward equation, don't you?'

She looked at my wrist on which my Rolex was coiled. I nodded, thinking I should have left the watch in my cell.

'You apply that to every aspect of your life, don't you?'

I was unsure what to say. 'Yes and no.'

'You could have come off a campus or a boardroom to be here today, the way you're presenting yourself. You're a puzzle John, you really are.'

The discussion became personal, interrogating the differences between the way I portrayed myself and my real motivations. Doesn't everybody, in every walk of life, exist within that paradox? How others see you and how you see yourself? What were they trying to prove? That I was human? It felt as if they were trying to push my buttons, to drag a reaction from me. I didn't let it work.

I had been through so much self-analysis already and had come to the conclusion that I am a goal-oriented person. My old goals had all been to do with goods, possessions, status and cash, but now they lay within the world of sport. When I focused on something, I didn't like things that stood in my way. Before that might have been security guards, in my new reality it would be competitors, but the essential process was the same.

Ultimately, after an hour of intense and uncomfortable questioning, they approved my request to be transferred to open conditions. I was already well over my minimum tariff, part of the heavy reality of serving a life sentence. Another parole meeting was set for 12 months' time, meaning that if all went well, I could be considered for release at that stage.

Buoyed by the positive result and expecting an imminent move, I returned to the wing in jubilant mood, but I should have known better. Prison bureaucracy had another trick up its sleeve. Days turned into weeks and kept ticking by. Three months after the hearing I was still at Lowdham.

I spoke to Darren, who went to the governor and did his best to hurry things along for me, to no avail. Eventually my solicitor had to threaten them with a high court review as they were keeping me in closed conditions unlawfully. As soon as this threat was made, my transfer miraculously came through. I would be heading to Sudbury, a cat D prison in Derbyshire.

On 12 August I cleared out my belongings and trollied them down to reception. Darren came to shake my hand as I waited downstairs.

'What you've achieved here has meant a lot to me,' he said, 'and I'll keep in contact with you, however I can.' Professional ethics meant he was unable to express too close a friendship but we both knew we had forged strong links. Prison officer or not, I would never be able to overlook the help and inspiration he provided. Darren had been there when I needed him and acted as a catalyst for my new direction. I would never forget that.

As was usual on these occasions, they left me in a holding cell for what seemed like forever before finally opening the door and asking if I was ready. I nodded and they led me out to the desk, where a group of other prison officers stood around. I could only tell they were prison officers because they said so. They were dressed in normal, civilian clothes.

For the final transfer of my prison career, I left Lowdham Grange in a Vauxhall Corsa. There was no bombproof lorry, no Perspex box, no helicopters and no machine guns. One guy drove, a female officer sat in the passenger seat and another sat in the back with me.

It was more than seven years since I found myself in a regular car and able to look out of the windows, to watch the landscape roll past. A simple pleasure but at that moment it was magical, like being at the movies.

'You're the guy that's broken world records then?' said the woman, as we pulled out on to the motorway. 'We've been told about you. You'll like it at our place. We've got a decent gym.'

Soon the others joined in too, chatting away, making jokes. They did not even behave like screws. I began to suspect that Sudbury would be quite a different experience.

21

Ergs Don't Float

I N some ways it was an unsettling journey. Freedom, I figured, is a bit like strong booze. If you haven't had any for years, even small amounts can make you dizzy.

The officers were friendly but I didn't know how to interact with them. They were talking to me as an equal, although that really wasn't the case, even calling me 'mate'. They told me that at Sudbury I would have the key to my own room and stressed that they referred to it as a room, not a cell, but they all carried master keys.

'It's based on trust,' the guy next to me said. 'There's no fence, there's no wall. If you want to, you can just walk out. Plenty do.'

'But do us a favour,' the driver chimed in, 'if you're gonna run off, please leave your keys behind. It's a real pain in the arse when keys go missing.'

The prison was located down a country road, the wrong side of Derby, and had originally been built as an Air Force hospital in World War Two. After checking me in at reception one of the officers walked me to my wing, except at Sudbury they didn't call it a wing. It was a 'billet'.

'The only rule is that from 8pm to 6am you have to be on the billet,' he said, as we walked along the path. 'Other than that, you can move around as you please.'

When we reached the door, he handed me my room key and said, 'You're in there.'

'All right,' I replied.

He turned around and walked off.

For a moment I lingered, watching him go, phased by the situation. What was I supposed to do now? I had a quick look from side to side. There was no one else in sight.

I put my stuff in my room, locked it and decided to go for a walk. What a strange sensation, to be able to *decide* to go for a walk! All the options made my head spin.

The gravel path around the billet crunched underfoot and I followed it to the rear of the building, where it brought me to something miraculous. My breath caught in my throat. Could it be true?

Having not seen grass, up close, for seven years, the small field behind the billet was a thing of indescribable beauty to my eyes, alive and green and natural, like a picture of paradise. I must have looked like a nutcase, but found myself laughing like a child, falling to my knees, running my hands through it, tearing clumps up then watching the blades scatter back down to earth. I rubbed it between my fingers and sniffed it. My eyes were damp.

When I felt able to continue walking, I discovered flowers, trees and insects. I blew a dandelion and saw the spores fly away. At one point a squirrel scurried across the path at my feet.

Intoxicated, I stumbled from one marvel to the next as if I was on some exquisite drug. For a man only two years out of high security, the Sudbury prison grounds were like Wonderland.

As I roamed around, exhilarated by it all, I bumped into a familiar face from Lowdham, a guy called Gerry who had been transferred a couple of months before me.

'What do you do here mate?' I asked, eyes wide. 'How does it all work? I don't even know where to get food or anything.'

'Dinner's at 5.30pm,' he said, pointing at the canteen. 'You queue over there. Have you got any utensils?'

'Eh?'

'Cutlery? Plates?'

'Mate, I've just got here.'

'Come to my cell,' he said. 'I'll lend you some of mine.'

I followed him to his room and he gave me a white porcelain plate and a stainless steel knife and fork. I was only used to plastic. I turned them over and over in my hands, feeling the weight of them. It was like being an actual person again.

Some daylight remained after dinner and I went for another stroll around the perimeter of the prison boundary, about three miles altogether. Birds sang in the trees and a smell of smoke hung in the air, as if someone in the village nearby was having a bonfire. I slept like a lamb that night, exhausted by sensory overload.

Knowing my background, the Sudbury staff gave me a job as an orderly in the prison gym and I began to take courses in personal training. A plan to become a pro athlete on release had half-formed in my mind, but I didn't know how to go about it or whether it was really feasible. PT work would give me a way to make a living while I sorted myself out.

The gym officers had been briefed and were well aware of who I was and what I had done. One of them in particular, a short, muscular ex-marine called Mark Sherriff took a keen interest. Mark could run a marathon in two hours 40 minutes, and his passionate explanations of training methods and diet piqued my interest. We developed an instant rapport as he told me stories of his time in the forces and sporting achievements.

Mark was very performance-focused. He did not just want to accomplish things and inspire me, he wanted to optimise execution at all times and spoke a lot about the ways to push your body to its absolute limits.

It was during one of these conversations that I first floated the idea of attempting the record for the longest continuous row. I already held the other two ultra-endurance indoor rowing world records and had the certificates to prove it, but if I picked that one up as well would hold all three simultaneously, a feat never achieved by a lightweight (under 72.5kg) rower before. Mark instantly liked the idea and made the necessary arrangements.

There was far less red tape than at Lowdham and clearance was given relatively easily. The prison even arranged for new rowing machines to be delivered as the ones already there were old and worn. I was given a day pass by the governor to accompany Mark in a van, to go and pick up two brand new Concept 2 machines from their warehouse in Nottingham. The company gave them to us for free, in recognition of what I had already achieved, a lovely gesture which was much appreciated.

Meeting the staff at Concept 2 was my first time freely interacting with people outside of jail since the start of my sentence. I enjoyed myself and was surprisingly comfortable, chatting and joking. The guys were eager to meet me and treated me as a minor celebrity because of my achievements, while Mark was impressed with the way I slipped back into social mode so easily. Perhaps it was a skill held over from my previous life. I had always been able to get on with anyone.

We brought the machines back and set up a special area in the prison sports hall. By then I had experience behind me and knew that this challenge would come down to sheer willpower. I would not need to row particularly fast, or with a great deal of intensity, I would just need to keep going and going and going. Breaking the record would require at least a day and a half of solid rowing.

I was allowed one fellow inmate to sit with me during the attempt and chose a guy called Neil Dunbridge. I enjoyed chatting to Neil, he was in for mortgage fraud and wasn't a hardcore criminal by any means, just a decent guy you could have a conversation with. I started in early morning and slipped into a rhythm straight away. Legs, then arms, legs then arms; soon I was in my rowing trance.

The officers arranged themselves in shifts with sleeping bags, to stay with me for as long as it took. Sixteen or 17 hours in, at about two in the morning, Mark arrived with a box of Kentucky Fried Chicken. Having eaten nothing but prison food for so long, those chips and greasy meat tasted like a dish from a Michelin-starred restaurant. In reality it is shockingly unhealthy stuff, of course, but in those circumstances you can get away with it. The protein, salt and fat gave me added strength to make it through the night, while the prison kitchen provided me with lots of high energy fruit like dates and bananas too. We knew that the energy requirements on my body would be extreme and after the problems caused by poor nutrition last time I wanted to ensure I was as prepared as possible.

I made it through the first 24 hours without a problem. Memory is a great help when doing something for the second time and I knew I could do it. Predictably, around 30 hours in, things began to get really tough. It was something more than exhaustion, like the beginning of a breakdown. My back was agony, all my joints hurt, I had a pounding headache, but the stubbornness and singularity of purpose I had felt before returned. There was no way I would stop rowing before breaking the record. I would pass out first. If my body could not do it, they would have to carry me out of there or phone an ambulance.

By 7pm on the second day I had rowed for 36 hours and the record was mine. 'Don't think about it anymore,' Mark said, passing me a flapjack. 'Forget about that number. If you dwell on it, you'll want to stop.'

Somehow, I ploughed on for another ten hours, finishing at 5am the next day. Mark and Neil couldn't believe what they had seen. Once again, I had not just beaten the record, I had smashed it and in doing so made a little mark in history. To hold all three of those records at once made a big statement.

Probably due to the sheer length of the row, the recovery period from that one was far longer. My body took nearly a week to return to its normal patterns, but as I ate and slept and ate and slept, my self-confidence exploded. I knew I could do all of it. I had proved it. From short to long, I had strength and endurance. I could cope with physical and mental extremes. *This* was my thing. Darren was right. I had a gift.

Within four months of arriving at Sudbury I had gained all my gym qualifications and the staff were very pleased with my progress. New possibilities began to materialise. In theory it would only be six to seven months before I was considered for release, so they began the process of reintroducing me to society.

Sudbury had a partnership with a Fitness First gym, based in Burton, about ten miles away, and requested a prisoner work placement for me there.

In the first instance I was sent for an interview with Jess, the manager, who explained that I would not be allowed to conduct one-on-one personal training but they would expect me to induct new customers. I had no issues with that and within a few days was notified that I passed the interview.

My work licence entitled me to be off prison premises until 8pm, so provided I reported back every evening, there would be no problem. I was also informed that occasionally officers would perform random checks, arriving at the gym to ensure that I was actually there. Unlike many inmates I had no intention to abscond and accepted all of this gladly.

For those who were still looking to escape, this sort of opportunity was a godsend. You could leave prison in the morning and not be missed until night-time. By then you could be halfway across the Channel, or even on a plane. It is for that reason that escapes from cat D prisons are so common.

At one time in 2007, 40 inmates ran away from Sudbury in seven months, a grim statistic for the governors, particularly when facing an inspection report. These sorts of figures often lead the media and members of the public to question the open prison system, but for someone like me, the rehabilitative qualities were crucial. If I had left somewhere like Belmarsh or Full Sutton and returned straight to society I would have found it tough to cope. Most in that situation do. You cannot put a man in a box for several years, control everything he does, then let him out and expect him to function in the world the same way as everybody else. It's not realistic.

My new routine saw me leave prison after breakfast, at about 6.30am, get the bus to Burton and arrive at work around seven. Already 29 years old, this constituted my first taste of a normal life, the kind that the majority of British adults lead. Suddenly I had colleagues and a boss and customers to deal with. They even gave me a uniform. I was in *the system*.

The salary for someone in my position was £23,000 a year, although as a prison inmate, I worked for free. That really emphasised to me how different this existence was. You could do this job for ten years and still make less than a top-end robbery, all the while having to pay rent, bills, living and travel expenses. There were no crazy highs, no moments of intense peril, just a routine and the reassurance that the authorities approved of you. It took a bit of getting used to, but I soon began to enjoy it.

The management made it clear from the beginning that if asked by any of the customers, I should not tell them I was a prisoner. It would be bad for business. Of course, questions did come up, from both clients and other staff. My accent aroused curiosity.

'So why is someone from London working in Burton-on-Trent?'

'It's just family reasons,' I would say, before changing the subject as quickly as possible. Occasionally it made things awkward, but was just how it had to be. Sometimes when the gym was quiet, colleagues spoke of their plans for Saturday night and asked what I was up to, if I would like to join them for a drink or a meal.

'I think I'll just stay in, thanks,' I would reply. They probably thought I was deeply anti-social.

After a few weeks of settling in, Jess threw me in at the deep end and asked me to take a short-notice 'legs, bums and tums' class on a Saturday morning, as the regular instructor was unavailable. I accepted, but was hesitant. Getting a qualification from the prison gym was one thing, but putting that into practice with members of the public was another altogether. I entered the room warily to find six podgy, middle-aged women wearing tights and leotards.

Despite all my sporting achievements, this was new territory. I was provided with a headset to wear so they could hear me over the bland, pumping pop music blaring from the speakers.

'Err...' I began. 'Okay, err... I want you to err...do some... lunges?'

It took me two or three classes to get the hang of motivational gym instructor speak, but in the end it really started to work for me.

'Feel the burn! Pump those knees, ladies! Better body, better life!'

Word spread and I was given the class on a regular basis. Within a month the room was full every week. Jess was thrilled with how well I did.

As the group grew in size I discovered something new. I had known for a while that I was self-motivated, but learnt that I also got a kick from motivating others. Seeing people enjoy my classes and derive benefit from them was an awesome feeling.

While all this went on, I continued my own training. As long as I did the required work, Jess was happy for me to use the gym equipment, so I maintained my rowing, doing at least an hour a day. I already had so much success with it and although I wasn't sure where it could lead, it seemed foolish to give it up.

Three months into the job, I was midway through pulling my daily metres when a girl approached. I had seen her sometimes around the gym.

She was tall and broad-shouldered, very athletic looking, always in lycra and professional training gear. She peered over my shoulder at the monitor on the rower.

'Excuse me,' she said.

I paused my session and looked up.

'Sorry to bother you, but have you ever rowed before? I mean, outside a gym.'

I shook my head with a smile and replied, 'No.'

She laughed. 'You're lying, aren't you?'

'No, really, I haven't.'

She stared at me quizzically.

'If you don't mind me asking, how much do you weigh?'

'Seventy-two kilos.'

'Wow, okay. That time you have just done is really, really fast for your size. You do realise that don't you? What do you do then, if you don't mind me asking? Do you use the rowing machine often?'

'Yeah, I work here, so I get on when I can and I've done some indoor rowing before.' I didn't want to boast. 'What do you do?'

'Funny you should ask. I'm a rower,' she said. 'I'm based at Nottingham national high performance centre for women. I come here to do my land training and at weekends I'm up there on the water. I'm gunning for international competition soon.'

Laura Wheeler was still a hopeful when I met her, but would later become a Team GB rower and if not for injury she would have been an Olympian. Whenever I saw her in the gym from then on we chatted and I told her about my indoor achievements. She was suitably impressed and soon we began training together, rowing on adjacent machines.

'Why have you never thought about rowing on the water?' she asked one day. 'It would be an obvious move to make.'

'I'd love to,' I replied, feeling uncomfortable. 'I'd love to do something with it. I've just never had the chance.'

'Well maybe I can help you with that. You've got great natural attributes, but if you want to row properly, you can't row like this.'

Laura taught me about rate caps, like restricting myself to 18 strokes per minute over 3,500m. She said I had to pick up the slack with my legs, straighten my body and then lock my arms out. Legs, body, arms, legs, body, arms. 'If you row any other way,' she said, 'you kill boat speed.'

'There's an old saying in rowing,' she told me. 'Ergs don't float. You can have incredible physiology, you can do brilliant numbers [known as ergs] on a machine, but the water is a whole new ball game.'

Over time she introduced me to other elements of rowing training, like specific weights exercises to target key muscles. It reached the point that we trained together nearly every day and when we did our standardised half-hours on the rowers, I would beat her every time. Being not only the top woman at the Nottingham high performance centre, but also capable of beating some of the men, Laura was not used to losing.

To make it more competitive, we started doing handicap rows, where I would pull 8,600m in the 30 minutes and she had to do 8,200m. In this way, the relationship became mutually beneficial. I learnt technical aspects from her, while Laura's times improved because she was competing with and being pushed by someone faster. When she went for race testing at Nottingham a few months later, her coach was amazed at the acceleration in her performance.

The bond we forged reached a point where I felt I had to break protocol and be open with her. She had invited me to her house, asking if I wanted to come and have dinner. I put her off several times and didn't want her to think I was rude.

'Look,' I said, after a session one day. 'I'm going to tell you something now. It's not easy for me to say but please listen.'

'Go on.'

'I'm in prison.'

She laughed her head off.

'I'm being serious.'

'What are you on about? I see you in here all the time.'

I explained to her about Sudbury and how it worked. She struggled to accept it, still unsure if I was joking and left in disbelief, but when I saw her the following day she looked pale and anxious.

'I can't believe it,' she said.

'What?'

'I looked you up on the internet. Your crimes are on Google. I even watched a video of you being arrested. I seriously cannot believe you are that person.'

I shrugged. 'I'm afraid so.'

To Laura's immense credit, her new understanding of my background did not affect her opinion of me and we continued training together. If anything, she became more committed. I truly appreciated that.

Before long the officers at Sudbury gave me a pass for Sundays, as well as my working week. It entitled me to go wherever I wanted within a 60-mile radius of the prison until 6pm. When I told Laura, she suggested I use the time to come with her to the local rowing club at Burton Leander, where she started as a child. I agreed and looked forward to the opportunity like a child waiting for Christmas. It could be the start of my future.

Having never been to a rowing club before I was hesitant at first, but was relieved to find it an unimposing place. The club was small but cheerful, with a little brick clubhouse next to the river Trent. It was full of kids, another strange experience for me, having not been around children for years. They were so noisy! Laura introduced me to everyone. None of them knew my past, of course. I found it liberating to meet people simply as John McAvoy, with no attached number or baggage.

'I guess we'll just chuck you in at the deep end,' she said.

Laura got me in a fine single scull for my first session, a proper racing boat, in which the base of the hull was shaped like a razor blade. It meant I would be very close to the water, which is great for speed but not stability. Any body movement would tilt the whole thing. Learning to balance would be key.

Laura asked me to get in. 'How hard can this be?' I thought. 'I'm a fucking world record holder.'

I seized the moment, stepped on to the narrow craft gingerly, sat down and capsized instantly. The river was glacial and I came up spluttering.

'Come back to the shore,' Laura shouted, laughing.

The water line only came just above my waist so I planted my feet on the bottom and dragged the boat back.

'Now get in again,' she said.

I followed her instructions and exactly the same thing happened. *Ergs don't float.* It was my first appreciation of how different water rowing would be to smashing records on the Concept 2.

'You just need to keep doing it,' Laura encouraged. 'Engage your core and find your balance. It's like riding a bike. Once you've got it, you've got it.'

Altogether it took me four attempts just to be able to sit in the boat without ending up in the river. Laura found the whole thing hilarious, as did the kids who watched, but she remained patient and reassuring.

Over the following Sundays and with Laura's unflappable guidance I gradually became more proficient. She began teaching me the basics of using the blades, how to turn around, to set myself, to push off. There is very little that is natural about water rowing. You either have to be taught it, or endure a lengthy process of trial and error.

Within weeks we had reached a point where I could row up the river and Laura would follow me on a bike on the bank, calling out tips and instructions. She asked her first childhood coach, a lovely guy called Ray, a local butcher, to help out too. Between them they improved me quickly.

A couple of months on from my first attempt, Laura and Ray entered me in a local 6km race. I was sceptical, not wanting to make a fool of myself, but ended up not only managing to stay in the boat all the way to the end, but coming third. I had beaten several guys who had rowed all their lives.

There would be a huge amount of work to do, but maybe, just maybe, I had a future as a competitive rower. Beginnings can come in many forms.

22

These Criminals Are All The Same

WITH the possibility of release looming, Laura asked me how I saw things panning out.

'I want to row,' I told her. 'I've got a talent and need to use it.'

She nodded. 'I was hoping you would say that.'

I was enjoying my time on the water, while also acknowledging a serious reality check. In a gym, on a rowing machine, no one could beat me. In a single scull on a river I was average club level, if that. I figured determination would see me through. If I wanted it enough, I could do it.

'You've got incredible natural aptitude,' Laura went on. 'There are guys in the Olympics who put out similar numbers to you. You could go far, although you'll need to learn quickly. Your only negative is a lack of height, but with your erg scores you can probably negate that. I think it might be useful for you to speak to Terry.'

Terry Williamson, Laura's sports psychologist, ran his own company called In Search of Brilliance and I saw him in the gym sometimes. A short guy, with an earnest, open face, I approached him one day as he warmed up on an exercise bike.

'Hi, I'm John,' I said. 'I was hoping to be able to speak to you.'

'Hi John,' he replied. 'What do you do?'

'I row and stuff.'

'Oh, you're the guy Laura mentioned?'

'Yeah.'

I tried explaining everything that was going on, but he stopped me short.

'Not like this,' he said. 'Let's make a time to meet and do this properly.'

Those introductions resulted in quite a long, deep conversation the following day. I found Terry easy to talk to and opened up about my past, not something I readily did with people I just met. He had a way of asking questions which made me think about myself, my motives for doing things. There was no leading or telling me what to say, but he allowed me to express myself freely. All the while he reinforced my belief in my own abilities too. I found him fascinating and energising.

'I tell you what,' he said, before he left. 'We can make this a weekly meeting if you like. You don't need to pay me. I see something in you. You have the power to do a lot of good in the world and I'd like to help it develop.'

From that point on, Terry became my mentor, coach and later, friend. Over the months that followed I saw more and more of him, sometimes meeting him on Sunday afternoons after rowing at Burton. He would buy me lunch and talk me through what I was doing. I developed trust in his judgement and would ask for advice on virtually anything. Like Darren and Laura before, it was as if he had been supposed to come into my life, to assist on my path, towards my new destination, whatever it was.

I really felt with Terry that he had absolute confidence in me as an athlete and as a human being. It became cyclical. His confidence fed into my confidence.

'You are going to succeed,' he would say. 'And you have got the possibility to help so many others with their lives.'

I got into the habit of speaking to him on the phone every day, even if only briefly. At the same time the date for my next parole hearing neared, at which there was a chance of release. Sudbury also began allowing me on home leaves to travel to London and visit Mum. Everything felt like it was coming together.

Laura fired off a message to a friend of hers who rowed at the famous London Rowing Club in Putney. LRC was known nationally as a high performance centre for lightweight men and often fed rowers into the GB squad. As a result, we swapped messages with the head coach, a no-nonsense Australian by the name of Phil Bourgignon. She did not mention my past or why I was based in the Midlands, simply saying I was a keen rower and would be interested in joining his club when I returned to London in the near future.

Bourgignon's reply was a little cold, stating that he generally didn't accept novices and enquiring after my erg scores for 2,000m and 5,000m. Laura sent them through, six minutes 20 seconds and 16 minutes 39 respectively, along with my weight of 72kg. The 2,000m cut-off point for the GB squad at that time was six minutes 33, meaning I was well inside it. Suitably impressed, Bourgignon suggested I come for a meeting when I was able. My path to a new life was clearing.

As all this was taking place, I received news that Johnny was getting married to his long-term girlfriend and wanted me to be best man. He had actually delayed the wedding until I was in an open prison so I would have a chance of attending. I was thrilled for him and applied to the governor for a weekend's leave. My request was granted, but on the proviso that I didn't drink alcohol.

I wanted to be there and looked forward to it. I knew it was important to Johnny, but at the same time, was a little tense. The wedding would provide the first major test of my new direction. There was no question that people from the game would be in attendance and it would constitute the first time since deciding to change the course of my life that I would mix with criminals. How would that be?

It was set for a big hotel in Oxfordshire and as I travelled down on the train, I had to admit I was nervous. I would need to handle myself very carefully. Under the wrong circumstances it could even be suggested that I had been associating with known criminals while on leave. In that eventuality, I would return to Sudbury and find a squad of prison officers waiting to handcuff me and send me back to a category B nick, which was the very last thing I wanted.

The hotel was already bustling and lively when I arrived. I found my room and put a nice, grey Paul Smith suit on, but as soon as I went downstairs I had to have a couple of drinks to take the edge off my nerves. It's hard to explain how good beer tastes when you haven't had one for eight years.

It was lovely to see some of the faces there, especially Johnny and his wife, but I couldn't help but feel estranged. That whole environment felt so alien. At one point a girl tried to kiss me and I pulled back, sticking my arm out to shake her hand.

'What are you doing?' she asked.

I didn't respond, but it seemed prison had subconsciously changed my response to physical and emotional contact. Maintaining a clear zone of personal space was important on the inside and I was unused to it being invaded. As I mingled during the course of the day, people kept trying to give me money. I turned it down.

'Come on John,' they would say. 'I'm sure you could use it. Get yourself back on your feet.'

Afternoon stretched into evening and more alcohol was consumed. We had a lovely meal and afterwards I found myself chatting to an old face called Gary at the bar. He was not anyone I had worked with before although we had many common associates.

'So what are you going to do when you're back on road?' he asked. 'Any plans?'

'I'm done mate.'

He paused.

'No, but really. What are you going to do?'

'I'm done.'

'Okay, but you'll need to earn a living, won't you? I'll help you out, put a few things your way. I've got lots of little bits and pieces going.'

'No, mate. You're not listening. I'll sort something out, it'll be fine.'

'All right,' he said. 'Just give it a couple of months and we'll see what happens. The offer will still be there.'

Not long after I returned to Sudbury, Gary was arrested, eventually going down for 23 years. It was further evidence, not that any was needed, that I had made the right decision. If I had listened to him that night and got involved it could have been the end of me forever.

Back in prison, Bourgignon's invitation made me increasingly anxious. I just wanted to get out and move on with my life but the bureaucracy of parole remained slow and indications were hard to come by. Once again I was slated to attend a series of sessions with a psychologist.

He wanted to talk about my views on society, how I saw other human beings, what my emotional responses to certain situations would be.

'Have you ever made fun of someone to hurt their feelings?'

'Have you ever touched someone's genitals without their agreement?'

'Have you ever thrown an object at someone and laughed?'

For three days I answered his questions as well as I could and he wrote his reports.

With that out of the way the internal probation officer checked through my file. My job at Fitness First had yielded positive reports. Jess had written a glowing reference. All my home leaves and the special arrangement for Johnny's wedding had been conducted without problems. Laura had written a lovely section for me, saying how inspirational she found me, how committed I had been to rowing and how I could only explore the sport fully should I be released. Terry had done the same. Never once, in my entire time at Sudbury, had I broken curfew.

My case was close to perfect, considering the initial severity of my offending. Keeping me in for another year could serve no logical purpose. Yet we were just days away when the administrative mix-up that had caused the delay at Lowdham Grange occurred again.

'We didn't realise you were on a discretionary life sentence,' an officer said. 'Sorry, but that changes everything.' It was difficult not to feel personally aggrieved. I was desperate to get out, there was so much I wanted to do, but again my parole meeting was delayed for four months while they arranged for a crown court judge to chair.

With sport operating as my new internal balance, I accepted the repeated situation as philosophically as I could. What else could I do? To pass the time I hit on another idea after reading a newspaper article. The London to Brighton ultra-marathon was something only the very fittest people could attempt, 67 miles, most of which was cross-country. I had been for a few jogs, doing laps of the prison perimeter, but running had not formed a huge part of my activities. Even Mark was shocked.

'Do you realise what this is? It's basically two and a half marathons back-to-back. You need specific training for that.'

Terry was the only one who believed I could do it, but undeterred, I applied for another weekend release and was granted. Despite my lack of running experience, the challenge appealed to my need to prove myself. It would mean being on my feet for 14 to 15 hours and using every bit of my physical capacity.

It proved to be one of the best decisions I ever made and a truly mind-expanding experience, the next best thing to freedom. Being out all day among nature, meeting and running alongside the athlete who won the women's race, just speaking to someone competing at that level as an equal – I felt honoured. My body seized up horribly afterwards, like an engine starved of oil, but spiritually I felt amazing.

I arrived back at Sudbury happier than I had felt for a long time, but barely able to move. My quadriceps had lost all strength and feeling and my back was knotted. The next day when I saw Mark at the gym, he was blown away, shaking his head in disbelief.

'I can't believe you did it,' he said. 'You'd never run more than 10km before and now you've run 110. It's literally unbelievable.'

Recuperating fully from the ultra-run took a couple of weeks, during which I refocused on my rowing, doing gentle sessions to loosen up. At last, my parole meeting was convened on a Thursday afternoon in the prison boardroom, attended by the criminal psychologist, a home office psychologist, two probation officers, my solicitor and a middle-aged, hawk-faced female lay-person.

Sitting before them I felt vulnerable and exposed. Again, it made me reflect. These were people I would not have looked at twice in my previous life. They would have been a complete irrelevance, but now they had absolute power over me. Whether or not I could be freed was in their hands. They all took their turns asking questions before the judge assumed control.

'What are you going to do if we release you?' he asked.

'I'm going to get involved in sport. I'm hoping to turn pro.'

He smirked. 'In all my years of involvement in these meetings, you are the first prisoner to say he intends to become a professional sportsman. We do note that in your last parole meeting, at Lowdham Grange, it was stated that your future plans were neither well developed, nor rooted in reality. Which sport interests you the most?'

'Rowing.'

'I see,' he nodded sagely.

As luck would have it, the judge had been a keen rower himself and had attended the same university as four-time Olympic gold medallist Matthew Pinsent. We had quite an in-depth exchange of views, talking about rowing on the Thames, different sorts of boats and equipment. He seemed impressed by my knowledge and I felt sure it had gone well.

'Thank you Mr McAvoy,' he said, before pausing. 'Thank you very much indeed.'

He shuffled a few papers around and pursed his lips, then looked up at my solicitor.

'He,' he said finally, jabbing his finger at me, 'is like the people I've dealt with for the last 20 years in Manchester Crown Court. These organised criminals are all the same.'

My heart sank.

'He has all the characteristics. The way he's come in today, the way he presents himself, the way he talks, I've seen it all before.

I'm not stupid. He has probably been thinking about this moment for the last eight years, planning what he would say and how he would appear. He knows exactly what we want to hear and that's what he's telling us.'

He turned back to me.

'You're a very calm and cool character, aren't you John? You're very confident?'

I nodded.

'Exactly how you would be if you were sitting in a car with a gun in your lap, waiting for a cash-in-transit van. It might interest you to know that previously I have presided over a case involving Kevin Barnes. He's a good friend of yours, isn't he?'

'Well…yeah.'

'And we all know who your uncle is. You've been raised into this way of life haven't you? It's been bred into you. You don't know any different, do you?'

I shrugged, unsure whether he wanted me to respond.

'And do you know what really concerns me in your file? In your entire time in the prison system you have only had one charge, for a sit-out protest at Full Sutton in which you participated.'

Again I was nonplussed, thinking that was a good thing. I had behaved well during my time inside, surely a positive?

'Do you realise that this is exactly what we would expect to see from high-status criminals? Men like you are puppet-masters. You get others to do your dirty work for you, don't you? For the first four years of this sentence you were in two of the highest security prisons in the country, surrounded by extremely violent men and you mean to say that you never had to defend yourself once?'

'That's right.'

'That tells me that you must wield considerable influence.'

When he finished speaking, he looked across at the psychologist.

'I would like to ask you a question,' he said. 'Do you think what we're seeing in this room today is all smoke and mirrors?'

'I can see what you're trying to say,' the psychologist replied. 'But if Mr McAvoy is pulling the wool over our eyes, he has taken it to the nth degree. We have to acknowledge that he has gone well beyond the minimum. We are not just talking about a few gym courses here. The man holds three world records and six British records and has a reference from a national level rower. He has just run a race from London to Brighton. These are not the sort of things that happen unless you are fully committed.'

The judge nodded.

'In my opinion,' the psychologist went on, 'this man is genuine. When he says he has effected a change in his life, he means it.'

'I did think that,' the judge said. 'But I have to explore all possibilities.' He turned back to me. 'Can you leave the room please, John?'

I plodded out. The wait outside was interminable. My solicitor tried to appease me.

'He was just testing you,' she said. 'He wanted to see if you would get angry.' But I remained convinced the judge had it in for me. They called me back in ten minutes later.

'We've finished with our questions,' he said. 'Have you got anything to say?'

I took a deep breath.

'All I can tell you is that everything I've said today was 100 per cent genuine. I want something different with my life. I'm sick to death. I've been around men who've spent decades in category A conditions. I've seen what it does to them. I've already wasted so many years in prison and I want to do something positive with myself. I've got a talent that I can use. I'm only asking for a chance.'

'Thank you,' he said. 'Hearing closed.'

I went back to my billet, on tenterhooks for a whole month, until one Wednesday morning the tannoy blared into life as I ate breakfast.

'John McAvoy to the main office please.'

Heart pounding, I walked to the office, collected my letter and stood on the corridor outside. Almost afraid to open it, I held the envelope in my hand for a while, staring at my typewritten name. I have no idea why, but I looked up and spoke to Aaron. In my mind I pictured the two of us back in Spain, in a different world, a different life.

'Please mate,' I said, out loud. 'Please say I'm out.'

Hands unsteady, I peeled open the envelope and began reading. 'The overriding factor is risk to the public,' read the first sentence. 'Every case must be considered on its merits.'

It seemed the panel had been concerned by what they described as my 'over-confidence' as well as my family background. Although they thought I was unlikely to re-offend, if I did, they suspected it would be at a very high level.

'The panel directs that you be released on life licence with the conditions laid out in this letter,' it concluded.

The feeling of relief was unimaginable, like coming up on pure MDMA. My fists clenched in celebration.

'Yes!' I shouted, as energy coursed through me. I felt like I could jump mountains.

'*I'm always there if you need me,*' said Aaron, from nowhere.

23

One of the Chaps

THE life licence meant that for the rest of my days I would have to attend monthly parole meetings and they would monitor my activities. If they even suspected me of involvement in further crime I could be recalled to prison without trial, but at that moment I did not care about any of that.

I had three weeks to wait and started giving away possessions to other prisoners. Clothing, books, shoes, all of it went. Those guys had more need for them than me, while I knew I would soon be able to get new gear. I spoke to Laura, who was thrilled by my news. She contacted Phil Bourgignon at the London Rowing Club again and arranged a time for me to see him.

When the big morning finally came, I walked down to reception and was given forms to sign, which barred me from ever coming into contact with guns or explosives (even fireworks), associating with any known criminals and possessing more than one mobile phone. My one phone number I was allowed had to be logged with authorities and initially I was only permitted to reside at my Mum's address in Chislehurst.

The officer on duty informed me I had ten hours from release to report to probation services in London or I would be considered 'in breach', then walked me down to the gate. I followed along the driveway, heading out of the prison, the same way I had every day for work. This time the journey felt different. This time I would not have to be back by 8pm.

'Good luck,' he said simply, as he showed me out. It was a tick under eight years since Currie and Foreman had frogmarched me through the doors at Belmarsh.

I ventured out into the car park and looked around for Johnny, who was meant to be picking me up. He was nowhere to be seen. Assuming I was the victim of one of his famous pranks and expecting him to appear grinning at any moment, I searched every corner. The bastard wasn't there.

After having thirsted for it for so long, my first 45 minutes of independence were spent standing by the side of a countryside B road watching cars come and go. The air smelt heavily of manure. It was like a bad joke.

At the back of my mind was the knowledge that if I did not get to London by the allotted time, my release would be very short-lived. Eventually my patience reached its natural limit and I walked to a nearby payphone, to call the hotel Johnny said he would stay at, in Nottingham. At first the receptionist was reluctant to put me through as I didn't know his room number, but I pleaded with her and she agreed.

'Hello,' the plonker said at last, his voice thick with sleep.

'Mate, what's going on? I'm standing outside the nick waiting for you.'

'Shit...I'm sorry...had a few drinks last night. What time is it? I didn't get in until late.'

Typical Johnny, I had to get a cab. He looked like a walking corpse as he opened his hotel door in his pants, reeking of booze, but I hugged the big tosser anyway. It was great to see him. We had a bit of lunch, he perked up, then drove us back to London. First stop was the probation office, down in Orpington in the south-east of the city.

'John McAvoy,' I told the young receptionist on arrival, pleased to have arrived within the timeframe. 'Just released.'

She checked her files with a bemused look.

'John who?'

Admin had lapsed and they were not even expecting me. I had to wait for half an hour for the officer to turn up.

Once she finally emerged from a door behind the desk, the probation lady, a small, talkative woman called Marilyn, took me through the terms of my licence. She warned me to avoid situations where I could get involved in anything, even minor things like a pub fight, as the last thing I needed was to compromise myself. She also offered a few words of wisdom about dating, which was something I had not thought too much about. Apparently the most common reasons for recalling licensed prisoners are bitter break-ups, during which the ex-girlfriend files a report of physical abuse for revenge. The allegations need not even be true for dire consequences to ensue. I thanked her in thoughtful mood, shook her hand and left. This wasn't freedom as other people experienced it. It was freedom with limitations.

Although I had been down to visit Mum a few times and had started the ultra-run in Blackheath, I hadn't looked properly at my home city for years. As Johnny drove us away from the probation office, from one south London street to another, it struck me how much everything had changed. Coffee shops had sprung up everywhere. People on the streets locked eyes on phones with huge screens. Cars and buses looked different. Pubs I knew well had closed down. New buildings had been built, old ones had disappeared.

'What the fuck is that?' I asked, pointing at an ugly collection of warehouse-style pre-fabs beside the road.

'Retail park mate,' Johnny replied.

'When are they gonna finish it?'

He laughed. 'Everyone says that. That's just what it looks like.'

It was as if I had been in suspended animation. From 2004 until 2012, the world had turned without me.

Johnny drove us around to Mum's who waited with my Auntie Kitty. Both of them were very emotional, which I expected, but I found all the hugging and kissing difficult. Eight years of prison had destroyed my natural sense of intimacy, even with family members. I found contact uncomfortable and stiffened up.

'Don't worry, Mum,' I told her as she clung to my neck. 'This time I'm not going back.'

After a couple of hours there, I went to see my cousin Bill, which also completely unnerved me. He had kids, a baby and a six-year-old. It was the first time I had seen either. The realisation of how long I had been away hit me again.

Johnny took me to a Lebanese restaurant for dinner where we talked about *work*, but for the first time outside prison, I meant that word in the same sense that regular people did. For the new John McAvoy, *work* did not mean bank jobs or drugs or handling stolen goods. It meant turning up at an office wearing a tie and earning a salary. Johnny had a position set aside for me in his company selling carbon offsets, whatever that meant.

After dinner we hit a nightclub in the West End. I knew what Johnny was trying to do so I played along. It was supposed to give me the chance to loosen up, but in reality made me feel old. As I looked around I had to accept that at 29 I was in the upper age bracket of the clientele. There were girls in there who were little more than kids, while all the lights and noise felt bewildering. The last time I had been to a place like that was back in Spain.

The music, garish colours and smells of booze and perfume overpowered me. The old John would have been in among it, throwing money around, but I kept my distance, sat in a corner and tried to soak it all in. I was due at the rowing club in the morning and it wouldn't make sense to get smashed or stay out late.

In the end I left Johnny to it at about 1am, with a sense of relief. That was more than enough freedom for one night. If I wasn't careful I would overdose on it.

When my alarm went off in the morning it took me a few minutes to accept my surroundings. My subconscious still lived in the billet at Sudbury, but a coffee and some porridge cleared my head.

My second experience of a rowing club was very different to my first. Where Burton Leander had basically been a shed with some gear in it, the London Rowing Club in Putney, not a part of town I knew well, dripped history and oozed class. Portraits of Prince Philip, the club patron, hung in several of the rooms which were decked out in polished wood and brass fittings. The main meeting room featured a grandfather clock and chandeliers. Trophies stood everywhere. Over the bar hung a boat that had been rowed to a silver medal in the 1936 'Hitler' Olympics in Berlin. I felt like I had arrived on the set of *Downton Abbey*.

As I made my way inside, a tall man with glasses approached me on the stairs.

'Are you okay?' he said in clipped, upper-middle-class English. 'You look a bit lost.'

'It's my first time here,' I replied, keeping my voice flat, disguising my culture shock. 'I'm here to see Phil.'

He shook my hand. 'Mike Hill, assistant coach.'

Mike introduced himself, explaining that not only did he work at the club, but he coached at one of the top public schools in the area. He was friendly and welcoming, showing me around, taking me to the gym equipped with familiar Concept 2 rowers, and then out to the boathouse, stocked with everything from single sculls to eight-man sweeps. He pointed out famous faces among the pictures on the walls, men who had been to Olympics and world championships.

'There's a lot of heritage here,' he said, smiling.

I nodded, internally processing this new environment. When I thought back to my time in Belmarsh or Full Sutton, among psychopaths like Byrne and McAteer, surrounded by junkies and violence, it occurred that this was the polar opposite.

On conclusion of his mini-tour, Mike took me back down to the riverbank where the crews were just starting to come in off the water after morning training.

'There's Phil,' he said, pointing at a slim guy in a baseball cap stepping off a speedboat. Mike led me over and introduced me.

From the first instant I met coach Bourgignon, I liked him. He had intensity, and a no-nonsense demeanour. He was a winner and I could see it. These were the sort of people I wanted to be around.

'What are your erg times again?' he asked.

'Six 20 and 16.39.'

He raised his eyebrows. 'That's right, I remember now. You're not even that tall either, are you?'

'Five foot nine.'

'Impressive, especially for someone so compact. Right, the next water session I'll let you go out on a launch with my assistant coach Brian Ulliott. You can have a look at how we do things, then we can have a chat.'

Meeting Brian helped put me at ease. A Yorkshireman who punctuated virtually every sentence with swear words, he was not a stereotypical rowing club guy. I headed upstairs with him and sat among the other rowers as they ate lunch between sessions.

Listening in to the conversations around the room revealed a surprising range of accents. A number were what might be termed middle- or upper-class voices, but there were also Aussies, Canadians, Kiwis, even a couple of Spanish guys, as well as regional UK dialects. The guys spoke about the typical things you would expect young guys to talk about, sport, work and girls. Of course it was different to jail, but I didn't feel out of place at all.

When the time came to head back out for session two, the rowers got their boats from the trestles and I boarded a small motorboat with Brian. He explained to me the rules of the tideway, which direction you are supposed to row at different times of day, how the lanes work. The guys rowed off down towards Westminster and we followed, with the sun high in the sky and Big Ben looming ahead.

'So where have you come from?' Brian asked, turning to me.

'I was err... working up north near Derby... but I've moved back down.'

'Oh, so what do you do for a living?'

'I work in carbon offsets,' I said. I was scheduled to start work with Johnny on the Monday. Thankfully Brian did not quiz me any further on that as I had no real idea what it was.

Soon we pulled up alongside a boat full of tousle-haired, pink-cheeked lads, who eased up for Brian to shout a few instructions. The guy at the front of the boat, known as the strokeman, listened to Brian then turned and said something inaudible to the rest of crew. Brian's manner immediately changed.

'Stop rowing!' he yelled.

They did. We were outside the Houses of Parliament and huddles of tourists stood taking pictures on the bank.

'Listen son!' he screamed. 'I'm the fucking coach. Got it? I tell you what to do. You don't fucking coach from the boat, not if you want to stay in it. Keep your gob shut and your mind on your fucking work or you'll be out on your arse!'

The kid looked down at his legs. 'Yes coach,' he said. Suitably chastised, they began rowing once more.

The scene jolted me. Up to that point I had felt fairly comfortable with what I had observed, but not then.

'That was disrespectful,' my inner voice said. 'No one speaks to me like that. If anyone spoke to me like that, I wouldn't have stood for it. Is this how they speak to people here? Do I have to accept this?'

Adjustments would clearly be needed and I remained deep in thought until we returned to the shore. Back on the bank, Phil asked me to jump in a single scull so he could watch my technique. I obliged and rowed out to Hammersmith and back.

My form was a bit ragged, but it went pretty well, although the waves made the boat twitchier than I had been used to at Burton. Rowing on the Thames would require an intricate, more developed skill set.

'Okay,' Phil said, when I returned. 'Not too bad. We'll start you from the bottom and bleed you into the squad gradually. We won't put you in crew boats until you've learned how to row well. You'll need lots of water sessions to bring you up to scratch. But I reckon in future you can be an asset to this club.'

We shook hands. I followed him inside and signed my membership papers. Within 24 hours I had transformed from an inmate, to one of the chaps.

24

There's Something You Need to Know

FOR the next three months, when not working in Johnny's office, I lived, breathed, ate and slept rowing. I saw it as a massive privilege. How lucky I was to train alongside such dedicated and committed people, men who rowed for their countries and went to the Olympics! I got to know the guys and many of them became friends. My social circle was transformed overnight, which was incredibly important. Without that, like so many ex-offenders I would have been at risk.

Without a change of scene, it only takes one exception. You can decide to go straight, but one tiny lapse, you choose to do something small for a couple of hundred, then something slightly bigger for a few thousand, then before you know it you are back in the game. LRC removed any possibility of that and I immersed myself fully in rowing club culture. I found it exciting and refreshing, but sometimes it still provided stark reminders of the contrast between my old life and my new.

I had only been at LRC for a couple of weeks when I found myself in the changing rooms with two older members. There were many of them around, former competition rowers who liked to socialise at the club and get out on the water occasionally. As I changed into my kit, these two conducted a conversation, in cut-glass accents, about court and which cases they had heard that day. The two old boys were judges, getting dressed a few feet from me! Having never seen a judge in his underwear before, I had to suppress a chuckle.

Alongside club training sessions I paid extra for private coaching from a former team GB rower called Steven Feeney. His wife was a policewoman and I spoke to her from time to time. We got on well.

Another copper at the club, a shaven-headed, stern-faced guy, known by other members as 'Mr Angry', was on compassionate leave from the Met after being involved in some serious operations. He suffered with post-traumatic stress disorder, making him prone to outbursts. Never one to be put off by a man's reputation, I found him surprisingly easy to talk to and we chatted often. He started helping me out with boat tips and coaching.

Six weeks into my new life I spoke to probation and asked if I could look for somewhere to live nearer to the club, to avoid the inconvenience of travelling up from Chislehurst every day. I explained that LRC was central to the life I was trying to build and the commute was killing me. They were okay with it as long as I had a stable address.

I put word around and a lovely girl called Oonagh, who worked as a make-up artist for the QVC TV-shopping channel, told me she had a spare room. Her sister, Lucy, was dating the tennis player, Greg Rusedski.

I liked Oonagh, a confident, attractive young woman, with a great sense of humour. Having her as a flatmate could work very well, especially as her place was in Putney.

'We can keep it informal,' she said. 'Don't worry about contracts, just pay me at the end of the month.'

Her kind offer was exactly the sort of arrangement I needed, but also stirred something in my conscience. In reality Oonagh knew nothing about me. She only knew John the clean-cut rower. If I was going to share her flat, I felt she had a right to know more.

I arranged to meet her for coffee one day after training, at a café in Putney and as we sat down I realised I was genuinely nervous. The possibility of a negative or even hysterical response worried me. No one at the rowing club knew of my past. More than that, Oonagh was good fun and I didn't want to lose her as a friend, but depending on her view of serious crime and those who commit it, it was a very real possibility.

'Oonagh, there's something you need to know,' I said. She looked at me curiously, but tenderly, the way girls do if they think you're about to get soppy. I think she may have thought I was about to tell her I was in love with her.

'I don't know how you're going to react to this,' I paused. It was taking a while to get the words out. Once it was said, it was said and there would be no going back. Tension built.

'Go on,' she encouraged.

'Well, I think you should know that I've been in prison.'

Her face dropped.

'In prison? What do you mean?'

'I mean I've only just got out of prison,' I repeated.

'What, were you drink-driving?'

Nerves made me laugh. 'No, no. I mean I've really been to prison.'

'What for then?'

Again I found it hard to say. Part of me didn't want her to know.

'Armed robbery.'

'You're joking!'

I shook my head. She searched me with her big, brown eyes.

'My God. How long for?'

'Just over ten years altogether. I've been in twice.'

She started welling up. Her lip wobbled. I didn't know what to do.

'Oonagh, what's wrong with you?'

'I can't believe it...you're such a nice person,' she said, dabbing her tears with a napkin. 'I can't imagine you being locked up for so long.'

'Does this change anything?' I asked when she regained composure.

'Definitely not,' she replied. 'I can tell you're a good person. I trust you.'

'Thanks,' I said. I meant it, too. The sincerity of her friendship genuinely touched me and I moved in a few days later.

Living with Oonagh made getting to and from the club far easier and I started arriving earlier and leaving later, determined to make every second count. I made it my business to absorb every bit of wisdom from Phil, Brian and all the others. My rowing improved drastically and my confidence increased, but the other side of my post-prison life was not going so well. When not at the club I continued working at Johnny's company, quietly acknowledging as time went by, that I truly hated being there. This created a strange divide in my life.

At the rowing club, no one other than Oonagh knew anything about my past. As far as they were aware I was just a guy who had worked at a gym in the Midlands and knocked out some impressive erg scores. At work, on the other hand, everyone knew I had been in jail. Before my first day Johnny had felt it was necessary to explain the situation to the team and had briefed them on my background.

The job entailed a lot of telesales and the office was full of cubicles, phones and young lads eager to prove themselves. They all fancied themselves as some sort of *Wolf of Wall Street* type, working hard and playing hard, hitting their sales targets then boozing and taking coke. Maybe eight or nine years earlier I would have enjoyed the vibe, but the atmosphere jarred with the new me.

Half the other guys were scared of me, because of who I had been, while the other half looked up to me as some sort of gangland hard-case. Unlike the rowing club, no one in the office seemed able to take me at face value.

I found the physical entrapment tough as well. Sitting in there for hours on end reminded me of sitting in jail. While there I became moody and detached. I knew I was so lucky to have a friend like Johnny and he had offered me a generous salary package to help me out, which meant I earned well without doing very much, but as I sat by the phone my mind would wander away from what I was supposed to be doing, daydreaming of boats and technique, catch and drive, economical blade entry, flutters and shunts.

'Have you managed to speak to anyone on the list yet?' my team leader, a young Mediterranean-looking guy, would ask, breaking my trance.

'Eh?' I would look up at him, meet his eye and both of us would know without speaking I had done nothing.

Yet it was important to me to make an honest wage and not be seen to be living off my old life. While inside I had spent lots of money, not only on prison expenses like extra food, but keeping a few bits going, girlfriends in particular. That meant when I came out I had very little left. There were things I could have sold, like watches and jewellery, but I hadn't wanted to take that option and gave everything away. If I was to live without crime I would need to live without the proceeds of crime and I thought the best approach was to start again with a clean slate.

Money management was difficult because living on a budget was so thoroughly alien to me. In my previous life it had been easy come, easy go. A £15,000 watch, a £50,000 car, you would get them, use them for a bit, give them away then move on to the next one. That attitude was ingrained and hard to shake off. I had to force myself to be thrifty. Nonetheless, despite all my efforts at normality, I could not get on with office work. After the first couple of months I went to see Johnny for a chat.

'I appreciate the help,' I told him, 'but I just can't do this.'

'Oh, mate...'

We both knew that the probation office would raise major concerns if I found myself unemployed. Lack of regular work had been earmarked as one of my expected triggers for re-offending and Johnny was keen to help keep me out of that trap. We talked over possibilities and hit on the idea of personal training. I had my qualifications from Sudbury and some experience at Fitness First, so I could begin by working with him and his family then see where it went.

Of all my decisions since release from jail, that was one of the very best. The work suited me so much more and blossomed quickly. Johnny's wife recommended me to friends of hers who then did the same. The whole thing snowballed and within weeks I developed a healthy client base. Meeting them for open air sessions at the rowing club or Hyde Park was far better than spending all day indoors. Importantly, it still earned me a decent living.

With the rowing club still at the centre of my sporting ambitions, it became the major feature of my social life too. I found myself invited for lunches or parties at the weekend where I mixed with an entirely new, middle-class, professional crowd. It felt that between that and the PT work, everything was falling into place.

My only issue was one of ongoing secrecy. Often at these gatherings, people would make innocent small talk. The question of what I had been doing before would come up, which was natural and unavoidable. As I had when working at Fitness First, I batted the questions away as well as possible while trying not to sound too defensive.

During this period of assimilation, becoming the person I wanted to be, my end goal of professional athletic status remained. It was nice to be perceived as a normal and productive member of society but I wanted *more*. I needed to make up for all those wasted years.

For that reason, improving my rowing was my top priority. I focused on it fiercely and in our daily chats Terry would advise me to temper my intensity, to ensure I did not zero in on sport at the exclusion of all else. Focus was good, obsession perhaps not. Balance, in life, was important.

Yet I wanted quick results. Money was a side issue and as long as I had enough to live and row, I was happy. The idea of becoming an international competitor remained lodged in my mind, with the 2016 Olympics in Brazil as a target. What an achievement that could be – from inmate to Olympian in four years!

Guys rowing at that level remained some way ahead of me, however, and I had to learn to accept that knowledge. Until I caught up technically, they would beat me on the water every time.

This fact was not something I found easy to live with. It was not in my nature to acquiesce to defeat, so I made it my business to destroy everyone in the squad at every single bit of land training.

If we were in the gym and another rower lifted 110kg, I would lift 115. If someone pulled six minutes 20 on the rowing machine, I would pull six minutes 18. If I went on a run with other rowers, I would wait for them to get tired, then push and push and push, leaving them all behind, so they would know, unequivocally, that I was the fittest guy there.

We would do capped 18km rows on the Concept 2s, where we had to maintain a rate of 18 strokes per minute, to test how much power we were generating. I smashed every lightweight at the club. The only one who could compete with me was a Cambridge graduate called Marc Aldred, who has since gone on to win at Henley and pick up a clutch of international medals. I even beat most of the heavyweights as well. That was my mentality. In terms of pure cardiovascular fitness, I refused to lose.

When we did circuit training I would partner up with the fittest guy around and make it my objective to break him. In taking that approach, I brought others along in my wake. Guys wanted to try to beat me, so it improved them. That was how I showed my worth, which was important. I did not want anyone thinking I was some shit-kicker who turned up and couldn't row, a hanger-on, a waste of space.

After three months of solid graft, of friendship building and new-identity-forging, Phil called me to his office. He had watched me sculling every day.

'You're wasted,' he said. 'Your training scores are through the roof. All your erg times are gold standard for Henley. We need to start stepping you up. From next week I'm putting you into crew boats with other guys.'

25

Ironman, Ironman, Ironman

I WORKED with such dedication and singularity of purpose, addressing my technical deficiencies – developing core movement after the 'catch' when the oar blade hits the water, learning the right moment to start driving with the legs, the angle to drop, but still I lacked refinement and knew that I would for some time. Like any sport, the best rowers don't have to think about what they are doing, they row on feel and instinct and are able to make adjustments on the fly. I absorbed all the information I could and watched videos for hours at home, fixating on minutiae, but rowing is so very, very technical.

Other club members gave plenty of encouragement and ironically, considering his profession, I formed a very close bond with Mr Angry, whose real name was James. When he had spare time he would often come out on the water with me to give me pointers.

Early one morning, I arrived at the club just after breakfast for a training run up the Thames. James spotted me, asked to tag along for company and soon we were conversing in the easy, breathless manner of gym buddies. He asked how work was going and what I hoped to achieve with rowing, then began to speak about himself.

'It's a funny thing John,' he said, as we jogged. 'You work all your life for something and believe in it, but it can kick you in the teeth. I only ever wanted to be a policeman, to serve society, but I've seen some awful things in my time in the force.'

He related a few tales of events that had affected him very deeply, colleagues he had seen injured, sickening crime scenes. I gained a new understanding into his character and the source of his rage. In many ways James inhabited the same world I had. Its poison had got to him too. Criminals are not the only ones who live with violence as a daily companion.

Spurred on by his new openness, I spoke up.

'I'm going to tell you something,' I said.

'What?'

'I've been to prison.'

Immediately, there was tension where there had just been chatter. He looked ahead, we ran on and neither of us spoke for several minutes. The silence soon became eerie, contrasted with the informality of before. As we neared Chiswick Bridge he finally said, 'What for?' He still didn't look at me.

'Armed robbery.'

He paused again, breathing heavily, as if those words required extra processing time.

'Really? Okay. Where were you?'

'Belmarsh HSU, Full Sutton and a few others.'

James fired a few questions about fellow inmates and prison officers I had known, checking to see if I was spinning stories. Suddenly, it all clicked, his stride slowed and he looked my way.

'My God!' he said. 'John McAvoy! You're Micky's nephew, Brinks-Mat!'

'That's right,' I smiled. He looked at me in wonder, as if I had just levitated or walked on water.

'I can't believe it. I can't believe we're running together, like this.'

'It's a funny world.'

'Yeah,' he laughed in disbelief.

'I'd appreciate if you didn't tell anyone,' I said.

'Don't worry John,' he replied. 'It's between us.'

That afternoon we went out in a boat and again, as with Oonagh, I felt moved by his reaction. It would have been easy for a man in his position to foster hostility against someone with my background. If we had met years earlier, he would have been my enemy and I his, but our friendship seemed unaffected by my revelation.

Confidence grew from the knowledge that I could be honest with people and still be socially accepted. As with so many things, I had been wrong. *The system* did have a place for me.

Meanwhile, I continued to row in the crews where my natural tenacity ensured I let no one down. Experienced guys even began asking if I could row with them at races, although I was not ready to get in a boat with the very top lads yet. Considering my starting point as a non-rower only a few months previously, I had to be pleased.

Yet when your goal is excellence, as mine was (and is), you sometimes have to ask yourself tough questions. Despite my swift progress and natural optimism, after half a year of solid, committed water training, doubts started creeping in. Something I had not fully appreciated at the beginning became clear – namely that rowing is a young man's sport. Among competitive rowers, you are considered a veteran at 26. At that age I had still been in the bedlam of Full Sutton.

Steve Redgrave may have won his last Olympic gold at 38 but he was very much an exception to the rule. Most of the other guys at the club were at least five years younger than me. Physically I was on their level, if not slightly above them, but while physiology put me with them, on the technical side I had to be realistic.

The 2013 Henley Regatta was just around the corner and I was slated to row with a crew of four, but as I had become more enmeshed in the scene and learned more about the art of rowing – and it is an art – as I spoke at length with the best guys in the squad, I began to contemplate a change of direction.

The facts as I saw them were simple. By some sort of accident of birth, I had an exceptional natural engine, something that could be described as a rare physical talent, but I was already 30. It would probably take another three or four years to master technique well enough to catch up with elite guys who had rowed since childhood. By then my chances of a top-level career would be all but over.

Of course, I could row to a top club standard and then in senior competitions for years to come, which is probably what Bourgignon had meant when he said I could be 'an asset to the club in the future' but that was not what I wanted.

I hadn't come into sport to attend regattas, wear a blazer, lean on the bar in the clubhouse and enjoy the ambience. I was competing to prove something to myself and the world, to make up for lost youth. If I did not achieve something notable, if I couldn't become a professional, I would feel I had failed.

Over the course of about a week I grappled with this dilemma and the change overwhelmed me almost unintentionally. Contemplating one evening at home, as I sat alone eating my regular dinner of mackerel, rice and broccoli, leafing through a magazine, I acknowledged that I enjoyed the company and competitiveness of the guys at the rowing club. I didn't want to separate myself from them, but as I turned the page and came across an article about Craig Alexander, the Australian three-time world champion, one word kept repeating itself in my mind, growing louder and more insistent – Ironman, Ironman, Ironman.

The ultra-endurance triathlon event had been on my radar since Lowdham Grange, since all those conversations with Darren Davis and the books he gave me to read. The TV programme I watched in my cell had ignited my imagination. Ironman would suit someone of my abilities. The best Ironmen were not necessarily the best swimmers, cyclists or runners, but athletes of enormous cardiovascular capacity who had the psychology to endure pain.

While rowing would not take me to the level my physiological gifts were capable of, due to my late start, many of the world's best Ironmen were in their mid-to-late 30s. Most came from other disciplines and entered the sport in their 20s or early 30s, like me. There would still be technical issues to master, particularly with cycling and swimming, but nothing as intricate as the finer points of boatmanship. The more I thought about it, the more it made sense.

The key component of Ironman success was stamina, which I already knew I possessed in spades. As I sat at home replaying Darren's words from my memory, I realised I had made my mind up. Rowing had been my saviour but I would take it no further.

Although I felt it was the right course of action, the idea of finishing my brief water career made me a touch despondent. I didn't want to think of myself as having given up but I knew my only chance of becoming a full-time athlete, which was my ultimate goal, lay elsewhere.

When I spoke to Terry on the phone, he understood my feelings and saw my point. Terry knew better than most about my inner motivations and made the two-hour drive down to Putney to discuss my situation face-to-face.

Among all his qualities, Terry has always been excellent at getting me to make my own decisions. He got me to compose a list of pros and cons, while attaching weight to the points I was making.

'What do you think I could achieve in Ironman?' I asked him.

'With your natural engine, the sky's the limit,' he said. 'You'll have to train for it though. What bike have you got?'

I shrugged. I didn't have one.

'How's your swimming?'

I shrugged again. Other than a bit of a splashing about in the Mediterranean nine years earlier I hadn't been swimming since childhood. Terry didn't need to say any more. I knew I had work to do.

As soon as he left I got on the internet and looked at possible events, seeking something to train and aim for. The Ironman organisation ran races all over the world, both at full distance and half, known as Ironman 70.3. Many were abroad, which at that stage, still only six months since release, I knew were out of the question. Ironman UK was scheduled for July in Bolton, just six weeks away. I entered without hesitation.

I bought a bike from eBay, a red and white Moda, for about £700. That's a lot of money for a normal bicycle, but dirt cheap for a competitive racing bike. It was about three sizes too big for me and I had to fiddle with the saddle and handlebars to be able to sit on it comfortably, but began going out on training rides into Surrey and Kent.

One of my favourites, which I still use today, was Box Hill in Dorking, which had been used as part of the bike course during the 2012 London Olympics. It presented a 2.5km ride, with five per cent gradient, nothing compared to the great climbs of races like the Tour de France but challenging enough to give your legs a workout, particularly if you perform repetitions. My fitness levels were such that although my bike experience was lacking, I was able to sprint most of the way up, come back down then repeat that several times.

I read that the Bolton bike course presented many technical sections. There would be lots of inclines and declines, lots of braking and lots of manoeuvring around tight and narrow corners. Also known to cyclists as 'Zig-Zag Hill', I believed Box Hill would provide some sort of preparation for that.

I bought some decent triathlon kit, an all-in-one suit that you wear throughout the day. It's made of lycra, with a padded inner-leg area for the cycling. You swim in it, dry off on the bike then soak it with sweat on the run.

I spoke to some keen cyclists from the rowing club who advised that there was no point trying to hit the full 112-mile distance in training, as we were too close to the race. I would just exhaust my body. They suggested keeping distances down to 30 or 40 miles at a time, but doing it often. In the absence of a coach, it was the best guidance I had, so I followed it.

I acquired a wetsuit for the swimming and hit the Lido in Hyde Park, a roped-off, 110m stretch of the Serpentine River. Oonagh came down to watch. I got in and splashed about, up and down, breathing on every stroke, chucking my head around, throwing up more foam than Niagara Falls, but I did that every day until I could swim the required distance with ease. My technique was awful, but I would get through it which was all that concerned me.

I would go from one end to the other, changing elements of my stroke, then checking my watch to see if I had gone any quicker. I would try keeping my head in one place, doing different things with my arms, kicking with higher or lower intensity. This trial-and-error, pot-luck approach was the best method I had at the time.

Meanwhile, with running it was just a question of ticking over. I knew I could hold the distance without concern as I had already run more than double that on the ultra-marathon, so I would go out around Richmond Park, or along the Thames, often in the evening, after training the other disciplines during the day.

The rowing club still provided a base for me and there were several guys in the same situation, ex-rowers who worked out in the gym and attended the socials, but no longer went on the water. I trained with some of them.

By that point, I had been a regular face at LRC for eight months and become well known among the regulars. Naturally, the clamour about who I was and where I came from had grown. People noticed that I tended to be evasive in those conversations and whispers came my way that gossip was circulating behind my back.

Up to then, only Oonagh and James, whom I trusted, knew definitively about my past, but with information about my criminal activities freely available on the internet I realised it would only be a matter of time before word got out, which I dreaded. The members at the club had accepted me as one of their own. How would they react when they knew the truth?

The idea bothered me to the point that I began to consider making some kind of public announcement. Terry agreed it was a good idea. That way I would be able to present information in a manner that suited me, rather than people hearing half-truths or starting wild rumours. He suggested writing a blog and offered to help put it together. I grasped the nettle and we did it.

When my blog went live, in early July 2013, the response was unbelievable. It was shared on rowing websites from all over the world and I received a ton of messages from people saying how much I inspired them. At the club everyone wanted to shake my hand. Nobody expressed negativity.

People may perceive rowing to be an elitist sport but in their attitude toward me, the guys at LRC could not have been more open-minded, even the older members. That is something I will never forget and always treasure.

I went to Henley with them all just to socialise and see what the fuss is about. Having pulled out of the crew it was just another chance to experience something new.

The whole thing was brazenly and unashamedly upper-class, like some sort of debauched aristocratic ball. Gentlemen in stripy club blazers and straw boaters, ladies in dresses below the knee, the weather was glorious and the bar well stocked. I behaved myself as I had my sights set on Bolton, but most attendees did not. A favourite Henley tipple is the Royale, one part Pimm's, ten parts champagne. Half of the punters were legless by lunchtime.

Following the three days of Henley and with the weight of secrecy off my shoulders, I could concentrate fully on the event ahead. Biking and swimming continued as daily activities, although not to anywhere near race intensity. My confidence grew and to some degree, the first part of my post-prison journey felt complete.

I had been accepted into a world by people who knew my past. I was earning an honest living. And I had a clear, athletic goal to aim for.

26

Competers and Completers

I FIGURED it would be important to get some sort of triathlon experience before attempting the most demanding triathlon event of all, having read that many parts of the race can trip you up, particularly the changeovers between each leg.

Transition, in which you remove your swimming gear to get on the bike, then later rack your bike to get out on the run is even known as 'the fourth discipline' by triathletes and can add minutes to your time if performed badly. It is not as simple as changing clothes and footwear, although that can be awkward enough when wet with water or sweat, coursing with adrenaline. For a full distance event, which I would be attempting, you would need drinks and snacks in place, sunglasses, a helmet, kit bag and race belt and everything would need to be pre-arranged to be as accessible as possible.

For a taster, I entered the Eton Dorney *sprint* event, the shortest triathlon distance. It only comprised a 1km swim, 20km on the bike and a 5km run but was enough to show me what I was in for. Within seconds of the start I had to stop swimming and resort to doggy-paddle because of the frenetic activity of those around me. The water churned and I became disorientated.

In the end I swam the course in 26 minutes, a very poor time. The bike leg was reasonable and I felt strong on the run, hitting 19 minutes for the 5k distance. All in all, enough of a performance to suggest I would be okay.

Three weeks before Bolton I attended a reconnaissance day at the course, arriving full of enthusiasm and hungry to learn as much about my new sport as possible. It quickly became obvious that virtually all the other athletes were far more experienced than me. As we assembled at the edge of the swimming lake I heard conversations about races around Europe and the States, triumphs and injuries. Many of them wore official Ironman T-shirts, which are only given to those who successfully finish.

In a full-distance event comprising 140 miles of continuous racing, simply getting to the end is an achievement, many do not, but to be recognised as an Ironman you have to complete the course in under 17 hours. Failure to do that gives a result of DNF – did not finish. In this way, several tiers of Ironmen are created, ranging from 'completers', whose sole ambition is to finish within the cut-off time, to 'competers', who are aiming for a high position, fast times and ranking points. At the very top of the pyramid are the professionals, who can accumulate considerable prize money.

It makes an interesting statement about our perception of human capabilities that in the first two Ironman races beginning in 1978, in which only the very fittest athletes in the world entered, all were merely completers. Most of the marathon runners, special-forces operatives, tour cyclists and open-water swimmers who contested those first events in Hawaii, failed to cross the line. Many considered the distance to be too extreme and the event to be one of pure insanity.

It was not until the days of Dave Scott, the American six-time world champion of the early 1980s, that Ironman turned into an actual race, rather than a straight-up personal ordeal. Yet as the event has grown in status and popularity into the 21st century, spreading all over the world, part-timers, some even carrying beer bellies, can get to the end. The bar has been raised and Ironman has shown us that psychological conviction is more important than physical prowess. Regardless of any of this, despite my novice status, within my mind I placed myself firmly in the competer category. I was not there just to make up the numbers.

To confirm my rookie position, by and large the other entrants even resembled each other physically. They were like some kind of Ironman sub-species – skinny and super lean. I still had my rower's physique, with a broad back, deep chest and thick limbs. I felt like a bulldog in the middle of a pack of greyhounds.

We studied the course and I sensed I would be fine. If nothing else my fitness levels and refusal to stop would get me around. Anything beyond that was a bonus, but if I could finish an Ironman, at the right end of the field, on just six weeks' specific training, that would be encouragement enough. Some guys train all year and still don't make it.

After returning from the reconnaissance day I developed Achilles tendonitis, which limited my running. It didn't bother me too much as I knew I had to focus on the swim, my weakest of the three elements. To perform respectably I would have to put myself in a position where I was not completely shattered getting out of the water. If I felt okay at the start of the bike, I knew I could fly through the rest.

I stayed at Terry's house for a couple of days before the event, another much appreciated gesture. Although by that time we had known each other for nearly a year, most people would not be happy letting an ex-convict stay in their home with their kids. It really showed me how much trust he had in me and I wanted to repay that.

Two days before the start, at the pre-race briefing known as a 'pasta party', an opportunity for competitors to mingle and do a bit of carbohydrate loading, I found myself sitting next to an Irishman.

'So is it your first Ironman?' he asked, making conversation.

I nodded.

'We've all been there! You'll be fine if you take it steady. So how many regular triathlons have you done?'

'None.'

'Oh…okay.' His eyes widened, betraying shock which he tried to disguise. He clearly had no idea what to say.

On race day I woke at 4am and caught the athletes' bus down to Pennington Flash, the lake where the swim would take place. Before heading down to the water's edge I had a last check of my bike in the transition area. My water bottles were still attached, as were the nutrition bars I had taped to the frame. Everything looked fine. Calm and ready, I walked from there down to the start line, where the scene that unfolded astonished me.

Two thousand competitors had gathered on the banks in a fidgeting, shuffling, rubber-coated horde. It almost looked biblical – a great mass of humanity wearing swimming hats and wetsuits, like seals in the pre-morning twilight, preparing to throw themselves into cloudy, unwelcoming water. What would aliens make of this if they observed it?

As we waited for the signal to start I conducted an internal MOT. I felt good, no nerves at all. My body was strong and ready. I didn't know fully what to expect, but whatever came up I could handle it. I was in a good place. Familiar coldness and steeliness overcame me. I looked around at some of the others, foreheads creased, eyes narrowed, hands shaking. A few of them even crossed themselves.

'This is nothing,' I thought. 'I'm out here in the fresh air. I've got the chance to use my body. Belmarsh or this? No contest.'

In 2013 the swim still had a floating start, meaning we had to paddle out to a line in the middle of the lake, then tread water until they gave the signal. The national anthem played over the tannoy system as we all bobbed around in water so murky that your hand disappeared from view at a depth of 20cm.

A man's voice came over the speakers.

'Three…two…one,' followed by the bang of the starting gun. Chaos.

I tore at the water like a jet-ski, thrashing at it to get the best possible purchase. All around me, 2,000 others did the same. The lake boiled, as if filled with a shoal of giant piranhas on a feeding frenzy, a human tsunami. Competitors clambered over each other and pulled each other back. A stray elbow caught me around the temple. A foot planted itself in my ribs.

I got stuck behind a couple of slow swimmers and almost had to stop to match their pace. Frustrated, I pushed my way between them, not caring if I impeded their progress. It was kill or be killed. When Charles Darwin spoke of 'survival of the fittest' he could easily have been describing an Ironman mass-start.

Three or four hundred metres in, it began to settle down. The natural order of things asserted itself as the stronger swimmers put distance between themselves and the rest, while the stragglers tailed behind. I got myself into a rhythm and completed the first lap comfortably, before hauling myself out of the lake. Bolton featured what was known as an 'Australian exit', meaning at the end of each lap you got out, covered a short distance on foot then plunged back in.

Crowd noise filled my ears as I clambered from the bitter water. Spectators shouted encouragement and rang cowbells, an Ironman tradition. I was not among the leading group, but they were not too far ahead. Pleased with how the race had begun, I leapt back in to continue.

As I swum the second loop the sun began to climb over the trees. Its warmth was welcome on my face and back, but I soon realised I had committed my first schoolboy error. My goggles were clear, not tinted and as I neared the halfway point of lap two, with the rays slanting over the water, I became totally blinded. The buoys I was supposed to follow disappeared in the glare.

Unpanicked, the only tactic I could think of was to attach myself to another swimmer. I became dimly aware of someone to my right and made sure I stayed close to their feet for the remainder of the lap, having to trust they would successfully guide me into shore. Fortunately, they did.

After completing the last two laps in that way, constant squinting had given me a small headache and red dots in front of my eyes, so it was a joy to emerge from the water for the last time, remove those useless goggles and head for T1, unzipping my wetsuit on the way. Sunproof eyewear would be top of my next shopping list.

Running to the area where my bike was racked, peeling my wetsuit down my torso, I checked my watch. My time for the 2.4-mile swim was one hour seven minutes, quite creditable under most circumstances, but considering I had gone from being a virtual non-swimmer to the race in six weeks, really encouraging. I had not expected to be so quick.

As I pulled on my cycling shoes, wheeled my bike to the mounting line and clambered on, it suddenly occurred that up to that point, the longest ride I had completed was a 60km jaunt from Mum's house out to Ditton and back, but my self-belief was firm. I set off in determined mood.

With the little bit of information-gathering I had done, I knew that the three-lap circuit of the Bolton bike course was regarded as a challenging one, involving 1,600m of climbing, including the infamous Sheephouse Lane and a lot of winding descent sections. Once the early hills were out of the way, you spent the rest of the circuit out on the moors, where the topography was bumpy, the roads were poor and northern winds could be fearsome. Those with Ironman experience regarded it as a pure cyclists' course, meaning that it suited riders with technique and plenty of road and bike handling experience, rather than athletes of power.

I was pleasantly surprised to find Sheephouse Lane not to be the destroyer-of-legs it was so often described as. Rather than one continuous climb, it was actually three separate uphill sections with small flat parts between. The individual ascents were testing, rising to a maximum 17 per cent incline in places, but the respite provided by the flats more than compensated.

An hour or so in, as I passed the 60km mark and embarked on new territory, I still felt fresh and strong. Despite the fact I had one of the worst bikes in the race, I found myself gliding past other riders. Outside of my immediate focus on what I was doing, excitement began to build.

'If I can sustain this performance,' I thought, 'maybe I can get up among the leaders.'

Unfortunately, Ironman has a way of crushing hubris and teaching harsh lessons to the naive and inexperienced. I was about to discover that a variety of elements need to combine to create a successful race. Preparation, equipment and natural aptitude are all important but one of the most indispensable commodities is luck. During nine or ten hours of racing, a multitude of mishaps are possible. If fate decides to conspire against you, you're screwed. Having navigated the swim and about a third of the bike course without too much trouble, that was about to be made abundantly clear.

At 75km, as I started out on the second loop, I felt a sudden irritation on my left eye which I tried to ignore. Within five minutes it had worsened into persistent and sharp pain spreading up from my eyelid to my eyebrow. I blinked repeatedly and felt a strange friction. The eye streamed. Allowing my pace on the bike to slow, I raised one hand and lifted my sunglasses. A bee flew out. Within seconds my left eye swelled completely shut. The pain was excruciating, but I lowered my sunglasses and continued. Cycling one-eyed caused further problems, however. On the downhill stretches wind blew into my face, making me squint. With my left eye closed, my right eye watered profusely, obscuring my vision on that side too. As I had on the swim, I found myself rendered almost blind.

Fearing for my safety and that of other racers, I slowed down, becoming aware of others whizzing past me. Fellow racers yelled, 'Get left!', 'Watch what you're doing!' or 'Move over!'

Without realising it, I had been veering all over the road and if seen by officials I could have been ejected from the race. The sensible thing to do would have been to pull over for a while, but something in me refused to stop. I also suspected if spotted by a race steward and they saw my eye, they would pull me out. There was no way I could allow that to happen.

By the time I finished the bike leg, I knew my chance for a high placing had gone. I had slowed almost to a standstill at times and been unable to recoup momentum at others. From then on my first Ironman was about salvaging as much pride as possible.

At T2 I removed my helmet and went to rack my bike. As I did so I pulled my sunglasses up and saw a marshal look my way with an expression of absolute horror. I pulled them back down swiftly.

'Did my eye look bad?' I asked him, as light-heartedly as possible.

'Yeah, what happened?'

'Nothing, it'll be all right in a minute,' I said and dashed off before he could speak again.

As I started the run, the eye actually opened up a crack, giving me a tiny sliver of vision on that side. It was still sore and wet but improving. Terry was there to cheer me on, as was Darren Davis, who had travelled up to support me too. It was great to have him there. In many ways he was the one who had started it all and seeing him raised my spirits. I saw them both on each of the three laps around Bolton town centre.

My legs were more tired than they should have been from all the stop-starting on the bike, which I also chalked up to experience. Constantly breaking inertia tires you out more than powering along, but I ran the marathon in three hours 59 minutes.

As I passed through the finishing chute and crossed the line a lump rose in my throat. Not only was I a free man, within limits, but I could now call myself an Ironman. At the same time, I could not help but be slightly disappointed that I hadn't managed to go quicker, but put those thoughts to one side. Finally, it had really begun. I was at the start of something.

My total time clocked in at 11 hours 49 minutes, putting me in 66th place in the 30–34 age group, not as fast as I had hoped for, but on six weeks' training and competing in my first real swim and bike, both of which I completed half-blind, I could not be too hard on myself. The average for a competitor in my division was 12 hours 12 minutes, meaning my time and placing were certainly enough to suggest I had a future at the right end of the sport if I could correct my mistakes and ensure I was better prepared.

Terry and Darren congratulated me on the finish, but already my mind ticked over with what I needed to do to improve. Training was key. I was racing against guys who had developed their athletic potential while I was locked up, so I would have to devise a rigid, professional programme and stick to it, no excuses. I would push myself to the extent of my limits, as I knew I was capable of doing. I would show myself no mercy. A year of that and there would be no stopping me. Internally I resolved to return to Bolton in 2014 and win it.

Those thoughts were still going through my mind as I checked into the medical tent, post-race. The doctor winced as he examined my eye. By that point yellow pus oozed from one corner and ran down my cheek.

'You're going to need to go to hospital,' he said. 'You've been stung on the eyeball and the stinger has remained in your iris.' He pulled it out gingerly with a pair of tweezers. 'If you don't get that sorted it could get infected.'

My first night as an Ironman was spent at the Manchester Royal Infirmary, with an antiseptic dressing covering one side of my face. I reflected on the race. It had not been that hard, physically. What was all the fuss about? Without the eye problems, who knows what I could have done? There was no question I could run and cycle considerably faster. My swimming needed further work. I laid there alone, looked up at the ceiling and made plans. Oh, such plans.

27

Sequel

A BIT of internet browsing told me that the sole requirement for obtaining a professional Ironman licence was proving you were competitive. If you posted results in age group races, showing you could keep up with the top boys, you were there.

Achieving that was my ticket towards prize money and sponsorship contracts. Until then I would have to race as an amateur and rely on personal training work to pay the bills. That wouldn't necessarily be easy, but is the way it is for athletes in most sports, below elite level.

The goal of every professional Ironman is to compete in and (for a select few) ultimately win the annual world championship race in Kona, Hawaii. Prize money for the winner is something in the region of £100,000, with another £600,000 or so available for athletes who place. Qualification is achieved through regional events like Ironman UK.

My personal target was straightforward. In the first instance I aspired to get myself among the best in the country. I wanted to arrive at races and other competitors to understand that I was a man to beat, an athlete of substance. I would not just be another guy there for a day out.

The winner of my age group in Bolton, a Kiwi by the name of Graeme Buscke, had completed the course in nine hours 40 minutes, two full hours ahead of me. I needed to match that sort of performance and in order to do so I would utilise every angle I possibly could.

My quest for professionalism led me first to search out and visit the human performance unit, a sterile-looking white room, part gym and part science lab at Essex University. The décor reminded me a little of prison. They were advertising an aerobic testing programme which could assist with training by setting challenging, yet realistic goals based on natural capabilities.

I signed myself up, to get a measure of where I was starting from. My baseline of fitness would be high, I hoped, from the years of rowing, but this would give me indications specific to cycling and running. At the end of it all they would define my VO2 max score, the most important single measure for any endurance athlete.

VO2 max refers to the amount of oxygen the body can consume per kilo of bodyweight. Essentially it is a measure of cardiovascular efficiency. While the average man will typically record a score of 40-ish, elite endurance athletes are often up in the 70s or 80s. Lance Armstrong, at his chemically-assisted, multiple Tour de France-winning peak, hit 84. To some degree this score is innate. You can train to improve it, but without performance enhancing drugs, it is unlikely to increase dramatically.

They made me run on a treadmill while steadily increasing the incline, until I could not continue. Then I performed a similar test on the stationary bike, all while wearing a breath mask attached to a bank of monitors.

My VO2 was logged at 78. Combined with a body fat percentage of eight per cent, it put me up there with international class athletes, especially considering I recorded it in disciplines I was not yet performing efficiently in. If they had tested me on a rowing machine, I may well have scored higher. That cemented it. The potential was there, it was scientifically proven and all I had to do was train and train until I couldn't train any more, then carry on training.

Step one was to get myself a proper bike. Regardless of how hard I worked, it would be nigh-on impossible to be competitive on the Moda. Johnny once again put himself out for me and lent me three grand to buy a time-trial bike. I promised to pay him back as soon as I could. Due to its lighter frame and superior gearing, the bike on its own would mean about 30 minutes of gained time in a race.

From there it was simple, I thought, no shortcuts, no easy routes, no excuses, just effort. I applied the single-minded mentality I trained with in prison, doing cell circuits and on the Concept 2, to my new discipline. A combination of determination and stubborn refusal to fail would see me through, just as it had in breaking indoor rowing records.

Scotsman Graham Obree, the former world record-holding cyclist, became my number one role model. His was one of the books Darren had given me to read in Lowdham Grange and his entire philosophy was built on solo training.

'The only person you can never lie to is yourself,' Obree said. With a coach, there is always room for deception. You can smash a personal best in training and delight your coach, while within yourself you know that you eased up at one point and could have gone even faster.

'My biggest fear isn't crashing this bike at 85mph and losing my skin,' Obree said. 'It's sitting in a chair at 90 and thinking, "I wish I'd done more."'

The levels of obsession and ruthless self-examination in his methods connected with me and I decided that like him, I would run my own sessions. I would demand the absolute best from myself. No one could push me harder than I could.

My approach, Obree's approach, worked wonders. My runs took place in Battersea Park, with my programme informed only by a bit of reading and some YouTube videos. Everything was high volume, high intensity. Rest days were for wimps. Within five months of starting I ran sub-three-hour marathons comfortably. Only 0.2 per cent of people who run marathons are able to do that. Sometimes I did one a day, every day, all week.

In the same vein, when I compared my cycling performance to other triathletes, I was streets ahead. Using the wattage output meter on the bike, I could hold power levels for an hour that most of them only managed for 20 minutes.

Through the internet I got in touch with an Ironman called Keith Sanders, who also lived in south London. A fireman by day, Keith was a strong athlete who had completed numerous events, achieving a personal best just outside nine hours, a good time. We went on some training rides together and discussed technique. I more than held my own with him despite my inexperience. He was impressed with my performance and enquired after my VO2 score.

'If you put those together with your bike wattage output,' he said, 'you could be a genuine competitor at this.'

My splits got quicker in swimming too, although I found it by far the hardest to master of the three disciplines. Raw fitness will only get you so far in the water and I soon saw that my performance plateaued. I was looking at a time of one hour six minutes for the 2.4-mile Ironman swim distance, which was reasonable but not markedly quicker than I had managed in 2013.

With the different loads being exerted on my musculature, my physique began changing and I lost bulk from my upper body. I drove myself and drove myself. If I became fatigued, I didn't care. I kept going. Nothing would stand in my way.

It reached a stage where I was training so hard, that even after dinner and a good night's sleep, I would wake the next morning feeling weak, drained, shaky and groggy.

'It's all part of it,' I would tell myself. 'Just battle on through. Pain is temporary.'

My head was filled with slogans that extolled the virtues of mental toughness, never giving up. I found them inspiring. They had worked for me in rowing and would work for me again.

After cereal for breakfast I would be back out on the bike, or in the water and once I started to train and endorphins kicked in, I felt fabulous. Each day I ran 15–20km and either cycled 100km, up and down hills, doing sprint sections, or churning laps in lidos or the Serpentine river for two hours at a time. I behaved like an addict, for whom a deep-seated need for success was the drug of choice. I was so fixed on my goal and had complete tunnel vision.

Of course my calorific output was huge and I ate accordingly. Breakfast could be five or six Weetabix. While out on the bike I would scoff energy bars at regular intervals. Lunch would be brown rice and mackerel, followed by a generous portion of fruit and nuts, to provide potassium, iron and omega three oils. An evening meal would be a couple of chicken breasts with brown rice again, followed by a banana with peanut butter.

I touched no alcohol at all. The only fluids that went into my body were sports drinks and water.

As my times for all three disciplines shrank, I became excited and super-energised. I used websites like Strava and Sportstracker to GPS log my performances and compare with other athletes, where I could see that what I was doing was working. My ultra-high volume approach garnered results that a coach would have said were impossible. On our joint sessions Keith sometimes said he thought I was going too hard, that I was risking burnout, but I wouldn't listen.

In that relentless build-up to Ironman UK 2014, I spent the vast majority of my waking hours alone. I still did my indoor training at the rowing club, where I conversed with other triathletes who worked out there and occasionally hooked up with Keith, but other than that my regime was spartan and detached. Requests to socialise came my way, which I typically ignored. Most nights I was in bed by nine. Distractions could dilute my focus and drag me off course. My mission was all consuming. I was fanatical.

Through the internet I began communicating with Hywel Davies, the Welshman whose British rowing record I had broken in Lowdham Grange, and early in the year he invited me on a cycling camp in the French Alps. Hywel's sporting achievements were highly respected, particularly with regard to Ironman, and he had been named triathlete of the year in 2008. Spending the week with him and his squad could only improve me.

I suspected that probation would not allow it as it involved foreign travel, but they were impressed by my sporting dedication and wanted to offer encouragement, so gave special dispensation under certain provisos.

'I have to tell you that I've been in prison for serious crimes,' I told Hywel on the phone, going through my now familiar confessional. 'Is it still okay for me to come?'

'Of course it is, John,' he said. 'You'll find that many of the guys have things in their past lives they're trying to get away from. We train as athletes, nothing else. Don't worry about it.'

It seemed the power of sport to heal and offer hope was real and among endurance athletes, many of whom seek validation through pain, I was accepted and welcomed. I looked forward to the camp hugely. Hywel had been a fantastic source of advice and encouragement in our online chats and his personal best for Ironman was eight hours 40 minutes, a world-class time. To be able to absorb his wisdom face-to-face and train alongside him was a fabulous opportunity.

Still, when I arrived in France and probably due to my own instincts, I felt acutely aware that to the rest of Hywel's boys I was an unknown quantity. They were all tremendous athletes. Some of them were Ironmen, some were cyclists but all of them competed at a very high level. Despite the fact I had already been pushing myself so hard for months, I was tenacious and refused to take a back seat.

This was not a series of sprint repetitions up and down Box Hill. We rode serious climbs like Col de la Forclaz, Col de la Colombiere or the Signal de Bisanne, an 84km loop, with 460m of elevation on an average eight per cent gradient. On some sections the incline rose to 11 or 12 per cent. These were all mountains that had been used in stages of the Tour de France and were seriously challenging. On most you would find yourself riding through cloud then emerging among snow-capped peaks at the top. The scenery was breathtaking, the air was crisp, but the riding was brutal.

Every day I beasted myself, aiming to beat the other guys and trying to 'drop' them on the mountains. I would ride alongside someone for a while, maintaining a pace before picking a moment to surge. As they tried to come with me I would keep surging, pushing and pushing it until they fell back. It was the attitude I always had in training.

Four days into the camp I woke with a cough, which I ignored, continuing the same way. Some of the other guys made comments about me overdoing it, that I should ease up. I didn't listen. I knew best.

When the week was done, I flew home on the Saturday night with a sore throat and a thumping headache, went straight to bed, then got up on Sunday morning and ran 35km around Richmond Park. I allowed myself no recovery time whatsoever. Six weeks out from my second stab at Ironman UK I did not feel I could afford respite. There was no way I would be under-prepared like 2013. Only 100 per cent effort was enough.

On the Thursday, four days after returning from France, I went swimming at Tooting Bec Lido and emerged from the water with sickening, choking pain down the right side of my face. Much as I tried, I could not shrug it off and by evening had lost the hearing in my right ear.

Waking the next day after a terrible night, my face pounding and my breathing laboured, it felt as if someone had filled my sinuses with quick-drying concrete. I had to accept there was something seriously wrong and saw a doctor, who confirmed my ear canal had closed up due to a massive viral infection.

He asked what I had been doing, I explained and he arrived at a simple conclusion. My body had been pushed beyond its limits and my immune system had been unable to cope. At first I struggled to believe him. My arrogance and determination to better myself would not let me accept that somehow I had screwed up.

I had believed that single-minded stubbornness would make me better. That my mentality set me apart from the rest, but instead I was being forced to face a grim fact that hits many endurance athletes at some stage – there is actually a paper-thin line between supreme fitness and total physical breakdown. Maximum effort is important, but you have to apply it intelligently.

The final stage of my carefully designed training programme was meant to be a half Ironman race in Staffordshire, about a month before Ironman UK. The competitive element would peak my performance at just the right time, allowing me to taper off and lighten my regime before the big one.

'Listen to me, there is no way you can do that race,' the doctor said. 'You need to rest. If you attempt it, it could even be fatal. Strenuous activity with a viral infection can cause terrible damage to the heart. In fact, when you see people drop dead running a marathon, more often than not it is because they were carrying an infection and didn't know.'

I left the surgery absolutely distraught that morning, my unassailable plan collapsing around my ears. It was six weeks until Ironman UK and I was unable to complete the final stage of preparations. It wasn't even clear that I would be well enough to compete.

When the Staffordshire race rolled around, my feelings of misery were compounded. Although it was only a half-Ironman event, a distance that some athletes specialise in, there were ranking points available. The winners of my age group were guys I knew I could beat. If I had been there, I could have begun building my reputation and gone to Bolton full of confidence.

On doctor's orders I eased up and endured a thoroughly boring few weeks. Resting and relaxation were neither restful nor relaxing for me. I felt twitchy and anxious and had no idea what to do with myself. Once or twice I went out on the bike, just for a gentle pootle around. I had to do something.

By 16 July I kidded my inner critic that everything would be okay, packed my gear and headed up to Bolton. I sought no further doctor's advice. If he had told me 'no' again it would have been too demoralising for words. I had trained so hard all year. The antibiotics must have cleared up the infection. Surely 11 months of training in the bank would still enable a good performance?

I saw Keith, who was competing in his last season and aiming for Kona, at the orientation meeting and discussed tactics with him. He said if he had a terrible swim or bike, for any reason, he would pull out and save himself for Ironman Wales later in the year. I nodded sagely, saying I would do the same, not confessing to the full extent of my health problems.

The next day, as I waited in my wetsuit to start the swim, among the broad shoal of fellow masochists in the timid morning light, I tried to ignore the warning signs from my body. I felt fatigued, light-headed and shakily weak before the race had even started.

The swim was tough, but not disastrous. The water made me a little woozy, which I put down to floating algae. By the time I dragged myself out of Pennington Flash after the third lap, I was well off the pace, 20 minutes slower than a year earlier.

'Come on, you can salvage this,' I told myself. 'The swim was slow but you can recover.'

I got my bike from T1 and climbed on. My mood blackened. From the very first pedal stroke, I knew. There was nothing in me.

Still, I kidded myself. Sometimes while training I had started sessions feeling washed out then picked up when endorphins and adrenaline kicked in. Perhaps that would happen again? But by the 40km mark I was gaining no ground on those in front. My body still would not respond. Bleakly, I pressed on.

At around 80km, all my remaining strength deserted me. I slowed terribly and tried to refuel with an energy bar and some fluid. As soon as I swallowed, my guts convulsed. Bile rose in my throat and I threw up. Thin, rancid vomit spattered my legs and the side of the bike. Feeling weaker and weaker, I tried again a short while later. The same thing happened. Whatever I put in my body came straight back out.

At 100km my stomach and lower back cramped and my pace slowed to a crawl. Spectators could probably have walked beside the bike and kept up with me, not that I would have noticed if they had. I saw only the handlebars and the road, framed in a dark circle, as if I were filming my own race through a fish-eye lens.

Deep within myself, I felt ashamed, because I desperately wanted to stop. An internal voice pleaded with me to pull over and sit by the side of the road. *Just have a few minutes, rest on the grass, you could even lie down, gaze at the sky and all this will be over.* But I could not bring myself to do it.

In a moment of clarity, I drew a stark conclusion. John McAvoy had come from prison to be in that race. John McAvoy would not fucking give up.

Quitting, especially so publicly in front of spectators, was not going to happen. Instead I would continue until I collapsed, which I assumed would be fairly soon. It's impossible to finish an Ironman with no energy intake so my chances of getting to the end were minimal, but I could not show weakness. They could scoop me up from wherever I dropped and take me to hospital. Let the chips fall how they may. *Pain is temporary, quitting lasts forever.*

From there I stopped bothering with food, but continued drinking. Every time I drank, I threw up. My tri-suit was soaked in it and I must have smelt terrible, but figured if I kept taking the 750ml bottles of energy drink from the marshal stations, even if I puked most of it, I might retain some. Somehow I vomited my way right to the end of the bike course.

Crazy as it sounds, off the saddle and in T2 I tried to kid myself again that maybe the worst of it was over. Maybe I would be able to run well? My pre-race target had been a sub-three-hour marathon off the bike. Perhaps that was my one target for the day I could still reach? *Come on!*

Determined, I set off on the road hard. For the first 3km I actually maintained three-hour marathon pace until, unsurprisingly, I threw up violently again. I stopped at an aid station, got some more drink and heaved that everywhere too. My ribs hurt from all the retching. A couple of marshals stared at me searchingly.

Every time I threw up, I would walk for a while then try running again, until I threw up again and so on. At around 10km I found myself in a village chundering over a wall. An old woman came over and put her hand on my back.

'I don't know why you people do this to yourselves,' she said. 'You're all barmy. But as you've come this far, don't give up, love.'

I wiped my mouth and looked at her. She had no idea how far I had really come, but she had a kindly, maternal face.

'I won't,' I said and pressed on.

At the end of the first 16km loop I saw Terry and Darren, so stopped for some words of wisdom. They had followed me on the athlete tracker and seen my splits fall away after a reasonable start. In my heart I wanted one of them to tell me to pull out. *Come on John, you've done enough for today, save yourself for the next one.* I needed to hear it from someone else, to validate what I was feeling, but Terry looked me straight in the eye.

'How will you feel if you quit?'

It was a simple question that pierced me to my bones. I knew the answer. I knew.

So that was it. I had no choice. I continued, running and puking and running into oblivion.

Nothing I have ever felt comes close to the physical and mental depths I sank to on the rest of that run. Finding myself at the Old Bailey at 18, receiving a life sentence at Woolwich Crown Court, even learning of Aaron's death, agonising as those things were, they did not compare. This was steady and irreversible annihilation.

As my body ran out of everything and I shuffled on, I was no longer an athlete, I was a zombie. I passed through delirium and into a semi-catatonic state. My world compressed to a zone two feet in front of me. Completers jogged past me. I crashed and burned.

I knew it. It was proven. I was a let-down. Darren, Laura, Terry, Oonagh, everyone who had helped and believed in me, I let all of them down. And myself, for whatever that was worth at that moment. I let John McAvoy down too.

In the game or in prison I always maintained composure, an appearance of being in control. They could threaten me, isolate me, deprive me, treat me inhumanely and I didn't give a shit. I was bigger than that and would show it.

This was different. I had fallen apart. Anyone could look in my face and see I was broken. I had shown weakness. I had failed.

Ironman UK 2014 was supposed to be my coming out party as a top class athlete, a triumph, a vindication of my new direction.

Instead it was an unmitigated disaster.

28

Allowed to Fail

AT some point towards the end of the race, I don't know when, I heard a guy talking in my ear.

'My wife's a professional,' he said. 'We've both been doing this for years and I've been in your situation several times. Just get to the end. If you don't you'll feel worse, trust me on that. You're allowed to fail. You're just not allowed to give up. Just get to the end.'

At 20 miles, still throwing up, I found myself next to a runner in a worse state than I was. He was six feet tall, long and lean. The veins in his arms and thighs all stood out on his flesh, like a map of his suffering. He was so pale he was almost transparent.

'I'm going to tell you something now,' he said, voice like a ghost. 'And I bet you won't believe me.'

'What?'

'I can run a marathon in two hours 35.'

I looked at my watch. It was four hours 15 minutes since I got off the bike. I tried to smile.

'Do you know what mate?' I said. 'You're right, I don't believe you!'

Both of us laughed through our torment.

Without knowing how, I kept putting one foot in front of the other. At one point, after what seemed like an eternity of further suffering, I found myself on the verge of passing out, doubled over, with my hands on my knees. The road under my feet looked yielding, so comfortable. The temptation to sink to it was compelling.

People around began to scream. 'You're there, you're there, you've nearly finished! Get going!'

I raised my head and saw I was actually at the mouth of the finishing chute. There were only 200m left. Eyes shut, I staggered through.

It would be nice to say I felt some achievement in completing that race, in crossing the line against the odds, but it would also be a lie. My only sensation was relief that the torture was over. I flopped on to a chair as a marshal handed me a water bottle. I swigged from it before throwing up in my lap, exhausted, dizzy and dejected. Darren and Terry came over to console me.

'Your Achilles heel,' Terry said, 'is the fact that you could suffer. Other people would have eased up on the training when you started getting ill. Your biggest strength was also your weakness.'

'I'm sorry,' I said to both of them. 'I'm so sorry.'

'Don't worry,' Darren said. 'We're still proud.'

He meant well, but I didn't want sympathy. I had no interest in my time or where I had placed. I knew both would be awful. A nurse checked me over and said I needed to see the doctor. In the medical tent he asked when I had last eaten.

'At 80km on the bike,' I said.

'So you cycled another 100km and then ran a marathon without eating? Is that what you're telling me?'

I nodded.

They conducted tests and found my blood sugar levels were dangerously low. I was also severely dehydrated. For several hours they kept me there for rehydration and stabilisation. When they finally let me go I had to leave my car in Bolton and Terry drove me to the hotel in Rochdale where I was staying.

That night I continued using the special rehydration supplements and reflected, with a new-found humility. I had not shown the race enough respect. It was as simple as that. Arrogance had tripped me up.

I had believed I could breeze through it, but it had breezed through me. Terry was right. The Graham Obree approach did not work for me. I was too intense, too driven. There was a chance of doing myself serious harm.

I spoke to Mum. She was disappointed for me. I floated the idea of getting a job.

'But if I go out and become a roofer or a plasterer,' I reasoned, 'I'll never do anything with my life. I'll never amount to anything.'

Her eyes filled with concern and love.

'You keep going with what you're doing, John,' she said. 'You just keep on going.'

Yet I knew if I did not change my mindset, this situation could repeat itself. Evolution was needed and I would have to swallow my pride, reach out, put my trust in someone else and work with a coach.

Almost as if it was pre-ordained, Keith phoned me as soon as I returned to London.

'What happened?' he asked.

I explained about my health issues and he sympathised, but suggested I would probably have been better off pulling out, recovering properly and entering another race later in the year. Keith had come second in his age group in a sprint finish. He had only missed out on first by two seconds and qualified for the world championships in Kona.

'I actually ran past you on the marathon,' he said. 'You didn't see me because you were in such a bad way. You over-trained, didn't you?'

'Yes,' I replied, feeling meek. 'Do you think I could have a look at your training programme?'

'Of course,' he said gently, 'no problem, of course.'

He e-mailed me some documents which I looked through but did not fully understand, so after he had completed his race in Hawaii, in early October, he offered to meet at a lido in Charlton to explain.

'Look,' he said as we sat by the pool. 'I've gone as far as I can go in the sport, I've done Hawaii, so I'm retiring from competition. I'm setting up my own coaching company, Perform Fitness. You're a naturally gifted athlete, so if you're interested, no obligation, I'll coach you for free.'

'Really?'

'Yeah. I've trained with you. I've followed your times online. I know how much you underperformed in Bolton. Maybe right now I'm the only one who does. If we can make you into a top Ironman and I think we can, it'll be great promotion for me.'

His words were music to my ears. 'You're on.'

'But listen, if you want to optimise every session, you also have to optimise the time between each session,' he explained. 'Recovery, hydration, nutrition, stretching, massage, all these elements are as important as what you do in the water, on the saddle or on the road. You have to pick targets and aim for them. It's like a world champion boxer with a title fight three months away. He needs to be at his best then. No one can peak all year around.'

From that day on, I put my trust in Keith. Terry remained my performance coach and sports psychologist but Keith looked after the physical side. With his wealth of experience, he could only improve me.

It was a while before we started work, because the terrible ordeal I had put my body through in Bolton disrupted the arrhythmia of my heart. My resting heart rate had gone from 38 to 64.

The cardiologist at St Mary's Hospital gave me a 24-hour ECG and concluded that my training should be capped at 20 minutes a day for a month. At the time it felt like some sort of death sentence but Keith said it would be good for me. I eased into it and used the opportunity to have a bit of downtime.

I went out with the guys from the rowing club, ate some bad food, drank beer, got plenty of sleep and generally enjoyed myself. My body fat had dropped to five per cent in the build-up to the race, so I had a bit of room to play with. I even went on a few dates, although I still found forming those kinds of relationships uncomfortable since leaving prison.

The rest was needed, much as I struggled to admit it and I began feeling healthier and happier than I had in a long time. Sometimes it's only when you step out of that bubble you realise how all-consuming it is.

Once we did begin, in November, refreshed and re-energised, I followed the sessions Keith told me to do, when he told me to do them. He placed critical importance on the concept of heart-rate zones.

I would do two hard sessions a week, for example a bike and a run, in which I would run to my threshold, meaning the upper limit of my heart rate. Other days I might do a longer activity, but at lower intensity, meaning I was keeping myself ticking over, without putting too much strain on my system.

My particular focus was on the marathon and Keith understood my reasons. The swim and the cycle had both been pretty poor, but it had been the marathon that crushed me. My aim was to go to Bolton again in 2015 and run one of the fastest marathons on the day. If I did, I knew I could place well.

Keith wrote my training programme on to Training Peaks, an app you can download for smartphones or laptops. After every session my heart rate readings, my bike wattage and times would have to be entered on to the chart, meaning Keith could keep a firm grasp on my exact fitness levels during each training block, before setting targets for the next one. This is the kind of coaching involved in Ironman training, which is very different to most other sports. The sessions are so long, often involving being out on a bike or running for half a day at a time, that a coach cannot be physically present for all of it, but they can still guide and give advice from afar.

At the highest levels endurance sport is tied up with intimate understandings of physiology and body chemistry, becoming scientific and mathematical. Up to that point I had avoided most of that, believing I could do without it, but Keith brought it into my regime.

On my training runs I no longer ran at one, consistent pace, or various speeds as I felt. Before I would go to Richmond Park with a particular distance in mind and simply try to run it as quickly as possible, but Keith would cap my splits, meaning that for the first half hour I would run each kilometre in four minutes 30 seconds, then do 30 minutes at four minutes 20 per km, followed by 30 minutes at four minutes per km. The numbers would vary from session to session but there was always adaptation involved, an element of change and a pre-set pace I would have to stick to.

On the bike too it became more about intervals and holding certain ranges for periods of time. The idea was to increase my top-end power, which was where my talents lay. My physique was naturally stronger than many triathletes, meaning I could put more through the pedals than most. Keith would give me periods where I would have to maintain Ironman race power, then maybe follow that with a period where I would have to up it to half-Ironman power (because the half-Ironman race is shorter, the power requirements are more intense).

In the water, sessions became more technical, and sprints and repetitions formed a major part of my approach. Keith brought his business partner, Bruno, down to watch me swim. A former naval special forces operative in Belgium, Bruno was a top-end endurance coach himself with a speciality in swimming. He asked me to do 20 100m repetitions, with a ten-second rest between each, to observe my form. I held a time of one minute 46 seconds per hundred, which was awful.

Keith and Bruno spent a great deal of time improving my technique, working on my body position in the water, the efficiency of my stroke, the strength of my leg kick. With sustained effort I improved to the point that I could maintain one minute 35 per 100m, without stopping, for the full Ironman race distance of 3.86km.

In April I headed back out to the Alps with Hywel and his crew, enjoying the challenge of real mountain-riding again. Unlike the previous year I felt more secure in my own position and resisted the urge to go flat out at all times. Once again, it was a great camp.

As the 2015 race approached, my confidence soared and my innate abilities turned up surprising results. It seemed the longer and harder the session, the better I became. We found that on a long cycle, even if I maintained my power output, my heart rate would remain consistent. Sometimes it would even fall slightly. I was then able to get off the bike and run at my maximum heart rate from the beginning of the marathon until the end. This wasn't something I had ever trained or developed, although I suppose the rowing gave me a solid base.

It was just something within my physiology. I thought about my previous ability to stay icy-calm before and during a robbery, to always hold my nerve. Maybe that was also attributable to the same thing?

All I still lacked was race experience, but of course, we knew there was only one way to get that. The coming years would be crucial. 2015 would still only be my third full Ironman event.

Three weeks before Ironman UK 2015 I competed the half-Ironman at Wimbleball. The weather was dreadful, slashing down with rain, but the race went well other than the fact I had decided to run tubular race tyres on my bike. 'Tubs', as they are known, have no inner tube and are the fastest race tyres you can buy, but as they are glued on to the wheel, puncture repair becomes problematic.

One of the features of the Wimbleball course, in common with many of the British Ironman events, is that the bike leg is very technical, traversing lots of narrow, winding country roads. Unfortunately, the rain had scattered loose soil, grit, leaves and twigs over the road surfaces and as a result, it was often impossible to see what you were riding on.

Ten kilometres into the bike stage the inevitable happened and I got a front wheel puncture. I stopped to attend to it, using Pit-Stop foam to reseal the tyre, but made a silly mistake of forgetting to spin the wheel when I did so. Without that, the foam failed to coat the whole inner surface of the tyre. I used a CO_2 canister to re-inflate, but my incorrect use of the Pit-Stop meant the puncture had not been repaired.

In a sense I was lucky. It was not a complete blowout, rather a slow release of pressure, but with progressively less and less air in my front wheel, my speed reduced dramatically and I finished the course riding on the rim, with only a thin coating of rubber preventing the carbon fibre from being worn down on the road.

From the moment the puncture happened, I changed my tactics and treated Wimbleball as another training day. I completed the bike leg in just under three hours, which considering the extra toll the puncture took on my legs was not too bad. On the run I moved freely, with no pressure. It was an extremely hilly course and I was able to claw back a few positions from those who struggled on the inclines. I ran a one hour 27 half-marathon, the fourth fastest time on the day, which left me in 28th place overall. I accepted it without too much over-analysis.

Keith and I had set an immediate aim of a top ten finish in Bolton, which would give me world ranking points and be very credible in only my third full race. Secretly, we thought there was a good chance I could win it. At that moment Ironman UK was all I cared about.

29

Return to the Scene
of the Crime

AT 6am on Sunday 19 July 2015, I looked out over the rippling expanse of Pennington Flash for the third time. Three years since my release from prison and each one punctuated with an Ironman UK event. Within myself I resolved to make this one count.

This was the course, after all, that had kicked my arse the previous year, the race that had beaten me to my knees and kept me there. This time I had confidence in my preparation. We had been meticulous. Like chess, or criminal activity, we had planned several moves ahead.

Darren stood next to me, looking edgy. With our shared time in prison long behind, we were side by side as friends, nothing less. Inspired by watching my efforts for the last two years, he had decided to race as well, to discover his own one-day limits.

'You're the only one here who looks happy,' he said, concern etched deeply on his face.

'Good luck mate!' I laughed.

'Have you got any last-minute tips for the swim?' he asked.

'It's too late for that now, Darren. Just rely on your training. Whatever you've done in your sessions, use it all now.'

Seven months of working with Keith had educated and stretched me. If I performed to my potential I knew I would be up there, challenging the leaders. The numbers said so.

Main competition in my age group would come from Brian Fogarty, who held the British 100-mile cycling time-trial record, and Michael Jolley, who finished third in 2014, along with the usual smattering of Germans, Americans and Kiwis who are always strong.

As they had been in Wimbleball, conditions were appalling. There are never guarantees with the weather in northern England, even in July, and as we all stood there in our wetsuits like mutant amphibians, thunderous rain turned the surface of the lake into a maelstrom. It occurred to me how nice it would be to do an event somewhere with decent weather for once.

For the 2015 event Ironman UK introduced a staggered swim start, as had many Ironman events, to try to avoid the mass frenzy of flailing limbs that usually characterised the beginning of the race. Stewards held up placards stating that competitors likely to complete the swim in under an hour should head for the line.

The staggered start had logic behind it, but would mean that as the day panned out, it would be very difficult to know where you were placed in your category. With all your competitors starting at different times, it became more of a case of internal racing, producing your best and hoping it was good enough to go faster than others.

I weighed up my options. The truth was that I was not that fast in the water, but I thought there was a chance if I went in with a group of better swimmers they would carry me along. Maybe I could get a tow, hang on their feet and produce my best ever time? I said goodbye to Darren and joined the small bunch of professionals and swim specialists heading to the lake.

In a typical Ironman race the swim only accounts for ten per cent of the overall time, but tactically it's very important. For those whose strengths lie in cycling or running, like me, a better-than-expected swim can set the foundation for a spectacular race.

As we padded down to the water's edge, the PA blared into life, piercing the dawn with the screeching guitar riff of 'Thunderstruck' by AC/DC, an appropriate track given the weather. 'Thunder!' screamed the shrill vocal. 'Thunder!' The song finished as we waited for the start, giving way to the first bars of 'God Save the Queen'. I got shivers.

'You are gonna smash this,' I said to myself.

The voice of Paul Kaye came on, the South African MC known as the 'voice of Ironman'. He introduced the race then counted down.

'Three...two...one!'

The gun sounded and we were away. The swimmers around me fanned out quickly and I soon realised I had misjudged. I was not fast enough to keep up and was left in no-man's land. Battling through the choppy water alone, by the mid-point of the second lap I was caught by the group behind.

Rather than attaching myself to guys who were quicker and swimming in their slipstream, those who were a bit slower were attaching themselves to me. I found myself dragging a whole line of swimmers along with me as if they were tied to my toes by a string. Tactically, it was not a huge error and I accepted it for what it was – yet another stage of my Ironman education.

Most swim times were slower than normal that day because of the conditions and the blunder meant I completed the swim in a disappointing one hour ten minutes but I headed to T1 with undiminished vigour. In contrast to 2014, every inch of my body felt primed and taut. I just needed to remember the basics, to eat and drink, use all my training know-how and it was there for me.

For the first two hours on the bike the rain continued hammering down. A turbulent wind squalled around too, which made for pretty miserable riding conditions. Once we were out on the moorlands, the rain stopped, but the wind got worse, often buffeting from the sides, affecting balance and at other times coalescing into a pitiless headwind. The only consolation was that conditions were the same for everyone. It would not be a fast race.

I held on to the power numbers that Keith prescribed for me to stick to, but that meant with the wind and all the twisting corners of the Bolton course, my average speed fell back. I felt so good physically, my heart rate was low and instinct said I had it in me to push harder, but at the back of my mind was my embarrassment from the previous year. What if I exceeded my power numbers, pushed on with the bike then blew up on the run, ending broken and defeated like last time? I would never have been able to live with myself.

By the halfway point of the cycle, I had overtaken many of the professional women which had to mean I was up there. Ironman is a sport in which the distances between the best male and female athletes are not that great, but I knew that the top men were still a distance ahead. Ignoring the desire to give it everything, I held stoically firm to Keith's pre-race instructions, pedalling mechanically and with restraint.

On the last 2km of the bike course, as I neared Bolton Wanderers' football stadium, I could see the first runners coming past on the other side of the road, more of them than I expected. A little hint of panic spiked in my guts and I figured I would need a strong footrace to achieve my goal of the top ten.

I sprinted into T2 from the dismount line, wheeling my bike. The realisation hit home that there were around 50 bikes already racked. That meant 50 athletes with a considerable head start for the marathon. I changed into my running shoes frantically, feeling flustered and threw my bike anywhere, not caring about my race number or racking it in the correct place. I downed an energy gel and headed off. Physically I still felt great. My legs were strong, my heart was steady and my energy seemed boundless.

I reset my Garmin to run mode and went at it, finding that from the beginning I picked people off with ease. It was as if I was running a 5km and they were doing a 100km. Within the first 8km I must have passed at least 15 runners. I was flying.

'You might beat me on the swim and you might beat me on the bike,' I thought, 'but none of you are beating me on the run.'

I checked my heart rate, which was comfortable, and settled into a rhythm. On road, my domain, I ate up the ground.

I ran away from the stadium, down Chorley Avenue and found myself at the base of the hill that led up into Bolton town centre. I knew that once I reached the top, it would be three loops of the course up there to the end.

As I neared the hill I caught up with a group of four men running together and ran past them, making it look casual, as if I wasn't even trying. There are a lot of mental tricks in endurance sport and I had spoken about it with Keith. If possible you want to gain a psychological advantage. One of them tried to come with me. I liked that. *Mano a mano*, pistols at dawn, me against him.

As we started on the hill, a pretty fierce one, 500m long with a six per cent gradient, I could feel him behind me. He was close enough for his breath to tickle my shoulder.

I attacked it, showing the slope no mercy, knees pumping, elbows tight. I overtook two others on the way up, looked over my shoulder and saw my erstwhile co-runner way behind, labouring. That lifted me further and I crested the top feeling fantastic, knowing I had to be in or around the top 30 already.

Obviously I knew that the higher up the field I got, the harder it would be to overtake and the guys in the first few places may already have been too far ahead to catch, but the run was going as well as I could have hoped.

I ran through the top end of Bolton town centre, over the timing mat and through a drink station where a girl tried to give me a cup of Red Bull, which I waved away. As I continued around the first part of the loop I saw Fraser Cartmell, a professional from Scotland who had won Ironman UK in 2010. Fraser was running with a race official on a motorbike beside him, meaning he was in the top three. At that point he was about a kilometre behind me on the loop, meaning it was likely he would be lapping me shortly.

I stuck to my plan, completed the first loop, ran down the hill to take me back to the beginning and looked over my shoulder. Cartmell was nowhere to be seen. I had put distance into him, rather than him eating up the gap between us. That was when I realised just how fast I was running.

Keith stood on the corner, smiling.

'How are you feeling?' he called, as I ran past.

'Great!' I replied.

'Keep to the plan, keep eating, keep drinking, keep fuelling,' he shouted. 'Fogarty was 20 minutes ahead of you after the bike, but you're catching him.'

Terry stood a bit further along, at the 'special needs' aid station (I prefer to bring my own gels and provisions rather than use the ones provided) with my energy drinks. He told me I was in 12th place in my division, which fired me up. I knew I was running strongly and felt sure I could make up further ground.

I grabbed some caffeine gel from him and went hard into the start of the second loop, still feeling real zip and power in my legs. About a kilometre in I noticed Bella Bayliss, a renowned coach, by the side of the road. She pointed at me as I passed, turned to the guy next to her and audibly said, 'Get his number.' I knew that meant she wanted to check which of her athletes I was competing against and her concern encouraged me further. If nothing else, I was making an impression.

After running past Bella, someone on the sidelines screamed that I was in fourth, but as far as I was aware I had not passed anyone from my age group since I had seen Terry. This is a common feature of Ironman races, in which confused spectators shout out misinformation. It's not malicious, and is meant as encouragement, but you have to learn to ignore it. With staggered starts, deciphering what is going on in a race from the roadside can be difficult. Different age groups have different coloured race numbers and you are given armbands to show which lap you are on. Mistakes are easily made. There was no way of knowing if either of them were right, so I stayed in the moment and continued running my race.

At the halfway point of the marathon I clocked one hour 26 and felt comfortable, with plenty of gas left in the tank. I completed the second loop and saw Keith at the bottom of the hill again.

'What's your heart rate?' he yelled.

I had a look, '157!'

'Fucking go then!' he grinned. 'You're in 12th. Just drop the hammer, give it everything!'

His words were like a jolt of energy, my adrenaline spiked and – *bang* – I went. With the shackles of sticking to split times taken away I hit 18 minutes 50 seconds for the next 5km, a really fast pace to set after more than nine hours of competition. Again I passed a clutch of other runners. I kept that up until halfway through the final loop when my legs finally began to tire, not that there was any trace of panic or breaking down like the previous time, but simply that I reached the end of my capability to go at that speed.

I settled back into four-and-a-half-minute kilometre pace and finished the run strongly. As I entered the finishing chute, the Irish accent of Ironman commentator Joanne Murphy came over the tannoy.

'And a great story, ladies and gentlemen, finishing in tenth place in only his third Ironman event, a remarkable achievement, John McAvoy. Just three years ago he was still in jail! What an incredible young man!'

The roaring crowd urged me over the line, where a sensation of absolute joy washed over me. I clenched my fists, raised my head and screamed at the sky like a lunatic. A time of ten hours six minutes in atrocious weather, with a tenth-place finish, was a solid showing that gave me a spot among the country's elite. I had run the second fastest marathon in the male 30–34 age group on the day. More importantly, I had put to bed my disaster of 2014.

As is obligatory on these occasions, I sank to the ground and lay on my back. A TV camera appeared, hovering above me briefly, and a realisation dawned as I lay there – I was not spent. If necessary I could have got up and run some more.

I enjoyed the celebrations and congratulations that followed the race. Terry and Keith were overjoyed, the feeling of having let people down was banished, but inside I knew I could still do far better, especially on the bike. What if I had pushed harder at that stage, given myself a smaller gap to close? Where could I have finished then? I reckoned I lost 15 minutes while cycling that I had not needed to lose. Fifteen gained minutes would have put me in second.

These sorts of modifications are hard to understand when you are new to the sport, but racing over such long distances – and Ironman events involve 226.3km of continuous competition – every small decision, mistake, tweak or adaptation accumulates. Each can become marginal gains or marginal deficits and when stacked up over the whole day, make massive differences to your outcome.

I waited around for a few hours, cheered Darren on as he completed his run, then went back to the hotel to rest. Already that night, while I sat in a restaurant with friends, toasting my future as an athlete, my mind turned over with plans for the next one.

30

Mind Games

'WHAT are we doing next year?' I asked Keith, the morning after the race. 'I know I can do better. The bike leg let me down.'

Keith shook his head and laughed. 'John,' he said. 'Have some time off, mate. Forget about competing, forget about training and enjoy a bit of downtime, then we can talk.'

If it was left up to me I would probably have been training the following day, but I had to admit that Keith's approach worked. It would be foolish to start ignoring it just when I was seeing some success.

In the quiet month that followed, I turned it over and over. It wasn't my fitness that was lacking, just experience and bike handling skills. The swim should have been at least five minutes quicker, while on the bike, the technical elements of descending and cornering needed work. Over 180km those little ten- and 15-second adjustments add up, even taking corners too wide could add time. You need to hold a racing line.

I got on the internet and checked out possibilities for my next competition. Kona was still out of the question. Even if I qualified for it, the strict USA visa requirements were a barrier. Perusing the list of crimes that disbar you from American travel, I had committed nearly all of them.

The only race in the world that came close to Hawaii was the European championships at Frankfurt in Germany. Held every year in July, it regularly attracted top Ironmen from around the world and was known to be a fast course. Having already been cleared to visit the Alps with Hywel, which by then I had done twice, I was confident probation would give me the all-clear.

'It'll be a good course for you,' Keith confirmed, when I mentioned it. 'The bike leg is much more speed orientated than technique based. It's very flat and straight, with only 1,000m of elevation. That suits power riders like you. It's about efficiency and you'll be able to utilise your power output much more efficiently. You can put as much through the pedals as anyone.'

A quick check of the bike split times proved Keith's point. The fastest time in Bolton had been five hours 50 minutes, while in Frankfurt in 2015 the best was four hours two for the same distance. That added up to an hour and 48 of difference, a clear demonstration of how much course variations affect the race.

The bike section is such a huge part of any Ironman, often taking up two-thirds of your whole time, meaning that a course that suits your strengths is a massive boost. On that basis, Frankfurt looked a good fit for me. I applied to probation well in advance and was delighted when permission was granted.

With the Staffordshire half-distance event early in the summer to prepare, it would mean a solid two-race season, giving me a great chance to gain recognition. More than anything, I wanted to improve. I wanted 2016 to show that I had emerged.

To keep myself ticking over I entered the London ultra-duathlon in Richmond Park in September, which involved a 20km run and an 80km cycle followed by another 10km run. I finished second on very little training, showing my condition had not slipped that much since Bolton.

Keith and I set specific targets as my programme got underway. Swimming improvements were a big part, enabling me to get out of the water and ride with better cyclists. On the first leg of an Ironman event, there is little variation from place to place. Doing 3.8km in the water is more or less the same anywhere.

Of course the weather can have an impact, but that can happen anywhere. In July and on the same latitude as the English south coast, Frankfurt usually had good summer weather. Sometimes it can be scorching.

The Frankfurt swim would be held in a lake called the Strandbad Langener Waldsee and a question mark hovered over whether we would be wearing wetsuits, as the Ironman governing body do not allow their use in water temperatures above 24.5 degrees. The Langener had only been that hot on two occasions in the last 20 years, but it remained a possibility. For me, if that happened, it would be a small disadvantage. The increased buoyancy of the wetsuit helps me to hold a higher water position and swim more quickly. Without it, I knew I might go a couple of minutes slower.

Nonetheless, I hoped for hot conditions and we geared my training towards that eventuality. Keith, Terry and I all agreed that sweltering weather would impact the opposition and suit my mental strength. Sweat jackets and thermal tops became regular features of my training as we worked on raising my core temperature to get used to potential extremes. On a three-hour training ride and an hour's run I could lose about a kilo and a half in weight. My body had to be able to adapt to such a possibility.

Most indications suggested that Frankfurt would present an air temperature of around 25 degrees, so we planned that I would wear a two-piece suit that I could roll up over my abdomen when running, to release heat. An athlete in my age group had actually died there in 2015 through a combination of overheating and drinking too much water. He made the finish, but was admitted to hospital with a swollen brain and died two days later.

People don't realise as it seems counter-intuitive, but in an Ironman event large volumes of water can be an enemy. You sweat so much that drinking too much causes your system to flush itself out. As that process continues, your body runs out of electrolytes, salt and sodium which can cause major complications. A well-balanced sports drink is key. If you haven't got that, you're asking for trouble.

Just before Christmas 2015 with training already in full swing, I met a girl for a drink at a bar in Beckenham, the kind of place I avoided going for years. The previous two years had shown me that it was important to try to keep some balance in your life. I knew I had a tendency to be consumed by my sporting goals and needed to guard against obsession. While I had still not had a serious relationship since leaving jail, I felt I should get out when I could.

My date had set on central Beckenham as a location. I tried to suggest other possibilities, but she wasn't keen, so headed out with some reluctance. She was a nice enough girl, but I figured it was highly likely I would see someone from the old days. Beckenham was right in the centre of my old world.

As ever, my sixth sense served me well. In the end I didn't even make it through the door. An old face stood outside the bar smoking a cigarette.

'John, John!' he called as soon as he saw me. I winced internally. 'How are you? Long time mate, long time! Do you want a drink? Let me get you a drink.'

'No, I'm all right,' I told him. 'I'm just having a quiet night out.' We walked in to find a table and he stubbed out his cigarette and followed us.

'No, honestly John, let me get you a drink, come on, and what about your girlfriend? What are you having love? It's good to see you John. Fucking hell, where have you been? We were just talking about you the other day. Do you remember Lenny?'

He chattered on, conversing with me as if I was still the same John he knew from years ago, ultra-friendly but almost apprehensive at the same time, respectful but afraid. I'd forgotten what that was like.

I tried to put him off. He insisted. When he returned from the bar with our drinks, he pressed a little piece of paper into my hand with his phone number on it.

'Give us a bell in the week,' he said. 'I've got all sorts of bits you'd be interested in.'

I smiled, waited for him to turn around, screwed it up and put it in the ashtray.

'What was that all about?' my date asked.

'Nothing,' I replied, watching him walk away. 'He's got me mixed up with somebody else.'

I ended up seeing that girl a few more times. She had a couple of kids from a previous relationship, which I didn't mind, but it all ended one day after I met them for tea and cake near Crease Park.

We were chatting and laughing, then out of the blue she asked: 'So are we together now?'

Her words filled me with sudden dread, as if I were being taken back to high security, as if she was after my freedom. She'd be watching me, limiting me and trying to tell me what to do. I left soon after and never saw her again.

Over the holiday period I discussed Frankfurt with Keith, Bruno and Terry. Between us, we saw the race playing out in simple terms, understanding it was unlikely I could swim the course in under an hour, as swimming was still my weak link, but we trained to get as close to the 60-minute mark as possible. Anything under one hour five minutes would mean an excellent start.

Then I would be straight on to the cycle leg and out on those smooth, flat, German roads, with a new custom-made bike from Wyndy Milla. Off the back of my strong showing in Ironman UK, I had been fortunate to attract sponsorship from some great companies due to the uniqueness of my story. Craft sportswear provided me with some top quality kit, while the new bike was a dream machine, for which I was (and still am) really grateful.

As I was a 'brand ambassador', Wyndy Milla purpose-built a bike to match my body dimensions, fitted with the fastest wheel set possible, a full disc on the back and a tri-spoke on the front. Those wheels are worth £4,000 on their own. The whole thing is valued at twice that.

The aerodynamics, gearing and mechanics alone would mean massive improvements and best of all, I would be able to run a bigger chain ring on the front, meaning I could push and push my speed. With a tailwind I expected to be able to hit 65–70kph.

The overall idea was that I could begin to use the experience of the last two and half years on race days, combined with steadily improving technique and top-of-the-range equipment, meaning I would not need to be so regimented on numbers. I could race more off feel.

Sessions became even more technical, with Keith basing many around my functional threshold power, or FTP, which is a measure of the maximum wattage you can sustain for an hour. A key signifier for cyclists, FTP is linked to your blood lactate threshold. The more lactic acid your muscles can process before becoming overwhelmed – which is what endurance athletes call 'blowing up' – the more power you will be able to sustain.

Once we had established what my FTP reading was (365 watts), Keith devised sessions designed to stretch it. He would have me ride at maximum FTP for 20 minutes, after a warm-up, then ease off for ten, then go back at it. On another day he might introduce intervals where I would actually ride above my FTP for periods, the idea being that if I got used to riding with a build-up of lactic acid in my muscles, my body would grow accustomed to it.

When Lance Armstrong was winning his Tour de France titles with the assistance of a banned performance enhancer called EPO, he was able to output a maximum of seven watts per kilo of bodyweight. If he hit that number, he knew he would win. Other riders would never be able to match him.

In May 2016, two months before Frankfurt, I output 5.2 watts per kilo, which for someone not a pure cyclist competing in a multidiscipline event (and racing clean) is very high. That meant on the day I knew I could ride at about four watts for the whole bike leg and get off with enough energy conserved for a strong marathon.

All of this was tailored into my programme, to enable me to get off the bike in as strong a position as possible. When I racked my bike in T2 and began the footrace, up and down the banks of the River Main, it would be my time.

'You're going to take a lot of guys out on the run,' Keith advised. 'So let's play up to that, make them wary of you. Talk to them. It's the best way to judge. Get on a guy's shoulder and start a little conversation, see if they're breathing heavy or they're laboured.

If they are, if they have difficulty speaking, then just go, leave them behind. The minute you see weakness, hit it. That's what competition is all about.'

We discussed how there would probably be a point during the run that I would switch my watch off, forget about zones and heart rates and just go. If the race demanded it, if I was halfway through the marathon and ten minutes behind my target, I would commit, balls-to-the-wall. I'm not afraid to roll the dice and never have been.

Our meticulous preparations covered every possible detail, even something which is necessary during an Ironman, but must be managed properly to avert negative consequences – going to the toilet. Ideally you want to evacuate your bowels before starting, as needing to defecate can present real problems. It has been known for Ironman competitors to crap all over their own legs while running, rather than stopping by the roadside and losing time. The racing mentality dictates that you do what you have to do, but I hoped to avoid that eventuality if possible.

I intended to pee before I swam. While on the bike, a good indication of being well hydrated is urinating another three times. Obviously, I would do that while cycling. There's no time to stop.

If all that went well, the idea was that I would not have to pee on the run. One skill I am yet to develop is the ability to urinate while running, which some athletes can. If the need was pressing, I would have to stop and in a competitive Ironman, pausing by the side of the road to pee for a minute can be a major barrier to success.

From May, we started building volume, doing five-hour bike sessions and metric Ironman drills, where I would swim 4km, cycle for four hours at power, then run off the bike for two hours at pace. On another day I would do a 100-mile cycle, throw an electrolyte drink down my neck, have a quick shower or bath to open my capillaries and flush the lactic acid from my legs, then go out for an hour's hard run.

By spending more and more time practising the disciplines, the efficiency of my body grew. Training distances that once seemed challenging became easy, enabling me to add extra intensity. In comparison to previous years 2016 became race specific, very time and power focused, which is why I headed into the season with such confidence.

My programme only tapered a few days before my warm-up event, Ironman 7.3 in Staffordshire in June, then again for a few days before Frankfurt. Other than that, I trained with absolute conviction for nine months. By the time I lined up in Staffordshire I felt like a whole new athlete, with my new, bright pink Wyndy Milla good to go.

Unfortunately, a small delay in production meant I had only been able to collect it on the Wednesday, four days before the race. I then discovered the cassette on the back wheel was too small and needed to be replaced, which meant I didn't have as much practice time as I would have liked. The bike also had several elements that were new to me, like Di2 electronic gears. Only hours in the saddle would make me comfortable with them.

To top it all off, my power meter broke, meaning I had no idea of my wattage numbers while I was riding. Despite all of that, the bike itself felt incredible and when conditions allowed I absolutely flew. Aerodynamically and mechanically it was by far the best racing cycle I had ever sat on. At times I hit 50kph without even pushing it.

A further, organisational issue arose with the way the staggered start was managed. The race was being televised and the feeling among most of the amateur, age group athletes, was that the organisers wanted to make sure none of them came in ahead of the pros.

Rather than having the male 30–35 category, traditionally the quickest, follow the pros, they let the pros go first, followed by older age groups, before we got in. In the end they had a 45-minute head start on us. The professional men were finishing the swim and heading out on the bike before we even got in the water.

When we did eventually get to start, we found that within a kilometre we were catching up with the slower swimmers from the older divisions, making for a messy race. There were bodies everywhere, right through the middle of the course, slowing progress. It even overlapped into the bike course and for the first 10km, the best guys from my age group were weaving in and out of others.

I had to remain philosophical. Even temperament is important. You cannot afford to be too hard on yourself when things go wrong, or get too ahead of yourself when they go well. So many factors combine meaning level-headedness, not frantic action, is key.

Despite these difficulties I had a good race and finished sixth, my best ever official Ironman finish, running the second best half-marathon on the day. The half distance does not suit my strengths and most of the guys I was up against specialised in that length of event. Regardless of a few teething problems with the new bike, it was great preparation and filled me with confidence for the big one.

I allowed my training to taper off and spent a couple of weeks cruising around Surrey on the Wyndy Milla to get used to it. By the time I began my journey to Germany, four days before the race, I did so with total focus.

31

Frankfurt

HYWEL picked me up in his VW Touran from the Dartford Hilton hotel at 5.30am on the Thursday before the race. The early start precluded much conversation and on the way down to Dover I reflected back on the specific plan Keith and Bruno had devised for me.

We knew my swim would not be mega-fast and aimed for 60–65 minutes. I would have my shoes attached to my bike pedals in T1 to quicken transition, then aimed to hold 260 watts for the first 75 per cent of the cycle, before opening up and pushing harder in the final quarter. With good weather, as we expected, those numbers should provide a time around four hours 50 minutes on the bike. The marathon was where we intended to exploit my strengths, starting off at a pace of four minutes 15 seconds per km. With the right conditions, if all played out well, it would bring me home in under nine hours. In 2015 the winning time for my age group had been nine hours nine minutes.

The ferry brought us to Calais and we set off through northern France, across Belgium and over the southern tip of Holland, near Maastricht. I enjoyed sitting back and watching the scenery roll by and as we entered the Netherlands I found my mind instinctively turning to Aaron and my own time there. It was the closest I had been to his place of death since then.

I remembered how much I enjoyed myself and what a happy period of my life it had been, how I felt so *free*. But putting myself back into that time and place from 13 years before seemed impossible. What is the past really? It only exists when you think of it, and when I thought of it, it was like thinking of someone else, or watching a movie with actors playing parts.

I remembered how I had been going to a meet-up with Aaron near Antwerp, probably with Eddie or one of his associates. We never used sat-nav because it can be tracked by police so Aaron had sat on the passenger seat with a map, claiming to be an expert navigator. There was nothing wrong with that in itself, but in his other hand he held a big, fat, cone-shaped spliff, wrapped up with some of the top-notch Northern Lights cannabis we had been moving.

Of course we got hopelessly lost, doing laps of the ring road around the city, getting increasingly wasted and riled.

'If you were a fucking tank commander, you'd have got us all killed by now,' I'd told him, shaking my head. He had looked at me, red-eyed over the corner of the map and dissolved into giggles.

The memory brought a smile to my face, along with a stab of sadness. Whatever you do in life, whichever roads you take, you can never escape memory. It's always lurking in the background. Soon we left the low countries behind and crossed the border into Germany.

Seven hours after leaving London we arrived at the Inter-Continental in Frankfurt, the official Ironman hotel. We didn't have a room there but wanted to store our bikes somewhere secure, as we were booked in a rougher part of the city.

As soon as we entered the lobby we found ourselves among a whole host of professional competitors, people I had only read about in magazines. Miranda Carfrae (female world champion) noticed me wheeling my bright pink Wyndy Milla towards reception and smiled.

'Nice bike,' she said.

I thanked her, feeling I had really arrived on the scene.

After storing our equipment at the Inter-Continental we made the short journey across town to the hotel Hywel had booked.

'What's our place like?' I asked.

'All I know is that it's cheap,' he replied.

It could not have been a more different establishment. Situated down a back street in Frankfurt's red light district, surrounded by titty bars, our hotel was conveniently located next door to the city's main needle exchange. As we arrived a group of about 12 heroin addicts sat on the pavement in front, fixing up with the clean works they had been provided with. Several had obviously made use of them already and slumped, gurning in the gutter, eyes rolling up in their heads.

'Blimey,' Hywel commented.

'It's like being back in Full Sutton,' I said.

Both of us were surprised to see such a scene in Germany, a country renowned for its cleanliness and organisation. Fortunately, we only had one night booked there, before moving to somewhere much more upmarket.

Over the next couple of days we went through all the usual pre-race procedures, briefings, equipment storage, race orientation. The town was full of tall, ripped Germans who looked like they trained 24 hours a day and had never tasted crisps or sweets in their lives. For some reason Ironman is a particularly popular sport in Germany (the Spanish, Belgians and French are strong too). Since the eighties, when all the top guys came from the USA, the Bundesrepublik has taken over as the sport's leading nation. For that reason, along with the prestige of the race, I knew my age group would be extremely competitive.

On the day Hywel was scheduled to set off with the pros, meaning he would be at least half an hour ahead of me on the course. My job was simply to put in as strong a performance as I could. It would be difficult during the race to gauge my age-group position. I wouldn't know my placing until the finish, but this one was simply about doing as well as possible in the second biggest event in the world.

On the way over to T2 to rack and prepare my bike, my power meter cut out again, which caused me to roll my eyes. Why couldn't everything just work properly? As I had in Staffordshire I spoke to Keith on the phone.

'You know what 260 watts of power feels like,' Keith said. 'You know how to race. Just do it on feel. It won't be an issue.'

Darren came out with his wife Tracy and we all had an early dinner the night before the race. It was interesting, sitting there with Hywel and some of the athletes he coaches, as no one knew that Darren was a prison officer. It was a lovely relaxing meal, on an outside table at a restaurant near the historic centre. Darren was there to support me, as he had been in Lowdham Grange all those years before and it didn't matter to those present who he was or how we met. To them, he was just my friend, which is what he had become.

With our passage down to the Langener Waldsee due to take place in the small hours I set the alarm for 4am, making sure I was in bed by 7pm. My night was only slightly interrupted by the Germany v Italy Euro 2016 quarter-final being shown in street-side bars outside. The constant night checks at Belmarsh had trained me to sleep heavily despite disturbance – a useful skill when there are pockets of football fans screaming every 20 metres outside your bedroom window.

Wyndy Milla had provided me a new white tri-suit and as I lined up in it the following morning, with the wetsuit over the top by the water's edge, I felt again the icy calmness that always came over me. The air was surprisingly cold at about 13 degrees and as I watched the pros swim away I reflected again on my lack of emotion. It wasn't just a case of being in control of my nerves, it was a total absence of nerves, as if I was somehow unaffected in the way others were. Guys were in tears. Some were shaking. In a funny sense, that worried me a touch. Is it ok to be so unmoved? Was I in the moment enough? Why wasn't I fearful and anxious like everyone else?

The next group to go were the hour-or-under swimmers who I allowed to go off without me, remembering my mistake from

Bolton. When my turn came I got into the water and settled into a rhythm straight away. The water felt lukewarm, pleasant to swim in, much clearer and with a nicer taste than Pennington Flash.

For the first kilometre and a half I stayed on the feet of a group ahead of me, but their pace wasn't stretching me enough. After the first turning point and a short Australian exit, I noticed a female swimmer with a very strong stroke powering on ahead. I made a concerted effort to catch her then sat on her shoulder. Again, after acclimatising to her rhythm I felt the need to press harder and with about 1.8km to go, I left her and caught a group of five men who I stayed with all the way in.

First impressions on climbing out on the beach were that I hadn't pushed myself as hard as I could. My shoulders were loose. My breathing was relaxed, but a glance at my Garmin told me I had finished in one hour three minutes, my fastest ever Ironman swim.

I went for a pee in transition, adding dead time and stretching my stay in T1 to five minutes, then as I mounted the bike I removed five chia-seed bars from the bike box and tucked them into my new tri-suit. This was a habit I had developed throughout my short racing career, meaning I could slightly unzip the suit and nibble at the bars while riding and remaining in an aerodynamic position.

Within myself, I felt strong, but something about the suit didn't quite seem right.

It's the sort of thing that will sound silly to people who aren't involved in the sport, but triathletes have to be pedantic over details. For a race I wouldn't usually wear anything I hadn't trained in many times, but Wyndy Milla had been so supportive and provided me with such an amazing bike, I felt I owed it to them to wear the suit, even though I was yet to properly try it out.

After throwing my chia bars in, the zip remained slightly lower than I would usually leave it and sure enough, at around 100km, after an encouraging start, I hit a pothole and the three remaining bars fell out. I watched them go with a twist in my guts. There was no possible way I could stop and pick them up, losing all my momentum, but I had 80km of cycling left, with only half a bar carrying about 200 calories to get me to the end.

'That's an hour's worth,' I said to myself, making mental calculations. 'And if I use my two emergency caffeine gels I've got taped to the bike frame that will get me to about four and a half hours, then I've just got to collect some drinks from the race stations. It will be okay, as long as I drop my power slightly.'

I wouldn't allow myself to overdo it on the bike and risk blow-up on the marathon, not in the European championship, so I pared my imagined power number back from 260 watts to what I thought would be about 230. Allowing my heart rate to fall to about 138bpm, I figured it would be enough to pull out a decent time without completely exhausting my reserves of available energy.

It did mean I was a little light-headed when I reached the end of the bike leg, as well as being slightly bothered about the *drafting* many other athletes seemed to be doing. Drafting, or riding in another competitor's slipstream, is not allowed in Ironman, but is rumoured to be rife among continental Europeans. If you're holding a position within 12 metres of another bike you can be given a time penalty, but despite that, race officials on the day seemed quite slack in enforcing the rules. Large groups of Europeans were assembling into pelotons, like the Tour de France, assisting each other hugely and getting away with it. To me, that was cheating. Maybe I needed to adjust my very British attitude of fair play?

In my mind this was what I had spoken about with Keith. I was utilising my race experience. Not everything will go well or how you want or expect it to. Your plan will fail in some areas and you have to adapt. The loss of nutrition probably meant my bike was 10–15 minutes slower than it could have been, but slowing saved me from the possibility of falling apart on the run, while the behaviour of other athletes was something I could not control. There was little point dwelling on it.

I did feel that my energy levels were lower than I would have liked, but knew there would be plenty of aid stations and Darren waiting for me at 'special needs' with my own nutrition. As I pulled my running shoes on, my mind quickly processed the race so far. One hour three minutes in the water and four hours 54 on the bike were both good times, personal bests in official events, although the bike was slower than I had hoped. The five-minute transition in T1 was a small issue, though. If I wanted to break nine hours I would need to run a two hour 57 marathon, not out of the question by any means, but again quicker than I had raced before.

While I made these assessments I studiously ignored an increasing sense of pressure from my bowel. All the extra caffeine gels had stimulated my system. I didn't know how I was placed in the race but stopping to take a crap was the last thing I needed, so banished the thought from my mind and set off.

I began at three minutes 40 seconds per km, a strong pace, good enough to record a two hour 50 marathon. Halfway around the first of the three laps I saw Keith and Bruno who told me to stay calm and ease into it. I slowed slightly, but still found myself overtaking large numbers of athletes. For a time I attached myself to a female pro from Portugal, but she wasn't going quickly enough for me so soon left her behind.

Towards the end of the first loop I began to really feel an energy dip resulting from the bike, then saw Darren at special needs at the start of lap two, scoffed another gel and was forced to face a grim reality. The downward pressure in my guts was increasing. I desperately needed a crap.

I soon found myself running shoulder to shoulder with Vincent Depuiset, a French professional. We stayed together for a couple of kilometres and were holding a high pace but by then my need to relieve myself had become urgent. If I waited much longer there was a danger I would soil myself and at that stage of my career it was not something I was prepared to do in public. (I have thought about it since and think if I was in a pro race and knew it could be the difference between winning and losing, I perhaps would.)

I dived into one of the athletes' loos by the side of the course which was an absolute pit of filth. Piss and shit had been splattered everywhere by desperate runners. I pulled my tri-suit down, timed myself and it took me 63 seconds to get in and out, not disastrous but also far from ideal. Another step on my learning journey.

I ran hard out of the toilet. The stop, combined with lost momentum, meant I needed to. Within ten minutes I was back on Vincent's shoulder and we maintained a good, steady rhythm until the 30km mark, at which point I saw Keith again.

'You're 12km out,' he shouted. 'Just go for it.'

I upped my tempo. Vincent stayed with me. We weren't speaking, but when you run with someone in that way you become strangely tuned in to their movements and breathing. At 38km, as we approached an aid station, he sighed. In my peripheral vision I was aware that rather than run through, he had stopped to get a drink. Vincent was walking.

'He's cracked,' I thought and motored on alone.

With only 5km to go every instinct told me to drop the hammer and bury it, but I had begun to feel a small twinge in my left hamstring. Before I would have taken a gung-ho approach, but experience kept me sensible. I maintained a strong pace, without losing control, staying in touch and in tune with my body.

As I entered the final kilometre, the realisation of what I was achieving hit me. 'Fucking hell,' I thought. 'I am at the Ironman European championships and I'm about to finish.' I looked at my Garmin and saw I was at two hours 59 minutes for the marathon. That toilet break had cost me the opportunity to go below three hours. Never mind.

Knowing that I had narrowly missed my target time, I resolved to relax and savour the experience. Massed crowds went crazy as I approached the finishing chute, creating a funnel of noise. This is what I had dreamt about for all these years since learning about Ironman at Lowdham Grange. Euphoria erupted within me.

As I entered the main square of the old town, I slowed to a walk, receiving the congratulations and love of the crowd. Hands reached out to touch me. Kids screamed. Women blew kisses.

With the line just ahead, I broke back into a jog, almost crying with joy. A lovely, blonde female official put a medal around my neck. At that moment she looked ten times more beautiful than she already was. I felt like kissing her.

I grinned at her. She grinned back. I had been out of prison for just three and a half years.

32

An End, But Not
a Destination

I LOOKED over my shoulder. The clock above the finishing line said, 'John McAvoy, UK, 9:10:17'.

Instinctively the words 'oh shit' escaped from my mouth.

It was a very good time, in a highly prestigious race, but wasn't quite what I hoped. Instantly I thought of the issue on the bike and the time wasted going to the toilet twice. That was all that had prevented me from joining the sub-nine hours club, a truly select group. That particular target would have to remain one for the future.

Then another thought flashed through my mind. Nine hours ten minutes? My age group winner the previous year had only been 30 seconds quicker.

'Do you know where I finished?' I asked the pretty official.

'Sorry,' she said. 'I don't, but nine hours ten is really quick.'

I went from person to person, asking friends in the crowd, other officials, with a curious mix of anticipation and excitement in my guts. At last I saw Darren.

'Where did I come, mate?' I pleaded.

He had the official results on his phone.

'Fourteenth,' he replied. 'It was a freak year.'

My instant reaction was one of slight deflation but that was soon assuaged by the friends who had come out to support me. As well as Darren, Keith and Bruno, Seb, Ben and Jack from the rowing club made the journey, along with Neil, my old mate from Sudbury. A number of personal training clients of mine came out too – Georgia, Lucy, Lisa, Carrie and Sophie. I greeted all of them as I passed through into the athletes' changing area. Their joy and pride rekindled my positive mood.

Afterwards, as I reflected, it dawned what an enormous triumph Frankfurt had been. As an athlete it represented such a massive step forward. I executed the race professionally, using intelligence and common sense to deal with problems as they came up. Despite any disappointment over the position, I had to be pleased with that.

The fact was that on the day, athletes smashed records all over the place. People had never seen anything like it before. The standout statistic was that I had been the top British finisher in my age group and the third overall, only behind two professionals (one of whom was Hywel who finished just five minutes ahead of me, while the other was Will Clarke who broke the marathon course record in a staggering two hours 42).

In finishing in nine hours ten I had beaten large numbers of professional Ironmen from all over the world, recorded best times in all three disciplines and really placed myself at the top end of the sport. People now knew my name.

My last three events had all been successful, while the results of my two races of 2016 gave me 4,682 world ranking points, placing me third in the UK in the male 30–34 age group, in mid-summer.

And the best part is that I know there is much more to come.

A month later I discussed the future with Keith. He was bowled over by my achievements in such a short space of time.

'You've achieved in three and a half years what I managed in 12,' he said. 'Your rate of progress is staggering.'

We agreed to up my training levels to pro volume for the 2017 season, meaning 30-hour weeks for 12 months. Keith believed the time was right to push things on. I was there. We would spend the winter focusing on swimming improvement. One hour three minutes in Frankfurt was a good performance, but with dedicated coaching Keith believed six or seven minutes quicker would be possible. My cycling would continue its upward trajectory while my running was already solid. I could really see it all coming together.

By January 2018, I would be turning professional.

33

Just Do It

IN THE months that followed my return from Frankfurt, my story snowballed from one media outlet to the next. I was interviewed by Trevor McDonald on BBC radio, hosted my own guest edit on Radio 5, had segments about my life on both national TV evening news programmes, was featured in a clutch of newspapers and received coverage from places as far-flung as Canada and New Zealand.

It was touching to see how my experiences connected with others. Terry and Darren's faith seemed vindicated. My tale of redemption did have the ability to inspire.

In November, I spoke to Terry on the phone, just our regular morning chat. He had kindly taken on the responsibility of fielding enquiries through my website and we talked about interview requests that had come in the previous day, as well as a few speaking engagements I had been offered. As we were about to finish he said:

'Oh, and one more thing.'

'Yeah?'

'I'm going to tell you something now that could change the rest of your life.' His tone was deliberately casual.

'In a good way or a bad way?'

'I've just received an email from a man called Dan Smith.'

'And?'

'He's the track and field and cross-category sports marketing manager at Nike. They've been following your story and love it. They want to know if you'd be interested in working with them, possibly becoming a Nike athlete.'

'Are you having a laugh?'

'I'm absolutely on the level John.'

'A Nike athlete?'

'Yep.'

'Like Wayne Rooney, Roger Federer, Mo Farah and all that lot?'

'It seems so.'

I thanked Terry and put the phone down, mind racing. My overriding feeling was one of disbelief. How could this be real? But that email began a chain of communication that led to my signing a sponsorship deal with the world's biggest sports company early in 2017.

The only downside was having to speak to my former sponsors, who had supported me from the beginning. It did twang my conscience, but Kraft were extremely understanding. They said what a pleasure it had been to work with me, that they couldn't possibly stand in my way and wished me luck as my career developed. I will always be grateful to them for the part they played.

All this culminated with an invitation to speak to the Nike annual conference at their European headquarters in Hilversum, Holland in April. They booked me to open up the event, a real honour. Once again, I found myself struggling to believe my new reality.

Probation gave permission for me to attend although the clearance came too late to fly. The overall experience was almost dreamlike. Nike hired me a Jaguar XE to drive over, so I roped in my friend Ben from LRC for company.

The Nike campus is an impressive place, with a lake and athletics track hemmed in by modern buildings. Each block is named after a famous athlete. On arrival we headed through the revolving doors of the Federer building and were confronted by huge photographic portraits of Paula Radcliffe, Neymar and Lebron James. Memorabilia lined the walls.

Dan was seated on a sofa by the reception desk, got up, smiled and suggested going for a run. The two of us left Ben in the café and spent an hour jogging around the campus, getting to know each other. Dan spoke about how the business worked and all the famous athletes he had worked with. He impressed me with his humour and affability.

By the time we returned to the building, Terry had arrived, having been chauffeured from the airport Eric Cantona's car. After lunch Dan brought us to meet Edgar Jorissen, Nike's vice-president of brand marketing in Europe. Dressed head to toe in black, Edgar managed the delicate balancing act of being very direct and forthright while also easy-going and friendly. His communication skills were impressive. I could instantly understand how he held a position of such influence.

We ran through a rehearsal of my slot, deciding my talk would take the form of a video intro, followed by a Q & A with Edgar. With that settled, all five of us headed out for dinner before staying the night at a plush Amsterdam hotel. The conference centre was booked nearby.

The following morning, I found myself waiting by the side curtain of an impressive auditorium, in which 1,500 attendees were seated. A troupe of dancing girls limbered up nearby, preparing for their routines between the speakers. I had been fitted with a headset microphone and watched with a sense of near-awe as Edgar introduced the day's theme to the delegates.

'To begin our 2017 conference,' he said, 'we are going to talk about our new range.'

The company logo appeared appeared above him on a huge screen. As he continued to speak, Roger Federer's face replaced it there, which then morphed into Rafa Nadal. Nadal's dissolved into Ayrton Senna's, which gave way to Mo Farah, then Paula Radcliffe, then Manny Pacquiao, Michael Jordan, Rory McIlroy,

Cristiano Ronaldo and so on. One giant of the sporting world followed another in a seamless procession.

Edgar smiled warmly at the audience.

'And now, ladies and gentlemen, I have someone very important to introduce to you. Someone who personifies what we are all about. Nike's first sponsored Ironman triathlete, John McAvoy.'

As he said that, Serena Williams' face faded away and mine took her place.

'Showtime', I thought, remembering my feelings from the Old Bailey years before. I walked out on stage and shook Edgar's hand. The lights were blinding. I could feel the crowd. We began.

The next 20 minutes passed in a blur. Soon we were wrapping up, thanking the audience who filled the hall with noise. As they clapped and cheered, I looked down at the front row. Terry was crying. Ben grinned from ear to ear. Aaron sat next to him, beaming with pride. He winked at me. Somehow, above all the cacophony, I heard his voice.

'I always knew we would make it. I felt it in my guts.'

Head spinning briefly, I did a double take, but of course, Aaron had disappeared.

As we walked off, one of the security guards slapped me on the back.

'What a story!' he said.

For the rest of the morning I received nothing but welcomes and enthusiasm from the people at Nike. They set up a table for me to sign copies of this book. I stood there and watched as a 400-metre-long queue formed. It was unbelievable. Some employees were close to tears, saying they found my turnaround deeply moving. It was one of the most emotional days of my life.

After leaving Amsterdam and driving home, it took me several days to come down from the high it had given me. I also couldn't help but reflect. Dan, Edgar and everyone I met at Nike had been so likeable. Yet in many ways their organisation represented everything Billy brought me up to hate. A huge, multinational corporation, with a turnover in excess of $30 billion a year.

As a youth, this sort of thing had been my faceless enemy, a perfect example of the system.

Yet demystified and viewed from within, it seemed the system was built of ordinary, hardworking people. People doing their best, as I was. And they certainly were not intent on causing harm or servicing greed at all costs. They were hospitable and warm. They wanted to help me. The employees at Nike had really connected with my story and how it could be used to help others, particularly kids.

So who really had been my great enemy all those years ago? What really was this system? I had to conclude it was something internal. Despite all my years of physical confinement, my most restrictive prison had been inside my own mind.

34

Don't Look Back In Anger

R EGARDLESS of all that has happened since that day
late in 2012 when I walked out of Sudbury, the life licence
does preoccupy me, of course it does. I also know that
because of my background, people will always doubt me. Who I
was remains part of who I am. I have to live with those things for
the rest of my life.

Someone else can afford to make a mistake, to have a car
crash for example and injure someone by accident. They might get
arrested but it would not necessarily be a big deal. But if anything
like that happens to me, I go back to prison. In my eyes (and in
the eyes of the law), I am not truly free. I am *serving my sentence
in the community*. It feels like having a black cloud over your head.
And every now and then it rains.

Sometimes I do think it's unjust. There are people who have
committed crimes far worse than anything I did; sex offences,
things against children. Some of them are released and get to live
a normal life, even receive state protection, but not me. Stealing
large amounts of money from financial institutions is worse than
paedophilia, apparently. I guess that tells you who really runs the
country but something about it doesn't sit right with me. Maybe
I'm biased.

At the beginning I have no doubt that they were watching me. Probably on and off for the first year. I find it strange to think that even after I finished my first Ironman and was so dedicated to my new path, obsessed with training, it is likely I was being observed. Police probably spied on me running around Richmond Park or cycling on the South Downs. Maybe they still do now.

If I could share one piece of advice with the world it would be that life is not about cars and watches and money. That's the life you're sold by the media, but it's a mirage. I want to inspire others, especially kids, to stop them looking up to the fake role models they admire. I can tell them – I have seen it.

I have seen so called *badman* gangsters come back to prison after court, crying like babies because they've got life. They're 25 years old and they're not getting out until they're 60. That is their reality.

When it gets to that stage, those guys end up turning informer, grassing each other up, selling out their mates. In desperation they do anything police ask. They aren't so *bad* then are they? But youngsters on the street, in their communities don't see any of that.

I have sat among real criminals, the top-end guys, as they say how they paid a kid a few grand to kill someone. When that kid is caught and faces years behind bars, they couldn't care less.

'Never mind, he's expendable,' they'd say, 'just some toe-rag off an estate. There's thousands more, we'll find another one.'

That's who these *badmen* really are. These boys who walk the walk and make lots of noise are small fry. They get used and taken advantage of. Yet that's who these kids look up to, because they are visible. If they knew who the really shrewd guys are, the ones making all the money, street kids wouldn't admire them at all. The real top boys are a bunch of middle-aged white men, who never get their hands dirty, look and talk like regular businessmen, but are wealthy and ruthless as fuck. They don't make YouTube videos or drive around in soft-top cars with music pumping out.

I guess I was lucky I avoided needless violence. If it didn't make money, I wasn't interested. If I had come out after ten years with vendettas against me, as many people do, it would have been very difficult to stay out of things. You have to defend yourself in those circumstances. It's life or death. So physically, I escaped that world. It means I had to cut off a lot of people, even relatives, which wasn't easy but was the only way. I probably still bear internal scars, though. And I probably always will.

My probation officer is so proud. I still see her every month. I enjoy it. She shows my media interviews to everyone in the office. Of all the people who got out around the same time I did, I was the only one who stayed out. Her other cases were all recalled within two years.

I've received letters from mums saying their kids look up to me. That now they want to go into sport. Darren told me there are guys in Lowdham Grange doing the million metres on the rowing machine because they've read what I've done. That drives me on, fires me up – my successes are not just mine.

That's great, because in Ironman you cannot just go out and take what you want. You have to work and work and work to earn it – then you still might not get it. Risk to reward is no longer a factor. Its work to achieve now. Work to improve, little by little. It's hard, but hard is good.

Maybe that's why, when I train and compete, suffering is so important. Interpret that how you want. But I like to suffer.

I like to prove to myself how mentally strong I am. I hate to show vulnerability.

All Ironmen know that after the swim, after the bike, they will go out on the run and at some point they will be in huge, inhuman pain. It might happen at ten miles or it might happen at 20, but it will happen. It scares them.

I long for that moment, that little slice of hell. I crave it. I run towards it.

It's therapeutic.

When it comes, I transcend. Questions disappear. It is only now.

I move one leg, then the other, heart and lungs, feet on earth. Blood cells buzz, hormones stir, genes conjure.

While the body screams, the soul rests.
At that time, I'm not a McAvoy. I'm not even an athlete.
I just am.
And that's the way I like it.

Epilogue

JOHN'S accomplice on his last attempted robbery, **Kevin Barnes**, was moved to an open prison in 2014, having slowly descended through the security categories during ten previous years of incarceration. He was there for approximately three hours before he jumped over a perimeter wall and disappeared, whisked away by a waiting car. Two weeks later he was rearrested in possession of a firearm and is currently back serving his life sentence. He is now 57 years old.

John's stepfather, **Billy Tobin**, now 65, also remains in prison and is lodging an appeal at the European Court of Human Rights. He has so far served 15 years of a 12-year tariff on a life sentence, but has refused at any stage to admit guilt or participate in any rehabilitation courses. Without a change of heart, he could remain in jail indefinitely.

Roger Vincent's situation is not quite so dire, but it is unlikely he will see daylight until old age. He still maintains his innocence and is appealing at the high courts against conviction, succeeding so far in having five years deducted from his sentence. John has been unable to have any contact with him since release, even in the form of letters, as to do so would be deemed by the probation service to be 'association with an organised criminal' and could potentially cause him to be recalled. This remains a source of inner conflict for John who still thinks of Roger as a very dear friend.

Following his period of fame, John's Uncle **Micky McAvoy** continues to live a quiet life in Spain. He has neither been arrested nor come to the attention of the authorities for any reason since the end of his last sentence.

John's former cell-block neighbour **Abu Hamza** was extradited to the USA in 2012, as he always expected would happen. In 2015 he was found guilty of various terrorism-related charges and sentenced to life without possibility of parole.

Darren Davis still works at the Lowdham Grange prison gym. He has a picture of John on the wall, which he uses to inspire other inmates. Many others have attempted the million-metre row for charity, but none as yet have shown John's natural aptitude or mental toughness. After completing Ironman UK with John in 2015 he intends to continue challenging himself in Ironman events.

Terry Williamson and **Keith Sanders** both still work with John as he looks to a future of Ironman competition. Their help and support always been and remains, invaluable.

John often wonders if **DCI Currie** appreciates the profound part he played in transforming his life. As far as can be ascertained, Currie still works for the London Flying Squad.

After his achievements in 2016, **John McAvoy** is looking forward to a bright future as a professional Ironman triathlete. He is also committed to education and outreach programmes, through which he aims to provide living proof to alienated youth that it is always possible to take another path. At the time of publication, four of the British records set during his years in jail still stood and he remained the only lightweight rower to have held all three ultra-endurance world records at once. In a different, but perhaps connected way, John is still *good stuff*.